BIRT 2.6 Data Analysis and Reporting

Create, design, format, and deploy reports with the world's most popular Eclipse-based Business Intelligence and Reporting Tool

John Ward

BIRMINGHAM - MUMBAI

BIRT 2.6 Data Analysis and Reporting

First published: July 2010

Production Reference: 1090710

Published by Packt Publishing Ltd.
32 Lincoln Road
Olton
Birmingham, B27 6PA, UK.

ISBN 978-1-849511-66-7

www.packtpub.com

Cover Image by Vinayak Chittar (vinayak.chittar@gmail.com)

Credits

Author
John Ward

Reviewers
Moncef Maiza
Meenakshi Verma
Jason Weathersby
Michael Williams

Acquisition Editor
Douglas Paterson

Development Editor
Dhiraj Chandiramani

Technical Editor
Gaurav Datar

Copy Editor
Sanchari Mukherjee

Editorial Team Leader
Gagandeep Singh

Project Team Leader
Lata Basantani

Project Coordinator
Srimoyee Ghoshal

Proofreader
Lesley Harrison

Indexer
Monica Ajmera Mehta

Production Coordinator
Melwyn D'sa

Cover Work
Melwyn D'sa

About the Author

John Ward is a consultant for Innovent Solutions, specializing in BIRT and e-commerce search and navigation solutions. Before he began working with Innovent Solutions, John was an Assistant Vice President for Citibank, North America, managing the training MIS group and overseeing developing of new technology-based training initiatives. John actively works with and tests BIRT—an open source reporting platform built on Eclipse. His work involves development work based on BIRT reports and the BIRT APIs. John also maintains The Digital Voice blog at `http://digiassn.blogspot.com`.

I'd like to thank my Wife, Claudia, for her love, support, and patience throughout the writing of this book; my Grandfather and Father for their wisdom and advice; and my Mother for her encouragement and support.

I would also like to thank Scott, Jason, Virgil, and Krishna, for years of working together to bring BIRT support to the community, and showing the community what is possible and bringing BIRT to new levels.

About the Reviewers

Moncef Maiza is a technologist, with years of experience in designing and building products and services that are used by some of the largest corporations in the world. Currently Mr. Maiza is a Principal at DataSieve, where he identifies, develops, and manages the technical products and services to further to achieve company's goals. Previously Mr. Maiza was the first employee at digiMine, where he played a crucial role in getting the company started and played a leading role in developing a world class infrastructure for the pioneering WebHousing Application Service Provider.

Prior to working with digiMine, Mr. Maiza served as the president and CEO of ISTC Corp—a software development and business intelligence consulting company. During his tenure at ISTC, Mr. Maiza lead the company in building applications, data warehousing systems, and on-the-edge reporting systems for companies such as Ford Motor Company, Liberty Mutual, UPS, 3M, and SEARS Roebuck.

Before that Mr. Maiza was of Director of Information at CPHA—a pioneering company in the field of medical informatics that hosted the data of more than 2000 leading U.S. hospitals. CPHA was later bought in part by HCIA Inc. Mr. Maiza played the lead role in moving the company to adopt modern data warehousing and management techniques. He also helped in developing innovative techniques to mine data from the enormous CPHA/HCIA data warehouses.

Mr. Maiza holds graduate degrees in mathematics and computer sciences from the University of Michigan in Ann Arbor.

Meenakshi Verma has a been part of the IT industry since 1998. She is experienced in deploying solutions across multiple industry segments using SAP BI, SAP Business Objects, and Java/J2EE technologies. She is currently based in Toronto, Canada and is working with Enbridge Gas Distribution.

Meenakshi has been helping with technical reviews for books published by Packt Publishing across varied enterprise solutions. Her earlier work includes *JasperReports for Java Developers, Java EE 5 Development using GlassFish Application Server, Practical Data Analysis and Reporting with BIRT, EJB 3 Developer's Guide, Learning DOJO, and Websphere Application Server.*

I'd like to thank my Father (Mr Bhopal Singh) and Mother
(Mrs Raj Bala) for laying a strong foundation in me and giving
me their unconditional love and support. I also owe thanks and
gratitude to my husband (Atul Verma) for his encouragement and
support throughout the review of this book and many others, to
my four-year old son (Prieyaansh Verma) for giving me the warmth
of his love despite my hectic schedules, and to my brother
(Sachin Singh) for always being there for me.

Michael Williams graduated with a degree in Computer Engineering from the University of Kansas in December of 2004. He has been working with BIRT since 2008. Currently, he works as a BIRT-Exchange Evangelist for Actuate Corporation named *The People Behind BIRT*, and spends much of his time creating technical content for the website (`www.birt-exchange.org`), attending conferences, and answering forum questions.

Table of Contents

Preface

BIRT is an open source business intelligence and reporting tool, built on top of the Eclipse Framework. BIRT is used by developers for building reports that can best represent data and tell a story of that data that is easy to follow. In addition, BIRT can be integrated into a product, to allow that product to provide reporting capabilities. This book will walk the user through the basics of building reports with BIRT and introduce them to the various sections of the BIRT environment.

What this book covers

Chapter 1, Getting Started, is an introduction to BIRT. It gives the reader an idea of the BIRT features, community landscape, and the various websites out there that are dedicated to BIRT.

Chapter 2, Installing BIRT, guides the user through the various ways of installing BIRT.

Chapter 3, The BIRT Environment and First Report, introduces the BIRT workspace environment by walking the reader through a simple report example.

Chapter 4, Visual Report Items, presents us with various visual report items that are available for use in a report design.

Chapter 5, Working with Data, discusses how to retrieve data from databases, flat text files, web services, and other data sources.

Chapter 6, Report Parameters, explains how to get input from the report user, along with how to apply these report parameters in filtering data.

Chapter 7, Report Projects and Libraries, looks at reusing report sections and sharing resources through libraries and report projects.

Chapter 8, Charts, Hyperlinks, and Drilldowns, shows how to build summary data using charts and linking sections of charts to reports. In addition, hyperlinking used in online reports to link and show detailed data in other reports is discussed here.

Chapter 9, Scripting and Event Handling, discusses report generation through event handling, as well as how to manipulate and format data using simple JavaScript expressions. Some advanced scripting examples are provided based on common requests.

Chapter 10, Deployment, looks at how does a developer can get reports out into the world for consumption.

We also have the following two chapters that are available for free download on Packt site:

- The chapter *Styles, Themes, and Templates,* demonstrates the various ways a report developer can format their report using basic formatting, styles and stylesheets, and themes, along with how to reuse report designs through templates. The chapter is available at `http://www.packtpub.com/sites/default/files/downloads/1667-styles-themes-and-templates.pdf`.

- The chapter *Practical Example: Building Reports for Bugzilla,* takes everything covered so far and puts it all together by looking at a project with reporting requirements, and builds a report environment from the ground up. The chapter is available at `http://www.packtpub.com/sites/default/files/downloads/1667-practical-example-building-reports-for-bugzilla.pdf`.

What you need for this book

Any of the following BIRT versions will work for this book:

- BIRT 2.2.x
- BIRT 2.3.x
- BIRT 2.5.x
- BIRT 2.6

In addition, all the code examples can be downloaded from Packt site.

Who this book is for

If you are a Java developer and want to create rich reports using BIRT, then this book is for you. You will need a basic understanding of SQL to follow along.

Conventions

In this book, you will find a number of styles of text that distinguish between different kinds of information. Here are some examples of these styles, and an explanation of their meaning.

Code words in text are shown as follows: "Create a new report project called BIRT Book Chapter 5 examples."

A block of code will be set as follows:

```xml
<?xml version="1.0" encoding="UTF-8"?>
<Employees xmlns:xsi="http://www.w3.org/2001/XMLSchema-instance">
  <Employee>
    <firstName>John</firstName>
    <lastName>Ward</lastName>
    <jobTitle>Developer</jobTitle>
```

New terms and **important words** are shown in bold. Words that you see on the screen, in menus or dialog boxes for example, appear in our text like this: "Under the **Data Explorer** pane, right- click on **Data Sources** and select **New Data Source** ".

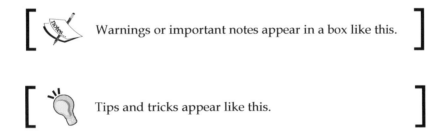

Warnings or important notes appear in a box like this.

Tips and tricks appear like this.

Reader feedback

Feedback from our readers is always welcome. Let us know what you think about this book—what you liked or may have disliked. Reader feedback is important for us to develop titles that you really get the most out of.

To send us general feedback, simply drop an email to feedback@packtpub.com, and mention the book title in the subject of your message.

If there is a book that you need and would like to see us publish, please send us a note in the **SUGGEST A TITLE** form on www.packtpub.com or email suggest@packtpub.com.

If there is a topic that you have expertise in and you are interested in either writing or contributing to a book, see our author guide on www.packtpub.com/authors.

Customer support

Now that you are the proud owner of a Packt book, we have a number of things to help you to get the most from your purchase.

 Downloading the example code for this book

You can download the example code files for all Packt books you have purchased from your account at http://www.PacktPub.com. If you purchased this book elsewhere, you can visit http://www.PacktPub.com/support and register to have the files e-mailed directly to you.

Errata

Although we have taken every care to ensure the accuracy of our contents, mistakes do happen. If you find a mistake in one of our books—maybe a mistake in text or code—we would be grateful if you would report this to us. By doing so, you can save other readers from frustration, and help us to improve subsequent versions of this book. If you find any errata, please report them by visiting http://www.packtpub.com/support, selecting your book, clicking on the **let us know** link, and entering the details of your errata. Once your errata are verified, your submission will be accepted and the errata added to any list of existing errata. Any existing errata can be viewed by selecting your title from http://www.packtpub.com/support.

Piracy

Piracy of copyright material on the Internet is an ongoing problem across all media. At Packt, we take the protection of our copyright and licenses very seriously. If you come across any illegal copies of our works in any form on the Internet, please provide us with the location address or website name immediately so that we can pursue a remedy.

Please contact us at copyright@packtpub.com with a link to the suspected pirated material.

We appreciate your help in protecting our authors, and our ability to bring you valuable content.

Questions

You can contact us at questions@packtpub.com if you are having a problem with any aspect of the book, and we will do our best to address it.

1
Getting Started

This is a very interesting time for open source. As soon as a novel concept is put forth by enthusiasts, new functionality is included into software that changes our lives, and a lot of it is built on open source technology. Having been an open source advocate for some time now, I have seen a phenomenal amount of change and progress in the quality and quantity of **Open Source Software (OSS)** projects. From the thoughtful minds of professional software developers, engineers, and hobbyists, tools have sprung up to support a number of disciplines, including programmers, authors, office staff, teachers, students, media, and graphic designers. While there was a time when there was only expensive proprietary commercial software available to use to perform particular tasks, now there are a lot of new and free alternatives based on OSS.

Open source projects start, and also die, all the time. Each project starts to address what a user, or group of users, perceives as a relative shortcoming in the current computing landscape. While OpenOffice.org was derived from StarOffice to address the lack of an open source office suite, Mozilla has grown from the ashes of Netscape to compete with Internet Explorer, leading to the creation of Firefox, which not only has provided an alternative to IE but has revitalized the browser wars, even garnering attention to its commercial competitor Opera. And there is no end to the innovations that PERL and PHP have brought about.

Even non-free software benefits from OSS. Many different projects take portions of fully functional open source software implementations to use in their products. Commercial routers from companies such as Linksys have embedded Linux in them, and even gamers are affected as the Sony PlayStation 3 and Nintendo Wii were both designed to run using Linux. Mono, the open source implementation of the .Net framework, has helped with growth in the .Net community.

But there has always been one area that has been severely lacking, and that is the area of business intelligence. While there are solutions such as writing PERL or PHP scripts, these really don't leverage full fledged Business Intelligence, the idea that reports and tools can be used by businesses to make strategic decisions based on short term and long term data and trend analysis. There has not been an open source tool that really addresses this shortcoming. Crafty developers can take the long approach and write scripts and programs that automate data reporting tasks, but this is a long and complicated process. Proprietary software for doing reporting tasks do exist, such as the report developer inside Microsoft Access for reporting off Access databases, Crystal Reports, and larger offerings such as Business Objects. These are tools that have been built to automate reporting tasks such as data retrieval, sorting, aggregation, and presentation into a format that is meaningful to the user. Such tools have been lacking in the open source community, and have only begun to gain speed in the last few years.

Introduction to BI

There are two major questions that need to be answered at this point of the book—what is Business Intelligence and why do we need it? Business Intelligence is a lot like many other technology buzzwords that get thrown around. Many people are just aware of this word and say it, and many people will give a complicated definition of it. But the answer is really quite simple.

If I had to give it a formal definition, I would say that Business Intelligence, as it relates to information technology, is any tool or method that allows developers to take data or information, process it, manipulate it, associate it with related information, and present it to decision makers. As for a simplified definition, Business Intelligence involves presenting information to decision makers in a way that helps them make informed decisions.

Consider this scenario. You are the manager for a chain of retail stores. You need to figure out what products you should push to the forefront for the upcoming holiday season. You have a two method approach. First, you get the latest buzz from your marketers, who tell you what the new and upcoming products are. Your second approach is to look at products that have traditionally sold very well. You could also look at web tracking data, usually from large analytics companies such as Omniture or Google Analytics.

In order to project how the current year may go, you need to look at the data you have at your disposal. What product categories have traditionally sold well over a five-year period or even a ten-year period? Has there been any sort of pattern to these sales figures. What individual items have sold well in that period? Are there any trends? When you look at these figures, can you give a projection of how well the products will do? What items should be put on sale in order to push for higher sales? These are the kinds of questions that a decision maker may need answered.

So, the first step in the process is getting to this data, which is usually located someplace such as a data warehouse. If you are looking at a regional level, you may have this information stored separately in a localized data mart, with specific data. If you are looking forward to working on the minutest of data, you may need access to transactional data. Either way, the first hurdle is getting access to the data.

What do you do once you have access to the data? How do you format and present the data in some meaningful fashion that can be used to assist in the BI process? In other words, what is the best way to use this data to tell a good story, one that is easy to understand and also gets you the answers you are looking for? This is where BI tools come into play. Using BI tools, you have the ability to write reports that can present this often time sporadic and confusing data into some sort of format that is useful to decision makers. Once this data is presented, trends can be identified, total figures can be aggregated, and decisions can be made.

The current state of the BI market

The current state of the BI market is similar to the state of any technology field. It can change at the drop of the hat. At the time of this writing, you can divide the major players in two categories—commercial offerings and open source offerings. Each route has its own benefits and drawbacks. Certain familiar names are associated with the commercial offerings, for example Actuate and Business Objects offers various tools aimed at different levels of business. Some of these tools are large enterprise reporting platforms that have the ability to process, analyze, and reformat large quantities of data. With commercial offerings, you get product support and years of experience. With the big guys, you often get professional services too such as consultation in developing your reports for a fee. One of the drawbacks of commercial offerings is the large price associated with them, both in terms of purchasing and running them. Some companies, in addition to the initial cost which, at times, can run up to thousands of dollars, also charge for yearly maintenance, upgrade fees, and have an additional cost of ownership that may be typically overlooked. There is also the cost of licensing. If you are building a large scale custom application, are you allowed to integrate these products into your application? If yes, then are there any restrictions? And finally, the years of engineering behind a product may leverage an obsolete methodology. Perhaps the technology behind these products is no longer viable or powerful enough to handle the demands of a growing enterprise.

Then you have your open source offerings. Currently there are three big names in the open source reporting realm—JasperReport, Pentaho, and BIRT. Two of these projects, JasperReports and BIRT, are run by commercial companies who make money doing professional services for these offerings to small scale, private projects. Again, there are a number of pros and cons associated with open source solutions. With open source, you have full access to the source code of the platform you choose. This allows you to add in functionality, embed it with in your existing applications, and actively participate in a development community that is often times very large and worldwide. There is little initial cost to open source in terms of purchasing because any open source tool is available free of charge. There are a few disadvantages too. There is typically a cost associated with finding individuals knowledgeable in open source. Sometimes open source is not very user friendly. And finally, there is often little to no support for open source products. This is not the case with large open source projects. However, with the large active development communities associated with open source projects such as Linux, Eclipse, and Mozilla/Firefox, answers to your support-related queries are only an internet search away.

The need for open source reporting

Some things are better illustrated with a story. So, let me begin this with what brought me to the world of Open Source Business Intelligence. My story starts on a late Sunday evening in 2001. I was then a student intern for a midsized network security monitoring operation. Here I am, landing a dream job for a college student, a paid internship at a high technology company, and working in one of the most exciting fields in the tech industry—network security. From this single department came some interesting projects and concepts such as Sguil (the Open Source Network Security Analysis front-end for Snort) and SanCP (a network session profiler). Concepts such as **Network Security Monitoring (NSM)** were being tested and proven over security appliances that promised a silver bullet to all security problems.

In this particular scenario, we are a department dedicated to providing customers with network security monitoring solutions using open source software. This entire NSM philosophy would later be expanded upon and described in *The Tao of Network Security* (Bejtlich 2004). And yet, here I am, with a broken keyboard, occupying a cubicle in my office where the A/C shuts off on a timer, so it's boiling hot, surrounded by great gadgets and cool blinking lights, flashing screens, and on the cutting edge monitoring of Internet traffic catching bad guys doing bad things. The whole setup is like a scene right out of a spy movie, with a lot of exciting things happening. Such a great opportunity for me, a young college student. Yet, on this particular evening, I was not enjoying my job.

My job here, this evening, was not to monitor the thousands of alerts, nor was it to inspect the exponentially higher amount of network packets in an effort to protect networks from the insidious under doings of the digital underground. Instead, my job this evening was to perform the most dreaded task in the entire operation—the weekly incident report.

Being a company dedicated to open source, we had tons of open source software, proving that the open source paradigm was a workable one. Our workstations were all Red Hat Linux systems configured and customized to help us achieve our mission statement. Our backend servers were all running FreeBSD. Our security console was a custom, in-house developed front-end, built on open source scripting tools (which was the base for what would later become the Sguil project). Our network sensors were all built on Snort and dumped all transactional data into a PostgreSQL data warehouse. Our office productivity suite was an early release of OpenOffice.org. Yet we lacked one important piece of a customer focused service group, a reporting system.

So, what tools did we use to address the area of reporting? We had scripts—lots of tedious, boring, manual scripts that generated lines of ugly text. The scripts took hours to run, mostly due to a lack of proper indexing on the reporting tables as the DBAs refused to listen to us and focused on the transactional databases that housed all our live data. As a result, the scripts were slow and their output was ugly. The scripts may have outputted RTF documents, but no formatting tags were actually used. Part of our job was to go through each of these reports, cut out duplicate lines, change the fonts and font weighting, and manually go through and confirm the accuracy of each of the counts in the summary. This was a time consuming, tedious, and boring task that was highly error prone and, as a result, required a longer validation time. Of course, due to the setup, the scripts were considered part of the Database Administrator and the system developers' tasks, so of course we didn't have access to change anything in the event of an issue. If a query was returning funny results in the reports, all we could see was an output page with no access to the code that generated it.

Now it's the middle of the night, we're tired, the other guy is griping about having to pick up the slack while I am doing the most tedious task of running reports. It is hot, and I'm pouring through hundreds of pages, cutting out duplicates, changing summary numbers to reflect correct counts, and changing the formatting. I am sitting here asking myself the same question I ask myself each week when we run these reports, "Isn't there a better way?".

Fast forward a few years. I have since moved on from BATC into a new role as a senior software developer for Citibank North Americas National Training Department. It's the 2004 Actuate Users Conference in Los Angeles, California. Always on the prowl for innovative reporting technologies since my encounters as BATC, I came to the conference to learn about the different products Actuate had to offer. But the one thing that always stayed at the back of my mind was that nagging desire to find an open source reporting solution. So, as a few days rolled on during the conference, I was getting a little annoyed at one of the product pitches. Therefore, on this particular day's keynote speech, the vice-president of some such department was speaking at a length about all the products that Actuate had to offer. Of course, as I was already starting to zone out, I started doodling in my notebook with little caricatures of him doing sales pitches. But suddenly, as if I had a moment of clarity from a drunken stupor, this VP said the most remarkable thing. He said, "Actuate realizes the importance for an open source reporting product, which is why we have started on an open source initiative with the Eclipse Foundation to make an open source report platform called BIRT".

It was as if he read my mind, and suddenly I couldn't help but listen to my new messiah. Apparently someone out there was listening, and someone had clued in to an untapped market. And thus was my introduction to BIRT.

While my story demonstrates the need for report developers, what about application developers? Well, let me give you a scenario. You work for the MIS/BI group in your company. For years you have leveraged hand coded, database-driven web pages for your reporting. You have come to the conclusion that development takes too long, and decided to leverage your existing J2EE platform because it is time to change your report development habits.

After extensive research, you have come up with a list of requirements. Reports must be accessible online and offer the ability to export to common desktop formats such as Microsoft Office formats and Adobe PDF. You need pagination and navigation as part of your reports. You also would like to take the hand coding of reports out of the loop to make them quicker to develop and deploy. Because you work in a development group, you need the ability to share common reporting elements among your group. You also would like the platform to be flexible and dynamic, and will also need charting capabilities. However, you have no budget at this time for an enterprise reporting platform, so you decide on an open source platform. After some research, you come across BIRT, and decide it is the way to go.

Why BIRT?

BIRT is part of Eclipse. It has a relaxed license in the form of the Eclipse Public License. As it is part of Eclipse, it has the ability to work with other Eclipse tools inside of a project. BIRT reports are simple, structured, human readable XML documents. When deploying BIRT, there are several options due to BIRT's flexible structure. It can be deployed in a standalone Java application, inside a J2EE application, and inside an OSGi/RCP application framework. It comes with a good set of tools to get you started such as a graphical report editor and an easily deployed report viewer for J2EE applications. BIRT Reports also do not require compiling. They are run and rendered from the XML report design file. The BIRT framework is also extensible. There are built-in extension points that allow application developers to add in new features such as new data sources, new rendered report output types, and new aggregations and report component types. And yes, BIRT is backed by some big players such as IBM and Actuate.

However, the thing that keeps me involved with BIRT is not the technical side. The thing that keeps me involved with BIRT is the community. There has been a very strong community built up around BIRT, centered around the BIRT Exchange and the BIRT news groups. The people who manage and maintain these communities work hard to provide the BIRT users with good examples, answering questions, and promoting the use of BIRT in their products. Users are always helping each other out and I have seen this community grow significantly over the past several years.

What is BIRT?

If you are new to BIRT, or are unfamiliar with Eclipse, you may be asking "What exactly is BIRT?" The first thing that comes to mind is a fuzzy puppet with a uni-brow. Well, this BIRT isn't related, although some may consider it fuzzy and cute. Others may think of it as mustached rouge on a race to win money, running from the law. Well, this tough guy also isn't what we are talking about.

So, what exactly is BIRT? This is a complex question to answer. Some would tell you that BIRT is a report designer built on top of Eclipse that provides users with a visual WYSIWYG design interface for rapid report development. Others may tell you it is a plugin for Apache Tomcat that allows you to view reports from J2EE web portals. And there are some who may tell you that it is a report engine that can be imported into Java applications. There is also a chart engine that may come up in some peoples answers.

Truth be told, all of these answers are correct. **BIRT**, which stands for **Business Intelligence and Reporting Tools**, is actually a development framework. Adding the word "Tools" to the title acronym is appropriate, as BIRT is in fact a collection of development tools and technologies used for report development utilizing the BIRT framework. BIRT isn't necessarily a product, but a series of core technologies that products and solutions are built on top of, similar in fashion to the Eclipse framework.

The focus of this book will be on the most visible and familiar product built with the BIRT framework, which is the BIRT Report Designer. The **BIRT Report Designer** is an Eclipse perspective built using a set of plugins, utilizing BIRT technologies that allow users to design reports in the BIRT XML-based document format. Inside this application, the Design Engine API, the Report Object Model, the BIRT Report Engine, the BIRT Chart Engine, and a number of other BIRT technologies are utilized to deliver a robust and capable report design environment.

Another product built with BIRT is the AJAX-based Web Viewer that comes with the report engine runtime download. This is a product that is plugged into a J2EE application container such as Apache Tomcat or BEA Weblogic that utilizes the BIRT Report Engine to run reports and output to various formats including HTML and PDF. Several other applications are built with BIRT as well. Actuate BIRT Report Designer and Actuate 9 platforms are centered around BIRT technology.

By looking at the earlier examples, we can see that the core BIRT technologies can be leveraged to build a number of business intelligence products. Hopefully this gives you an idea of what exactly BIRT is. For shorthand, we will refer to the *BIRT Report Designer* as *BIRT* throughout the book.

The origins of BIRT

While the story I narrated in an earlier section of this chapter is good for telling my introduction to BIRT and demonstrates the need for open source reporting platforms, it is not the official origin of BIRT. For that, we need to turn to Actuate, and give a story that eventually intersects with my story.

Actuate has been a big player in the reporting arena for many years. Previously they specialized in the realm of enterprise reporting applications. However, seeing a ripe opportunity to address a growing market, the idea of an open source reporting platform was proposed.

Most applications have some sort of reporting requirement, and typically the success or failure of a product is hinged on how well that reporting works. The problem with this is that often times reporting in the real world is a challenging issue. Data is typically spread out and not formatted for reporting purposes. There are several different sources such as data warehouses, transactional systems providing website analysis, points of sale, data marts, and all sorts of different collections of data. To top it off, reporting requirements often change based on user requirements and market influences. Because of all this, creating flexible reports becomes a challenge.

Actuate decided to address these kinds of concerns, leveraging their years of experience to create a more modern framework for report development. Keeping in mind the issues that come across, the Actuate developers focused on addressing these issues in a manner that can assist report developers and reach a level of adoption of reports close to total. The Actuate philosophy has been stated on a number of occasions—creating products that allow its customers to get to "100% adoption" of reports. The success of reports can be measured by how well these reports are consumed, and often, if a report is successful, users will ask for more.

The decision was made to create an open source reporting platform. However, the open source market is a funny industry and so Actuate joined forces with an existing open source development community, the Eclipse Foundation, to leverage their existing framework as a base for its application.

BIRT has grown due to support and feedback from the community. The developers pay close attention to the groups out there and listen for comments about the strengths and shortcomings of BIRT in order to improve it. Unlike a lot of open source projects that have only part time developers, BIRT has a team of full time developers dedicated to improving the BIRT platform as a whole. BIRT even has a few "evangelists" dedicated to promoting the understanding and use of BIRT in the developer community.

Features of BIRT

What does BIRT stand for? Certainly it's not everyone's favorite fuzzy uni-browed Muppet in the title slide. BIRT actually stands for Business Intelligence and Reporting Tools. Although not as cute, doesn't the definition just fill you with the same warm fuzzy feelings as a Muppet? It is an open source report development environment built on top of the Eclipse framework. I have emphasized the term "environment" as some of us already know that Actuate doesn't just build "products", they build full fledged platforms for report delivery, and BIRT is no exception to this.

BIRT is what the Actuate corporation sees as the future of its product line. While some may consider it in its "infancy", BIRT is actually a fairly mature product built on top of, and in conjunction with, the Eclipse Foundation and the Eclipse Platform. In the years since BIRT's introduction at the 2004 Actuate Users Conference, BIRT has grown and matured to a full fledged reporting platform, which is something that the open source community has been severely lacking. Their announcement in 2004 really peaked my interest as I was looking for a reporting platform to integrate into Sguil. Ever since my early introduction into the world of MIS and BI, I had to struggle with the lack of a decent open source reporting product, and BIRT delivered on that and more.

At a high level, BIRT can be broken up into two main categories. The one most often considered to be"BIRT" is the report development environment that is used to design and develop reports. The graphical designer runs inside Eclipse and leverages a highly customized workspace. It uses a familiar graphical development paradigm similar to what Macromedia's Dreamweaver would use for designing web pages or Visual Basic for designing programs. It contains a number of drag-and-drop visual and data components.

The second component of BIRT is the Java APIs. This is where BIRT gets so much flexibility from. This allows BIRT to be embedded into any number of Java or J2EE applications. For instance, these APIs provide the Java Servlet Report Viewer that allows for implementing a BIRT report engine into Apache Tomcat. I have provided examples of this, and how to use these APIs on my website.

Some of the features that the BIRT Designer provides out of the box as of the 2.5 release are as follows:

- JDBC Database Reporting
- Extensible data capabilities through the Eclipse ODA Data Connection and the ability to instantiate Java objects within reports
- Joined datasets to allow for multiple data sources in a single report
- Web deployment
- Templates for rapid development of similar formatted reports
- Libraries for sharing common report elements among reports
- Scripting for adding business logic and manipulating report elements and runtime behavior
- Instantiation of Java objects in reports via Mozilla Rhino
- A full blown chart engine with line charts, bar charts, pie charts, and a number of other chart types
- Crosstab reports using the new BIRT cube designer

BIRT provides connections to existing database platforms via JDBC. So, database back-ends such as Oracle, MySQL, and Postgres are all environments that you can connect to and start reporting. Even some of the lesser known platforms that provide JDBC drivers such as HyperSQL (the engine that Sun's Open Office uses) can be used.

For environments that don't provide JDBC, BIRT can leverage the Eclipse Foundations ODA for building custom data connections. For example, Hibernate objects can be reported on via ODA, which is an example that Jason Weathersby from the BIRT Project Management team has demonstrated. If necessary, **Plain Old Java Objects (POJOs)**, can be used as data sources via ODA and through BIRT's scripted data source.

BIRT also allows for joined datasets. This feature allows a user to join two separate data sources, regardless of physical data location, into one logical dataset. So, say for instance you have an HR database with employee information and a training database with corporate training data, these two can be combined into a single logical dataset for use in BIRT reports.

BIRT reports can be distributed via the Web through Apache Tomcat or any J2EE platform such as IBM WebSphere, using the BIRT Report View applet. While the BIRT Web Viewer is an example application, it provides a full set of report viewing features such as page navigation, export to CSV, and PDF format exporting. Additionally, as it is open source, its features can be extended to include authorization. It offers users a set of URL parameters for customizing report calls, or you can simply include the Report Viewer classes in your existing J2EE applications. This is useful for implementing reporting into your own custom portal using technologies such as Ajax and Reportlets or to extend existing applications.

For the interface designers, things that we have come to expect from large projects such as libraries and templates are also features that BIRT has to offer. And of course, for the fan boys out there, including myself, it's open source. And those are just out of the box examples. BIRT is also extensible, with extension points available not just for ODA, but for output formats (Emitters), graphical components, aggregations, chart types, and scripting functions. For example, let's say you need your report output to go to a specialized XML format to be used in an XSLT transformation. You can create a customized Emitter plugin to output that XML.

Eclipse framework

If you've never been exposed to Eclipse before, it can seem somewhat overwhelming. In fact, I'm sure some seasoned Eclipse users would still agree. The Eclipse framework is an interesting one to work with. What started as an **Integrated Development Environment (IDE)** for Java programming has grown into a full fledge framework for application development. With Eclipse, it is possible to develop applications utilizing the already pioneered area of graphical development using Eclipse's SWT and extend Eclipse functionality utilizing Eclipse's Plugin architecture. Applications developed on top of Eclipse can then be deployed as extensions to an already existing Eclipse installation or distributed as **Rich Client Platform (RCP)** standalone applications.

There is a series of core classes that are included with each Eclipse or RCP application. These classes contain all the necessary classes for building and managing the application and the application interface building. The core application is then extended using plugins. Things such as the **Content Versioning System (CVS)** browser, Java IDE, C++ IDE, and various tools in the Web Tools Projects are all plugins to Eclipse.

This is how the BIRT Report Designer works. The Designer API extends the core Eclipse functionality by providing the BIRT perspective with the report palette, the report designer, and ways to execute the BIRT Viewer for report previewing. From the BIRT perspective, this provides some really interesting deployment strategies. For shops that are purely focused on report development, a BIRT RCP application can be deployed to the desktops for developers to work with and not be burdened down with any of the other Eclipse features. This is beneficial where simplicity is key and developers might be confused with Eclipse concepts such as having to change perspectives to access the full features of an Eclipse plugin.

For the more robust development house, the plugin approach would be more ideal. This is beneficial for, let's say, building a larger enterprise Web application utilizing the Eclipse **Web Tools Project (WTP)** for J2EE, and being able to switch over to and utilize BIRT to handle data reporting tasks for this application. This way you can get the best of both worlds, you would have the impressive set of features that WTP offers such as web service creation wizards, server deployments, and the ability to debug applications in Eclipse, and be able to have the WYSIWYG report editor of BIRT for rapid development of data driven user facing interactivity.

This also allows users to develop Java applications that leverage the BIRT Report Engine and quickly switch over to the report designer for you to have your entire development process under one roof. Additionally, you can get the added bonus of utilizing Eclipse's internal tools such as the CVS tool for team project management, or using the free Subclipse third-party plugin for subversion repositories.

Currently, BIRT already leverages ODA for data extensibility, so this is one example of how building on top of the Eclipse framework has benefited the BIRT project. By utilizing the Eclipse Data Tools Project, BIRT can leverage the already existing driver framework and not have to repeat the development cycle.

While previous versions of BIRT included WTP Integration, 2.5 has this as a separate download. This add-on provides several additional project types and deployment wizards that simplify building WTP-based projects that integrate BIRT technologies. There is also a set of JSP tag libraries that make it easy to work with BIRT in JSP pages.

BIRT distributions

As it stands right now, the BIRT report designer comes in two flavors. The distribution I will be discussing in this book is the Eclipse BIRT designer, available at `http://www.eclipse.org/birt`. The Eclipse version of BIRT, which is an open source release under the Eclipse public license, is the fly by the seat of your pants version of BIRT, with all the latest bells and whistles, actively supported by the BIRT community — this is where all the action is if you are interested in the development of an application. If you are a computer tweaker or you like the latest and greatest features, a stable distribution is always available. This is the most popular version of BIRT.

The second version of BIRT is the Actuate BIRT designer. Actuate BIRT is a corporate branded version of BIRT, released by Actuate—the parent company behind the BIRT project, Actuate. This version contains all the same features of the Eclipse BIRT, plus some features that are specific to the Actuate platform such as integration into Actuate Iserver. Actuate's next generation of business intelligence solutions, Actuate 9 and 10, is build on top of BIRT technology, with Actuate's BIRT Report Designer, Business Reports Tools, and Iportal products all being heavily coupled with BIRT.

For the shirts out there who won't consider a product unless there is a professional support unit to call in the middle of the night and scream bloody murder when things don't work, this is the option that you are looking for as the Actuate BIRT is fully supported by Actuate. Actuate BIRT is always based on the latest stable version of BIRT, with additional service fixes. It is also a standalone RCP product. While the Eclipse version is integrated into Eclipse and you can actively use other Eclipse products, the Actuate version is BIRT only.

Conventions used in this book

The purpose of this book is to familiarize users with the BIRT Report Designer. In order to do so, I have decided to alternate between two different scenarios in order to demonstrate the capabilities of BIRT to familiarize you, the reader, with BIRT features, and to allow you an opportunity to follow along.

One set of reports will be built using the Classic Cars example database that comes with every BIRT distribution. This gives us an opportunity to allow you to follow along with examples and try them out on your own. The data schema used in Classic Cars is a simple schema, but it will require at least a basic understanding of SQL to follow along. This will allow me to give you some basic reporting examples such as listing reports, drill down reports, some basic charts, and some of the other BIRT features such as parameters, scripting, and the BIRT report emitters.

However, unlike most other books, I am also providing you an opportunity to follow along with a real life reporting scenario as well. With cooperation from the Eclipse BIRT Project Management Committee, I am also including examples of reports for the BIRT Bugzilla database. I feel these are beneficial to readers not only as a source of learning, but as an example of how the BIRT platform can be used in a real world scenario. This lets the user know that a whole lot of theory and sales pitches aren't the only thing BIRT is good for, but also demonstrates some real world usage of BIRT. This also gives us a chance to demonstrate some of the more advanced capabilities of BIRT itself.

Summary

In this chapter, we looked at the concepts of Business Intelligence and open source software, along with a brief introduction to some of the other players in the open source business intelligence community such as JasperReports and Pentaho. Finally, we got a little background information on some real world requirements for open source reporting projects.

2
Installing BIRT

I'm sure that after discussing the features of BIRT, you're excited to jump right in. Well, you're in luck, as I am equally excited to show how these features will help you. BIRT is a powerful application to meet one's reporting needs, but the first step is to get BIRT and install it. This can be a bit daunting, as BIRT comes in so many different flavors.

In this chapter, we will discuss the various methods of downloading BIRT and installing it. Specifically, we will cover the following:

- Installing the standalone BIRT report designer
- Installing the BIRT Eclipse Plugin through the Eclipse update manager
- Installing the BIRT Eclipse Plugin Manually
- Building BIRT from source

BIRT prerequisites

BIRT has a fairly small set of requirements to run, depending on one's needs.

Software requirements

There are no specific operating system requirements to run BIRT as it is a Java application and it should run on any platform that Java will run on. For the BIRT Report Designer, any platform that runs Eclipse will work. I have successfully run and developed reports under Windows, Linux, and Mac OSX.

 A fair word of warning to the Mac folks: In the past I have run into some performance issues running BIRT under OSX. It has been a few years and this may not be the case anymore, but I would like to put this forth as a cautionary note. If performance of BIRT is poor under OSX, it might be advisable to try to run this tool under a Linux or Windows setup using Parallels or VMWare.

Hardware requirements

As far as hardware requirements, I would recommend at least a Pentium 3 processor with minimum of 512 MB of RAM for the BIRT Report Designer to function without problems. The standalone report engine has much less stringent requirements as it does not run a full blown instance of Eclipse. For the standalone report engine, 256 MB of RAM should suffice, depending on the requirements of the application it is being embedded into.

Where do I get BIRT?

Our first task should be to download BIRT. The typical location for everything BIRT related is the Eclipse website. Browsing to http://www.eclipse.org/birt will take us to the BIRT homepage. Here, we can get the latest news about BIRT, including status of upcoming releases, news on books, conferences, and access to the BIRT newsgroups where we can ask questions about BIRT. The newsgroups are an excellent resource for BIRT questions as they are frequented by the BIRT developers and BIRT Project Management Committee members. The following is a screenshot of the current BIRT project homepage:

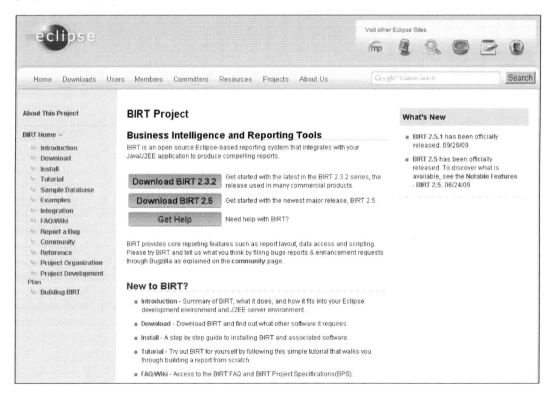

The homepage is also where one can get the various BIRT distributions such as the All-In-One Eclipse package. This distribution contains a prepackaged version of Eclipse, which is configured with BIRT, the BIRT Standalone Report Designer, and contains information about retrieving and building BIRT from source.

At the time of this writing, 2.6 is the latest BIRT release, which is what we will be referring to throughout this book. The same steps will work with all previous versions of BIRT, unless otherwise noted

There are several installation paths to choose from. The one I highly recommend is the BIRT All-in-One package. One can also install BIRT as a plugin to go into an already existing Eclipse installation or one can retrieve the BIRT Standalone RCP package. The chapter will give detailed information about each one of these packages along with the benefits of, and the reasons to use each method.

In addition to the BIRT homepage, we can also retrieve BIRT from the BIRT Exchange. The BIRT Exchange is an Actuate sponsored website that contains information on all things, including open source BIRT, commercial BIRT, and BIRT-based products. The BIRT Exchange also has a helpful community section with message boards where users can ask questions regarding BIRT, post and download examples, and participate in contests for the most useful submissions of the month. It is located at `http://www.birt-exchange.com`.

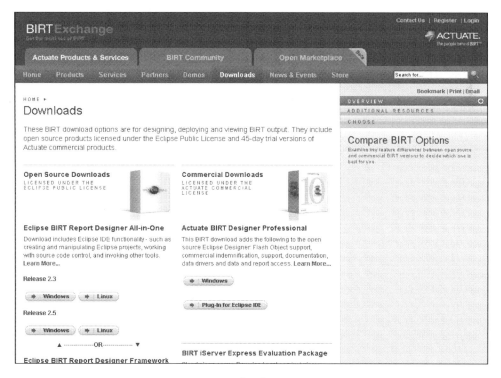

Installing BIRT from the All-In-One package

The BIRT All-in-One package is the easiest BIRT package to install, so it will be the first one we will go for. The BIRT All-in-One package is a BIRT distribution that contains a full Eclipse installation preconfigured with BIRT. I usually use this as the base installation for Eclipse and add plugins accordingly. BIRT can have some tricky issues with configuration that I have come across in the past, and since then, I avoid these by installing the All-in-One package.

As with most BIRT installations, the All-in-One package is available from the **Download BIRT** link. This will typically take us to the current, stable release of BIRT. The developers seem to agree that the All-in-One package is the typical way to go as it is the first link on the page. The following is a screenshot of what the BIRT download page looks like:

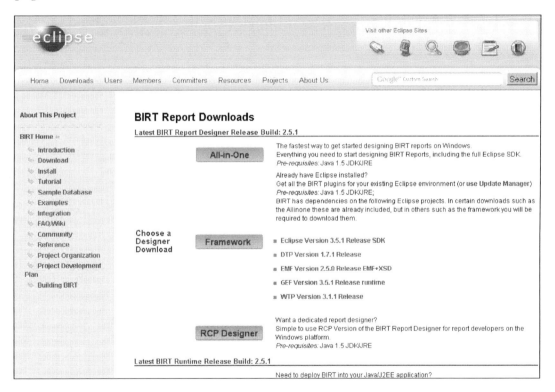

Additionally, older and pre-released versions of BIRT are available from the "More Downloads" section of the BIRT's download page, under the "full BIRT 2.x Download Page", where x is the subversion, such as 2.3, 2.5. or 2.6. From this link, you can retrieve older releases, current milestone builds, and the latest nightly release for those who want to stay on the cutting edge

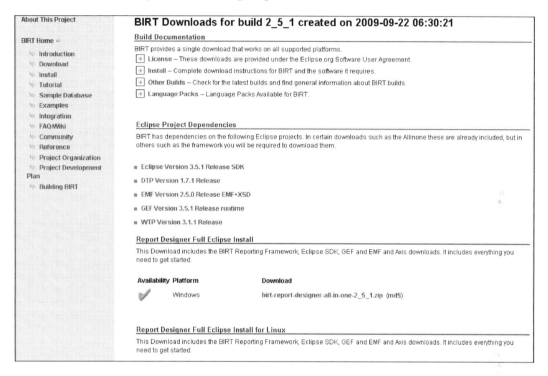

This screenshot is the full download page for BIRT 2.5.1. From here the various installation packages can be retrieved such as the RCP Standalone Report Designer, the BIRT Source Code, and various other runtime libraries and demo databases. Because we are installing the All-in-One, we will download the release for Windows.

The BIRT All-in-One installation package is a large ZIP file (roughly 150 MB), so for individuals who already have an Eclipse installation and are limited by a small amount of bandwidth, this may not be an attractive option. But for individuals with access to a high-speed Internet connection or those who do not have an existing Eclipse installation, this will work out fine. This ZIP file contains a full Eclipse installation with the BIRT plugins already installed and preconfigured for use.

Installation of the BIRT All-in-One package is as simple as opening the ZIP file in an archiving utility such as WinZip and extracting the contents to an installation directory of one's choice. I typically use C:\Eclipse as my base installation directory.

Installing BIRT All-in-One under Linux

On Linux, installation is similar. The archive file containing the All-in-One package is a standard Linux tarball file. One recommendation for the Linux installers is to use Sun's Java instead of the GNU Java. The GNU Java is compliant to an older specification of Java than BIRT requires, and some features will not work correctly under Linux. Installing Sun Java under Linux can vary based on the distribution of Linux one uses and the distributor's views of the Sun license for Java. I have chronicled my experiences getting Sun Java to work under Ubuntu Linux (a free desktop-based distribution of Linux based on Debian) as well as CentOS (a free alternative to Red Hats Enterprise Linux) on my blog.

 OpenJDK contains a version of `js.jar` that needs to be replaced with BIRT's version in order for BIRT to work correctly.

Also, based on the version of BIRT we run, we will need one of two different Java versions. For BIRT versions prior to 2.2, we will need Java 1.4, and for 2.2 and later, we will need Java 1.5. This is the same for Windows or any Unix-like operating system.

Once installed, we will extract the BIRT All-in-One archive to our target location. This will vary based on file management philosophy implied and the purpose of the system in question. For example, on a multiuser desktop system, we may choose to extract this archive to the `/home/yourUserName` folder so that no one except for the logged in user can have access to BIRT. If we wish to set this up on a single user desktop or set it up for multiple users, we may set this up under the `/`, `/usr`, `/usr/local`, or some other dedicated folder location.

Installation of BIRT through the Eclipse Plugin update program

This section covers the installation of BIRT using the Eclipse plugin manager. Suppose we already have an Eclipse instance that we use regularly. Because Eclipse can typically be a rather large package, installing a separate instance may not be feasible due to disk space constraints, I.T. policy, or some other limiting factor. In cases such as these, it is more appropriate to add to our existing Eclipse installation.

If one takes it upon himself/herself to install BIRT as a set of plugins, he/she must also install all the prerequisite plugins that the BIRT designer is built on top of. This is part of what makes the All-in-One installation method preferable to the manual installation of plugins. Another reason is that this is the avenue in which I have traditionally encountered the most installation problems such as dependency issues.

In order to proceed, we must first make sure the following dependency packages are installed with BIRT.

BIRT 2.6	BIRT 2.5.2	BIRT 2.3.2.2
HYPERLINK "http://download.eclipse.org/eclipse/downloads/drops/R-3.6-201006080911" Eclipse Version 3.6 SDK	Eclipse Version 3.5.1 Release SDK	Eclipse Version 3.4.2 SDK
HYPERLINK "http://download.eclipse.org/datatools/downloads/1.8/dtp_1.8.0.zip" DTP Version 1.8.0	DTP Version 1.7.1 Release	DTP Version 1.6.2
HYPERLINK "http://www.eclipse.org/modeling/emf/downloads/?project=emf" EMF Version 2.6.0 EMF+XSD	EMF Version 2.5.0 Release EMF+XSD	EMF Version 2.4.2 EMF+XSD
HYPERLINK "http://www.eclipse.org/gef/downloads" GEF Version 3.6.0 runtime	GEF Version 3.5.1 Release runtime	GEF Version 3.4.2 runtime
HYPERLINK "http://download.eclipse.org/webtools/downloads/drops/R3.2.0/R-3.2.0-20100615235519" WTP Version 3.2.0	WTP Version 3.1.1 Release	WTP Version 3.0.4

These requirements can be installed separately alongside your BIRT plugin installation, given that one includes the appropriate repositories. Plugin installation is done through the **Eclipse Software Update** menu, located under the **Help** toolbar menu, under **Install New Software...**.

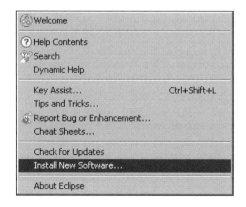

Once in the software update tool, there are two options we can select. We have the option of searching for updates or to install new features. If we do not already have BIRT installed, we should choose **Install New Features**. Otherwise, we can get updates to our existing BIRT installation by choosing **Search for updates**.

If we choose to update existing software, the software update tool will prompt us to verify which repositories or mirror sites to check for updates from. If we chose to install new updates, we will have to complete an extra step in choosing the list of repositories to search for new software in. As BIRT has been a member of the Eclipse consortium since 2004, it has been listed under the sites to include in one's search; one doesn't need to add BIRT as a new repository to search under. This makes things much easier.

However, as BIRT is collaborating with a number of other Eclipse projects such as the Web Tools Project for site deployment and the Data Tools Project for a future revision of the query editor inside of BIRT, in order to leverage their tools, we will need to include their repositories in our update search path.

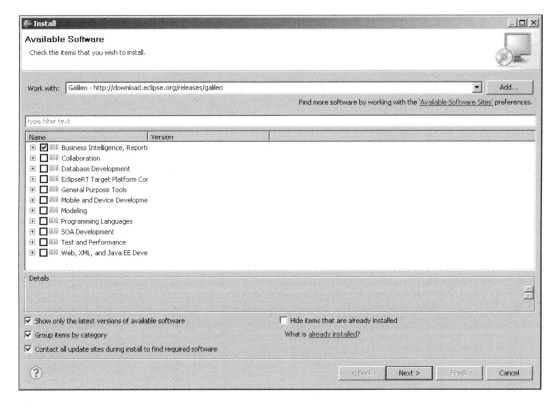

Now, with the correct repositories and projects selected, we click **Next**. A list of details about the installation will be shown. Once we verify that the correct packages and dependencies have been selected, a license will be presented and we must agree to it. When we click **Ok**, the installation will continue. Installation can take anywhere from 10 to 30 minutes depending on network speed.

Building BIRT from source

There are instances when it is desirable to build BIRT from its source distribution—if we are modifying BIRT, investigating a bug, or want to enhance the core of BIRT in some way. These are rare cases, but it is good to know how to build BIRT from source just in case. The following will walk you through building BIRT 2.5.2, but will work for 2.6 as well.

The first step is to retrieve the BIRT source code. The BIRT source is available from the BIRT Eclipse hompage. For 2.5.2, this is under `http://download.eclipse.org/birt/ downloads/build.php?build=R-R1-2_5_2-201002221500`. The source package is located under the section labeled BIRT Source Code. Note the instructions saying there might be other libraries to install. We will probably need to download the Eclipse Data Tools project source code as well. We retrieve the ZIP file, but do not extract it. One will need a working copy of Eclipse in order to proceed. Here, we will be using an already extracted version of BIRT 2.5.2. It is recommended to have a version of the Java 5 JDK installed and set up as the compiler in an Eclipse workspace, and that the compiler settings are set to a level of Java 5. Also, under **Window/General/Workspace**, it is better to set the **Text File Encoding** to **UTF-8**.

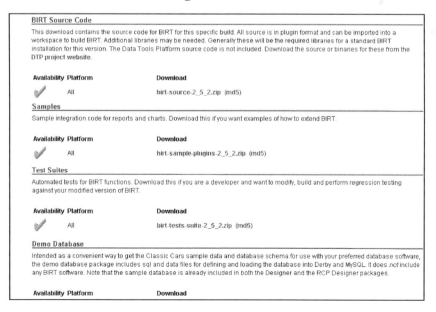

Let's open our copy of Eclipse. When prompted, we create a new workspace called BirtSourceCode_2_5_2 in the directory of our choice.

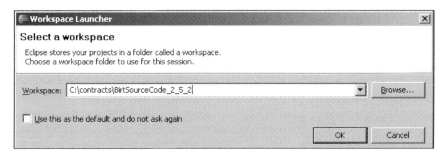

Next we right-click on the **Project Explorer**, and select **Import**, and then **Import...** from its context menu.

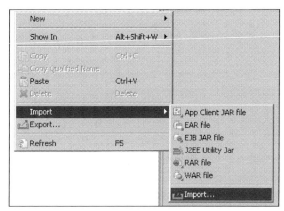

Under the **General** section, we select **Existing Projects into Workspace**.

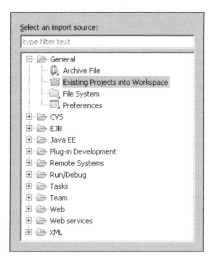

Let's selectelect the **Archive File** option and point to the location where we downloaded the BIRT 2.5.2 source ZIP file. We now select all of the projects within the archive and click **Finish**. If we get prompted by the install process about duplicate projects for WTP (Eclipse Web Tools Project), we just need to click **Yes to all**.

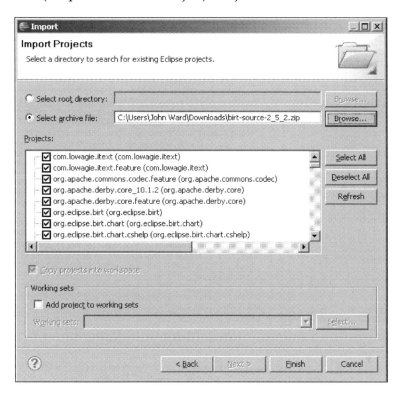

Once imported, Eclipse will start building the workspace. This can take from up to an hour depending on the speed of machine.

There will be a bunch of errors that may appear on machine. All these errors are related to the .nl projects. For our purposes, we do not need these projects. If we see an error saying that there is an invalid character constant in the Excel emitter, we will need to go to **Window/Preferences/General/Workspace** and set the character encoding to **UTF-8**.

To remove these errors, we open the window listing the log of errors, select all the errors, right-click, and select the **Show In | Package Explorer** option.

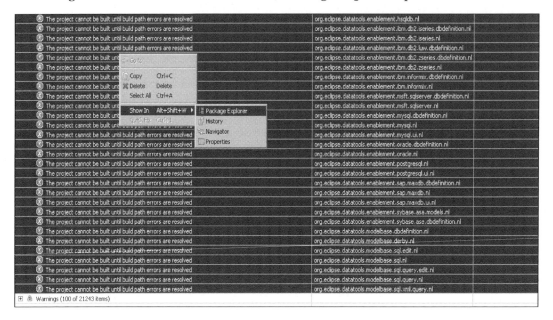

The projects with errors will be highlighted in the **Project Explorer** view. We can right-click on any one of the projects and choose **Close Project**.

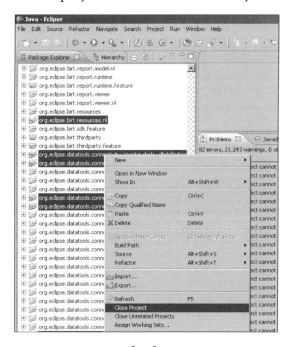

Once the workspace is generated, we will have the BIRT core JARs built and ready. From here, there are a number of things one can do. One can select the **Run Configurations menu** option, and choose to run the BIRT Designer RCP run configuration to have a standalone BIRT designer application.

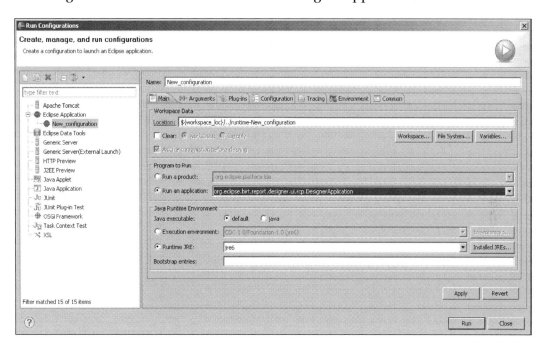

Summary

In this chapter, we looked at a number of different installation methods, including:

- The All-in-One package
- Installing through the Eclipse Software Update

We have seen where to get BIRT, how to install it, and a list of the requirements needed to run BIRT. Now, before getting into the heart of BIRT report design, we should first get acquainted with the BIRT development environment.

3
The BIRT Environment and First Report

Now that we have BIRT installed BIRT, what next? We have heard so many great things about the BIRT Report Designer and are eager to jump into creating some reports. For someone who hasn't worked with eclipse or BIRT, the BIRT Designer can look a little intimidating and, in some cases, we may not even see the BIRT Designer on first run. That's fine. In this chapter, we will get acquainted with the BIRT working environment—also known as the BIRT Perspective in Eclipse Lingo—and get started with creating a basic report.

A basic scenario

When I teach people about development topics of any sort, I like to use scenarios. This book will be no different. The scenarios provide a basic context for the learner to relate the topic information to, and hopefully help in facilitating information retention.

So, in this chapter we will look at a simple scenario in order to get us started with our first report. Assume you work for a toy company called Classic Cars. Classic Cars specializes in selling models of classic cars and motorcycles. Classic Cars uses a centralized database for all company operations, such as employee listing, offices, customers, products, and sales history. This information is in a relational database that is stored locally on your machine, as Classic Cars is a small company.

In this chapter, I will walk you through creating your first report that will be a list of all products that a particular customer has bought in the past. I choose this for a number of reasons. First, it is a fairly simple database query to build and understand. If you are not familiar with the SQL language, don't worry; I will provide you with the queries. However, I do highly recommend that you get some basic familiarity with database concepts, and SQL in particular.

While going through this report, I will introduce you to the BIRT working environment and show you where to get access to the various portions of the BIRT Designer. Finally, I will show you where you can refer to another guided tutorial, accessible right within the BIRT environment. You might as well have access to all available resources for further learning.

The BIRT perspective

We are ready to begin. We have defined a clear objective for our basic report, and now is the time to jump into the basic concepts of the BIRT Environment.

Once we start BIRT/Eclipse for the first time, we will be asked to select a location for our workspace.

A workspace is the location where projects get stored. This is very useful for Java developers who may want to reuse projects. However, for a report developer, a single workspace should suffice. In our case, we will set our workspace to `C:\eclipse\birt_book_workspace`.

If you're running the BIRT All-in-One package, you will start up in the default Eclipse screen and will need to change to the BIRT report perspective. Eclipse uses different "perspectives" as interfaces for different functionality and tools for particular tasks. For instance, if we are writing a Java program, we would use one of the Java perspectives available. This would allow us access to outlines, class views, and other relevant tabs. If we are debugging a program, we would use the debug perspective. This perspective gives you access to a tab with variables, tools bars for controlling the flow of programs, breakpoints, and other debugging functions.

For our purposes, we will use the BIRT reporting perspective, which will give us access to the BIRT report building elements that we need in report development. The BIRT report perspective can always be accessed from one of the few ways to open perspectives in Eclipse. One such is from the menu bar under **Window | Open Perspective | Report Design** (if available), or under **Other... | Report Design**. Typically, the **Open Perspective** icon is on the upper right-hand side for quicker access.

The BIRT workbench

In Eclipse, the main work area is called the workbench. Once we open the BIRT perspective, we will be looking at the Eclipse workbench with the BIRT perspective.

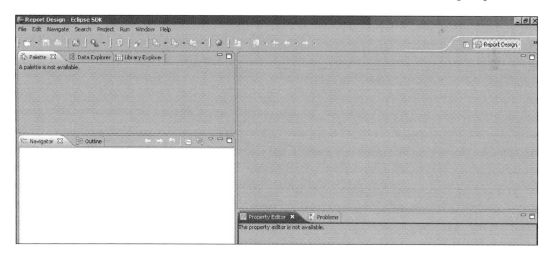

The BIRT perspective is broken up into several different sections by default, which are all customizable by the user. For this book, we will keep the defaults. But if one wishes to change the layout, he/she needs to only drag-and-drop any of the workbench tabs to another section.

The Navigator

The first section under the BIRT workspace that we will discuss is the Navigator. The Navigator is fairly universal among Eclipse perspectives, as it is used to browse the current workspace for contained projects. Under the Navigator, we can create and manage projects, reports, libraries, templates, and various other files that would be contained in our projects. If we want to rename the folder or create folders to organize report elements such as file locations, this can all be done under the Navigator. The Navigator can be used to do many of the same functions that we can perform under the **File** menu bar. If our workspace contains many different reporting projects, we can use the **Navigator** to go into those projects so that other projects are not visible during editing.

In the following screenshot, I have a single project called **StyleSheetExample** with a single report design file and a report library, which we will discuss later in the book. From this menu, you can see that the right arrow is available that will allow me to go into the **StyleSheetExample** project, which is like double-clicking on a folder in Windows Explorer. I also have the Sync with Editor double arrows clicked 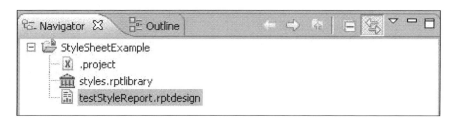, which allows me to automatically give focus to each of these items if they are open in Eclipse.

So, when shall one use multiple reports in a single project, or why would one want to break out projects instead of storing all their reports in a single project? This is really a matter of preference. I typically store reports based on real-life projects. So if I were doing an earnings report for the fourth quarter, I would create a single project called Fourth Quarter Earning Reports with a summary report containing graphs, high-level areas such as regions of the country, and all my detailed reports that would get linked when a user clicks on a portion of the graph or region in a single project. This allows me to keep report projects separated. If I were building an online reporting portal that used many shared components, I would also put them in their own project with a library housing the shared components. This is useful as online reports have the tendency to require multiple subreports and very rarely can be captured in a single report. We will discuss libraries in depth in *Chapter 7, Report Projects and Libraries* and linked reports in *Chapter 10, Deployment* .

The Outline

Next on the agenda is the Outline. Now if there was one portion of the BIRT perspective that is often overlooked, and yet provides a good return value when used, it would be the Outline.

The Outline provides a hierarchical view of a report structure that we can use to select and edit properties, view events, and edit scripts. Often, it is the best way to get access to particular elements of a report for editing with precision and without the hassle of attempting to select them in the graphical editor. It is easy to expand high-level elements and select contained report elements such as rows, cells, and groups. Rather than having to muck around with the Report Designer to find the element we are changing, we have it right at our fingertips with the Outline. It also makes things easier when we begin scripting to ensure that we are writing a script for the correct components. I can tell from experience that it is an incredibly useful view, and learning how to use it can save time and headaches in the long run.

The following screenshot shows an expanded view of a simple report demonstrating the different elements of reports that are visible in a report outline. We can see the data sources, datasets, the fields in the dataset, the visual report elements, libraries, and library components.

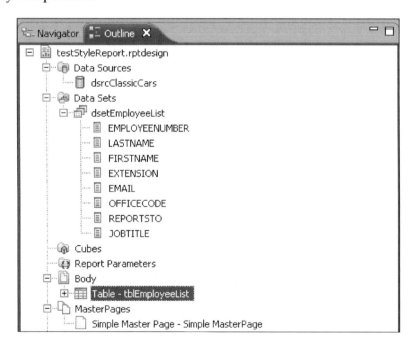

The Palette

Now, taking a page out of the book of many other visual IDEs, BIRT provides a component palette that contains visual report design components. Just like in Visual Basic, one can drag-and-drop components such as buttons, textboxes, and labels on to a form. BIRT allows us to drag-and-drop visual report components such as labels, data text items, HTML text items, graphics, and layout modifiers such as grids and tables. In the next chapter, we will cover the various report components, their purpose, and how each one is used in a report.

One new element in BIRT 2.3 and above is the inclusion of an Aggregation element. Previously, all aggregations were done through expressions. However, now we can add new aggregations to a visual element in BIRT report designs. This element is also extendible using the BIRT aggregation extension point as demonstrated in my IBM Developerworks article "Using BIRT Extension Points: Aggregations" at `http://www.ibm.com/developerworks/opensource/library/os-eclipse-birtextpts/index.html`. If you have Java experience, this approach provides significant options.

We will discuss aggregations in greater depth in a later chapter.

Now although we have not gotten into the topic of scripting in BIRT, it is worth mentioning that the palette does change when you open up the script editor in BIRT to give a simplified view of the different low-level script objects that are available. If this is a topic that we have not gotten to, why do I mention it here? Because this is one of those things that I wish I had known about early on in my BIRT development experience, and which I didn't find out until later and kicked myself for not knowing about it. As strange as that sounds, you will thank me when we get there. The following screenshot shows the BIRT **Palette** when editing a script, showing available functions and objects:

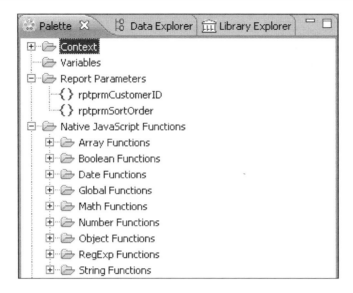

The Data Explorer

A report development environment would not be very useful if it didn't have any means or mechanism for managing data connections. The **Data Explorer** view provides this capability.

The **Data Explorer** provides several different data-related functions from where we can manage data connections to our data sources. For example, this is one of the locations where we can manage our database connections and drivers, and any sort of custom data adapters. We will also manage our data queries from this pane. And finally, this is the place where we will manage the **Report Parameters** that the report consumer will use to interact and pass in data to our report for processing.

Introduced in BIRT version 2.2 is the ability to manage cubes, which we will cover later on in the book. This option did not exist in the previous versions of BIRT. By adding this feature, we have the ability to maintain multidimensional data cubes for use with the Crosstab component.

It is important to note that this is not the only place one can manage his/her data-related objects. One can also manage these items from his/her report outline. This gives a little bit of flexibility depending on which views are open in designer.

New to BIRT 2.5 is the **Variables** section. This allows a report developer to create a variable inside of a global array for use in BIRT scripting and events. Although there is already a mechanism to do this via the Rhino JavaScript engine, this provides a visual element. This comes in handy when working with BIRT scripts as we do not need to remember where variables are declared and what they are called; we can reference this section to ease development. This is also different from global variables created in scripts. The variables created here are stored in an array called VARS. The variables are also useful when creating auto text elements to display on the Master Page(s). We will cover this more in depth in *Chapter 9, Scripting and Event Handling*.

Resource Explorer

Depending on the version of BIRT we are using, this is either called the Library Explorer or the Resource Explorer. The **Resource Explorer** has been expanded to show all the resources within a BIRT reporting project. With it, we can see libraries within our project, image files, scripts, and stylesheets. Using the **Resource Explorer**, we can include these for use in our report.

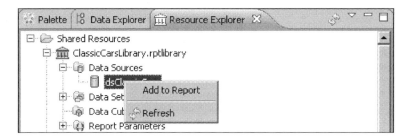

Property Editor

Now with any visual development IDE, we have the ability to change and manipulate various properties for visual components. BIRT provides this ability through the **Property Editor**. The properties we would expect such as font attributes (for example, size and weighting), alignment, and color are available through the Property Editor. But there are other features of the Property Editor such as value formatting, hyperlinking, table of contents entries for online reports, element to data binding, the ability to set conditional visual properties known as highlights, and enumerated value replacements called Maps that are all available from the Property Editor.

For example, let's say I was doing a financial report. Now with a column of financial data, I would want to right-justify it so the decimal numbers line up. I would also want to make the font of my column headers bold, set the values to display as currency with a preceding dollar sign, and display only two decimal places. This is all set through the Property Editor.

In addition, if an account status is stored as a number and I want the report to display an actual text representation—assuming that there is not a table in my database that contains this mapping—I would assign a map to my display element with the possible values and their display representation. I would also make bold the font of the accounts that were in danger of defaulting.

The Property Editor is particularly a large beast that we will be revisiting many times throughout the course of this book. As I indicated in the outline section, which is also a helpful hint, the Property Editor and the Outline make a very useful combination when setting report parameters—especially with visual elements in complex reports.

The **Properties** pane allows users to set various properties for report elements. Things such as font size, boldness, and italics can be set here for text-based elements. Data bindings for list elements and table elements are set here, and really tricky things such as highlighting conditions for setting up alternating colors for rows are accessed here.

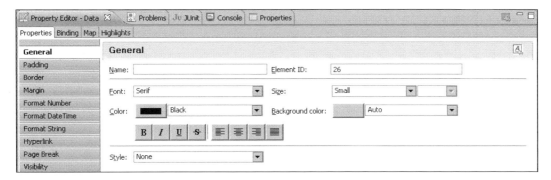

Report Designer

In any visual IDE on the market, there is a part of the user interface that allows a developer to manipulate the look and feel of what they are developing. In programming environments such as Visual Basic, this would be the Form designer. In web development environments such as Adobe Dreamweaver, this is the designer tab. In BIRT, we use the Report Designer. The Report Designer is the section of the BIRT workspace that takes up the most real estate by default. It is denoted by the title of the report design that is currently open and has multiple tabs along the bottom.

Reports need to have an interface to the user in which the report can be constructed, and this is that location. This is where we drag the visual components from the Palette in order to work with them and get the correct look and feel necessary to display the required information. Working with the Report Designer can be a little tricky if one has no idea of what to expect, so let me set your expectations now. BIRT is not a pixel perfect, what you see is what you get (WYSIWYG) development environment. So, if one expects to design perfect visual layouts for reports for use in print, or a pixel-perfect design interface such as Visual Basic, BIRT does not provide this out of the box. BIRT is designed as a primarily online report technology, and as such it is heavily HTML driven. So it uses a design interface similar to the one Dreamweaver or NVU has. BIRT, out of the box, does not provide layers. In the Report Designer, components will be resized, shaped, and adjusted to give an approximation of how an HTML engine will render it. Most of the alignment and an idea of the proximity of report items is demonstrated in the following screenshot:

The designer also has several other tabs associated with it. The **Master Page** tab will open a designer that allows users to design a constant header and footer layout that will remain persistent on multipage reports. These would be separate from the table headers and rows used in the Layout Editor.

The Script tag is for the more advanced report developers and allows for overloading report events associated with report elements. BIRT uses an event-based model for report rendering. So overloading particular events allows the user to control and manipulate at a much finer level the way a particular report will be displayed to the user. This also allows report developers to add in advanced business logic to report designs. BIRT utilizes the Mozilla Rhino JavaScript engine to accomplish this. In addition to the internal report script, BIRT also allows developers to provide event handlers in external Java objects.

The following screenshot shows the BIRT script editor overriding an event for a Table object. Notice that the drop-down box displays the event method that is being overridden. Next to it is a button labeled **Reset Method**, which will delete all the code in the editor and bring the event handler back to a default state. And next to it is a label indicating the name of the element that we are setting an event handler for.

It is important to note from experience that again the Outline provides an invaluable tool for script editing. It allows a developer to validate that he or she is developing an event handler for the correct component. Too often with report development in BIRT, a developer will select an incorrect component using the Layout Editor. Also, as the Layout Editor is not visible when the Script Editor is open, the Outline provides a convenient mechanism to switch between elements.

```
hideTable.rptdesign  ×

onPrepare                                          ▼  Reset Method   Table
//We only want to add this into our code when the value is set to true to
//hide the report table
if ( params["rprmAddGroup"] == true )
{
    //Bring in the BIRT Report Model API scripting elements for using the StructureScriptAPIFactory
    importPackage( Packages.org.eclipse.birt.report.engine.api.script.element );

    //Create a dynamic sort condition
    var groupCondition = StructureScriptAPIFactory.createGroup();

    groupCondition.setKeyExpr("row[\"A\"]");

    //set condition to ascending order
    groupCondition.setSortDirection("asc");
    groupCondition.setSortType("asc");

    //Add to the table
    this.addGroup(sortCondition);
}

Layout  Master Page  Script  XML Source  Preview
```

For those who are gluttons for punishment, we can view the actual XML source for a report page. Personally, I rarely use the XML source viewer except to copy report source code when helping individuals in the BIRT newsgroup.

And finally there is the **Preview** tab. This is a convenient way to preview how a report will look like without having the application to launch a separate window with the report viewer. This is different to actually running the report using either the **Outline** or using the **Run** options under the **File** menu. For one, it does not provide pagination, so report previews will come out as one continuous HTML page. Additionally, no navigation elements are available when using the report preview function.

Setting up a simple project

Now that we are familiar with the different aspects of the BIRT Workspace, what next? What does it all mean, how does it all work together, and how do we use it? Well, that is what we are going to explore next as we build a simple report. As far as the components are concerned, we will describe them in detail in the next chapter. So for now just follow along and see how to navigate in the BIRT environment.

The first thing we want to do when setting up our simple report project is to define what the project is going to be, and what our first simple report will do. Our first report will be a simple dump of the employees who work for Classic Cars.

First, we need to set up a project. To do this, we will use the Navigator. We need to make sure we have the BIRT report perspective open as described previously. We perform the following steps to create our project:

- Open up the **Navigator** by clicking on the **Navigator** tab.
- Right-click anywhere in the whitespace in the **Navigator**.
- Select **New** from the menu, and under **New** select **Project.**
- From the dialog screen, select **Business Intelligence and Reporting Tools** from the list of folders, expand that view, and select **Report Project**. Then click the **Next** button.

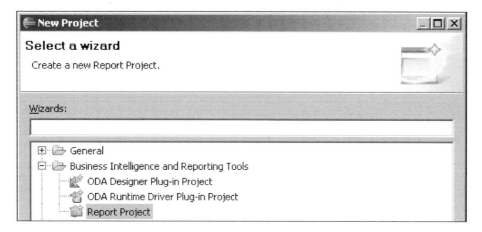

- For the project name, enter **Classic Cars BIRT Reports**. We can either leave the **Use Default Location** checkbox selected, or unselect it and enter a location on our local drive to store this report project.

Now, we have a simple report project in which we will store our BIRT reports that we will built in the first few chapters of the book.

Creating a simple report

Now that we have our first project open, we will look at creating our first report. As mentioned previously, we will create a basic listing report that will display all the information in the employees table. In order to do this, use the following steps:

1. Right-click on the **Class_Cars_BIRT_Reports** project under the **Navigator**, and choose **New Report**.

2. Make sure the **Class_Cars_BIRT_Reports** project is highlighted in the **New Report** dialog and enter the name as EmployeeList.rptdesign. I chose this name as it is somewhat descriptive of the purpose of the report, which is to display a list of employees. As a rule of thumb, always try to name reports after the expected output, such as QuarterlyEarningReport.rptDesign, weeklyPayStub.rptDesign, or accountsPayable.rptDesign.

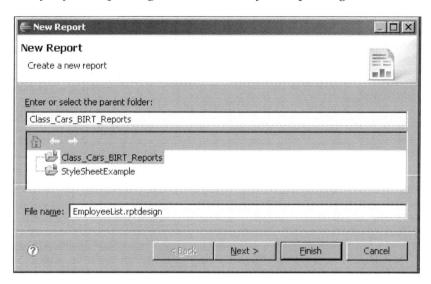

3. The next screen has a list of different report templates we can use. We will select **Simple Listing** and then click on the **Finish** button.

4. Go to the **Data Explorer**, right-click on **Data Sources**, and choose **New Data Source**.

5. From the **New Data Source** dialog, select **Classic Models Inc. Sample Database** and click on the **Next** button.

6. On the next screen, the driver information is presented. Ignore this for now and click on the **Finish** button.

7. Under the **Data Explorer**, right-click on **Data Sets** and choose **New Data Set**.

8. On the next screen, enter the **Data Set Name** as dsetEmployee, and make sure that our created Data Source is selected in the list of data sources. Then click the **Next** button when this is finished.

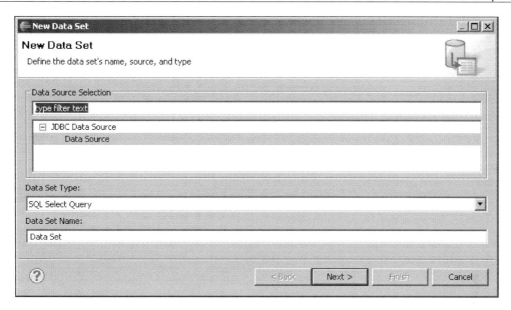

9. In the **Query Dialog**, enter the following query and click the **Finish** button:

    ```
    select
    *
    from
    CLASSICMODELS.EMPLOYEES
    ```

10. In the next screen, just click the **OK** button. This screen is used to edit information about Data Sets, and we will ignore it for now.

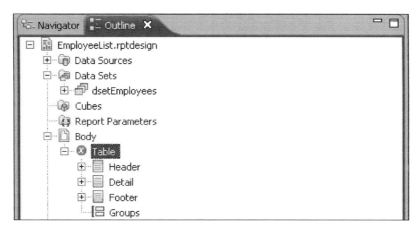

11. Now, from the Outline, select **Data Sets** and expand it to show all of the fields. Drag-and-drop the **EMPLOYEENUMBER** element over to the Report Designer and drop it on the cell with the label of **Detail Row**. This will be the second row and the first column. You might see an error in the table. Ignore it for now. This will be here until we finish dragging elements over and save the report.

12. We will notice that when we do this, the header row also gets an element placed in it called **EMPLOYEENUMBER**. This is the **Header** label. Double-click on this cell and it will be highlighted. We can now edit it. Type in **Employee ID**.

13. Drag-and-drop the **LASTNAME, FIRSTNAME**, and **JOBTITLE** to the detail cells to the right of the **EMPLOYEENUMBER** cell.

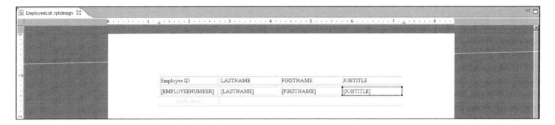

14. Now, we want to put the header row in bold font. Under the **Outline**, select the **Row** element located under **Body | Table | Header**. This will change the **Property Editor** contents. Click on **Font**, and then click the **Bold** button.

And that's it! We have created our first basic report. To see what this report looks like, under the **Report Designer** pane, click on the **Preview** tab. Alternatively, we can actually **Run** the report and get an idea of what this report will look like in the BIRT Report Viewer application by going up to **File | View Report** in the web browser. This option is also available by right-clicking on the **Report Design file** under the **Navigator**, choosing **Report**, and then clicking **Run**.

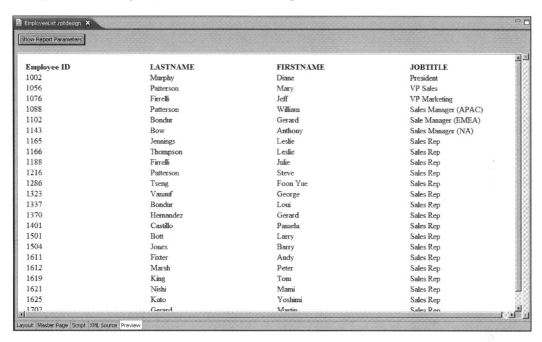

Although it may be a simple report, this exercise demonstrated how a report developer can get through the BIRT environment and how the different elements of the BIRT perspective work together.

The hidden views

BIRT includes two additional views that are not open by default. These views can be used for reference—the Report Examples View and the Chart Examples View. These two views include example reports that can be used as a starting point for many different types of reports and chart types, or as a reference if we want to use a particular feature in our own reports.

These views are available from the **Window** menu, under **Show View | Other**. They are located under the **Report and Chart Design** section.

Once opened, the views will appear in the same area as the **Properties Editor**. When the desired report is located, we can right-click on it and choose **Open**. When we do, it prompts us to create a new reporting project and store the example report there.

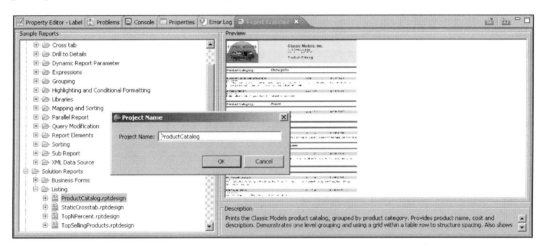

One can use this feature to familiarize himself/herself with the different report types and reporting features that BIRT offers, which we will be covering in this book.

Getting access to cheat sheets and the simple listing report tutorial within Eclipse

You may have noticed an area to the right of the screen in the previous exercise with instructions on how to build report. This is called a cheat sheet. Cheat sheets show up by default whenever a report template is used. Cheat sheets are accessible from the **Help | Cheat Sheets...** menu.

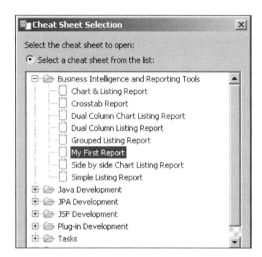

If you'd like access to another tutorial similar to Simple Listing, which we did earlier in this chapter, there is one available under **Help** from within Eclipse. It is also available as a cheat sheet called **My First Report**.

- Open the **Help** menu.
- Select **Cheat Sheets....**
- Select **My First Report**.

- Click on the **Click to perform** link.

- Once completed, we will be in the Eclipse Help file. Follow the instructions in the Eclipse Help File to go through the tutorial. It never hurts to practice report building skills.

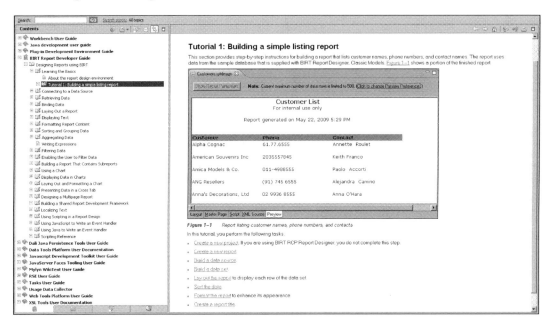

Summary

For a very simple report design, we utilized all of the major areas of the BIRT perspective. We used the Navigator to create a new report project and a new report design, and the Data Explorer to create a data connection and dataset. We dragged elements from the Outline to the Report Designer to get the data elements into the right place, and we used both the Property Editor and Outline cooperatively to make the font of the text in the table header bold.

In the coming chapters, we will build more complex reports, and in the process, explain what the various BIRT report elements are, and what they can do.

4
Visual Report Items

The previous chapter looked at the BIRT workspace. One should be familiar with the environment he/she will use to build BIRT reports. This chapter will take a look at each of the individual BIRT report elements, some of their uses, and some of their common properties. By gaining some familiarity with these components, we can save ourselves a fair amount of headache while working with BIRT. A surprising number of questions come up while performing some of the more common functions using BIRT components such as how to format numbers as currency or limit decimal places, and how to format dates, along with a few other questions that can be influenced by using simple BIRT properties.

BIRT report components aren't radically different from other visual components used in other visual development environments and report designers. We have some of our more common visual components such as text labels, data bound text elements, and graphics. For those who are already familiar with a web development environment, there are some formatting components that you might already be familiar with such as grids that are similar in function to HTML tables. Then there are some more advanced components such as graphs, tables, cross-tabs, and aggregations.

This chapter will take a look at a number of these components and some of their common uses.

Labels

In almost any development environment, you have static text elements—the elements that won't change for one reason or the other. Common uses of static text elements are as field identifiers in online web forms, identification of what some piece of data is, instruction for how to use an application, on screen prompts, and titles. Reporting is no exception to this rule. In reporting, one can see this type of static text content used as column headers for listings, report titles, and as footer information such as copyright lines. BIRT provides this in the form of Labels. The following is the icon used on the development palette for the Label.

In the previous chapter, we saw Labels used as the column headers in our employee listing report, although we didn't have to create them explicitly. We got to see one of the properties for Labels when we changed it and made it bold. This illustrated one of the most common properties of the Label component—font information. This will be the most common property to work with when one works with labels, although it is not the only one.

The Label report item is one of the most common and least technical report items to work with. We are going to create a simple report to demonstrate the properties used with this component. Follow the sequence of steps:

1. Right-click on the Class_Cars_BIRT_Reports project under the **Navigator** tab and choose **New | Report**.

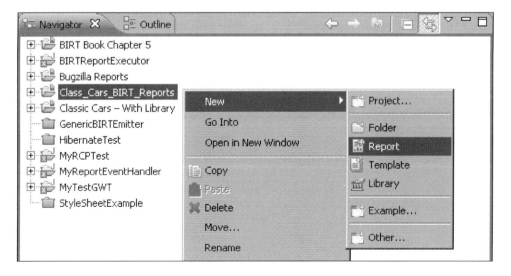

2. Make sure the `Class_Cars_BIRT_Reports` project is highlighted in the **New Report** dialog box and enter the **File name** as `HelloWorld.rptDesign`. Notice that we haven't used a space in the filename. This is because some operating systems have issues with spaces in names and it is considered bad etiquette in others to use spaces even if they are allowed.

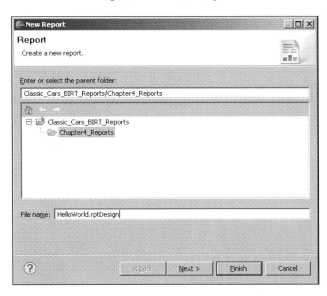

3. Select **Blank Report** from the list of **Report templates** and click **Finish**.

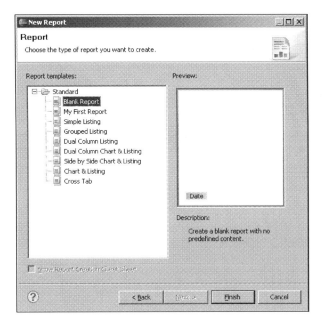

4. From the **Palette**, click on the **Label** and drag-and-drop it over to the **Report Design** pane.

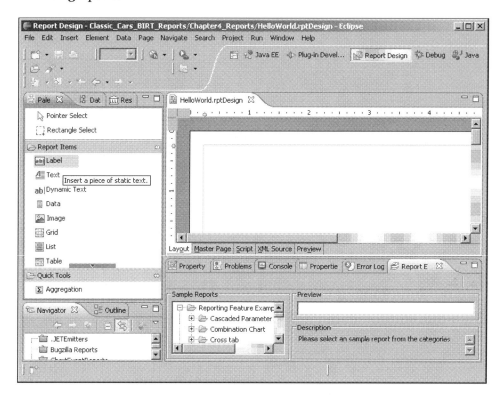

5. We will have a blinking cursor on the Label component we just dropped on to the **Report Design** pane. If we do not have a cursor, double-click on the Label component and type **Hello World**.

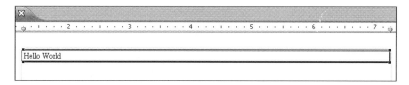

6. Under the **Property Editor**, the **General** side tab should be highlighted. If it is not, go ahead and click on it. The **General** tab is where elements such as the element's name, font selection, font color, alignment, stylesheet selection, and so on are located. Under the **Name** option, type in **lblHello** to name the component.

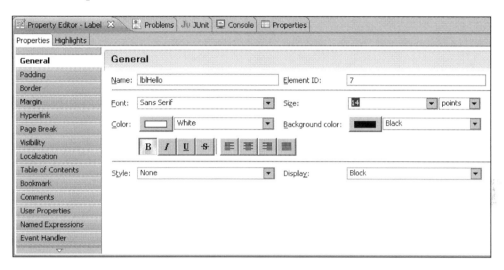

7. Under **Font**, choose **Sans Serif**. We can use any font we would like here; I chose Sans Serif because it is a commonly used font for reading text on a computer screen.

8. Under **Size** choose **14** points. This will make it easier to read.

9. Click on the button next to the **Color** option and select **White** from the available color options. We want a slightly different contrast than black on white to make it stand out a little.

10. Click the button next to the **Background color** option and select the color **Black**.

11. Click on the bold button to make the text bold.

12. Click the **Preview** tab under **Report Designer** to see the finished report. The following screenshot shows a finished report:

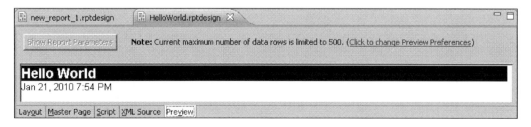

We were easily able to manipulate some basic visual elements of the Label component using the **Property Editor**. There are a number of other elements such as conditional hiding and hyperlinks that will be covered later in more detail. The important thing to remember about the Label is that it is a text component that is not bound to data in any manner.

Images

The next component we will talk about is the Image component. The Image report item is a mechanism of putting graphics such as company logos into a report page. The BIRT Image component has a lot of capabilities that allow for static or dynamic image usage based on data, including image data in report designs for easier distribution of single reports and using image files from a resource location or library to allow for single images to be used across multiple reports. We can even use BLOB data stored in a database if the data is an imageWe will discuss a lot of these features later in the book. The icon for the image report item looks like the following:

In the following exercise, we are going to insert a logo from the Eclipse home page at the top of the Hello World report.

1. Open the `HelloWorld.rptdesign` file from the `Classic_Cars_BIRT_Reports` project.

2. From the **Palette**, drag an Image object over to the **Report Design** pane, just above the **Hello World** label.

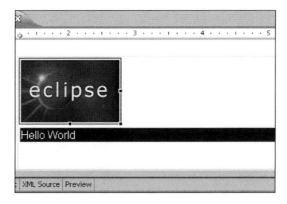

3. The **Edit Image Item** dialog box pops up. In the **Edit Image Item** dialog, there are several options for putting images in reports. We can put in a URL for a remote image hosted on a web server. We can add an embedded image from our local file system that will get stored in the report itself as a base64 encoded image. If we have an image stored in your resources (more on that later), we can add it from there. We can also set a dynamic image based on script or data conditions. This is useful if we want to pass in a value for different companies and have different report headers to be displayed. For this exercise, keep the **URI** option checked for the **Select Image from** option and enter the following URL: `http://www.eclipse.org/artwork/images/ eclipse_bckgr_logo_fc_sm.jpg`.

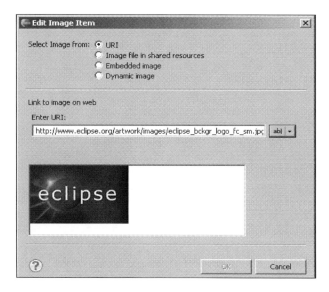

4. Click **OK**. The report preview is illustrated as follows:

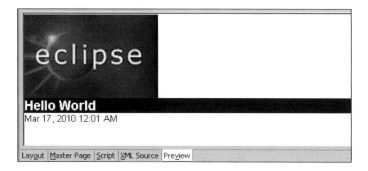

The finished report shows the image, the **Hello World** label, and the report footer.

Text and Dynamic Text

Text components are similar to Label components. They provide much more flexibility than Labels, in that they allow HTML formatting inside of the definition for the text. They also allow for some special tags that will display data from a JavaScript environment. This becomes important if we want to add AJAX or dynamic DOM manipulation to our report. It is even possible to put in images without using the BIRT Image component and anchor tags.

For the following example we will build on to our Hello World report by adding in a list that will be formatted with HTML. The items will be Item 1, Item 2, and Item 3 respectively. Item 1 will be set to bold using HTML, whereas Item 2 and Item 3 will be left alone. For the purpose of this example, you do not need to be familiar with HTML as I will walk you through the steps. A detailed tutorial on HTML is beyond of the scope of this book.

1. Open `HelloWorld.rptdesign` from the `Classic_Cars_BIRT_Reports` project.

2. From the **Palette**, drag a `Text` object over to the **Report Design** pane, just below the **Hello World** label. The `Text` element icon is illustrated at the beginning of this section.

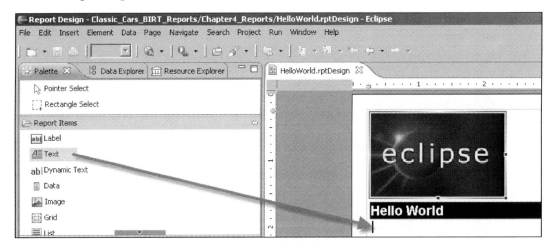

3. The **Edit Text Item** dialog box will pop up. Here we can edit the type of text we want to appear, control the HTML formatting of the text, and get access to quick menus that will allow us to see a small sample of HTML code we can embed in a text object. At the very top of the dialog box, change the type of text from **Auto** to **HTML**.

4. Go ahead and play around with the different types of formatting menus here; a drop-down menu with the name **Formatting** appears. Change the option from **Formatting** to **Lists**. Press the **<DL>** button that appears to the right of the drop-down list. We can see the editor will automatically create both the opening and closing tags for the list.

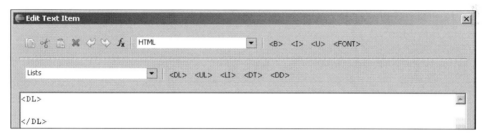

5. Now click on the **<LI>** button. Do this three times. In between the `<LI>` and `</LI>` tags, put the following labels in order:
    ○   Item 1
    ○   Item 2
    ○   Item 3

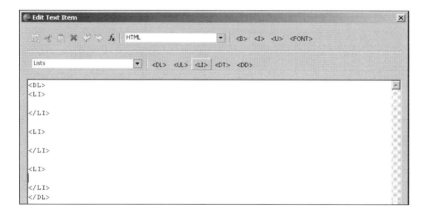

6. Now, using mouse, highlight the **Item 1** text between the first `<LI>` and `</LI>` tags. With **Item 1** highlighted, click on the **<B>** button at the top of the **Edit Text Item** dialog. This will automatically surround the **Item 1** text with the tags `<B>` and `</B>`.

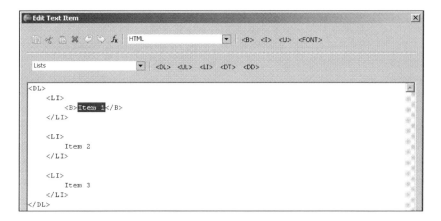

7. Move the cursor below the `</DL>` tag. Select the **Dynamic Text** tag from the drop-down list. Click on the **<VALUE-OF>** button, which will insert a `<VALUE-OF>` and `</VALUE-OF>` tag where the cursor is. The `VALUE-OF` tag is a special BIRT tag that will insert dynamic text based on any number of values such as JavaScript results or data values at the time of the report generation.

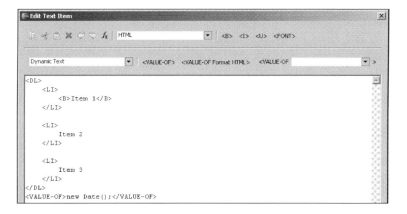

8. In between the `<VALUE-OF>` and `</VALUE-OF>` tags, type in `new Date();`. This is a small piece of JavaScript code that will retrieve the current date.

9. We will also want to format this date. Move the mouse cursor to inside of the first `<VALUE-OF>` tag, just to the right of `VALUE-OF`.

10. Now under the `<VALUE-OF>` tag on the top, with the drop-down box next to it, open the drop-down box and select **Format DateTime**.

11. Select the date format that reads "MMM DD, YYYY".

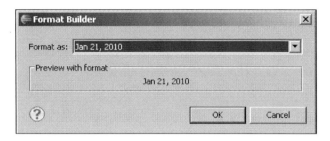

12. Click **OK**.

13. We will see that a format was inserted next to the `VALUE-OF` tag. Go ahead and click **OK**.

14. Now click **Preview**. We can see that the **Item 1** text is now in bold, and the place where the VALUE-OF tag was located now contains the current date and time.

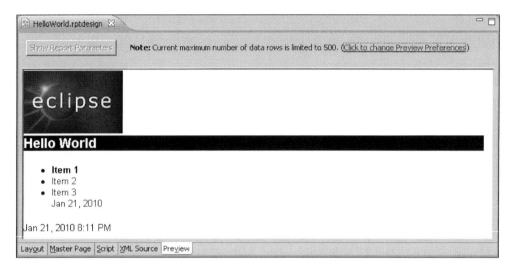

We can go back and change the formatting to use any standard Java formatting expression. In the example, instead of using the format dialog, we can change it using the format="YYYY-MM-DD", VALUE-OF tag attribute in the **Edit** dialog, and the date will be displayed as shown in the following screenshot:

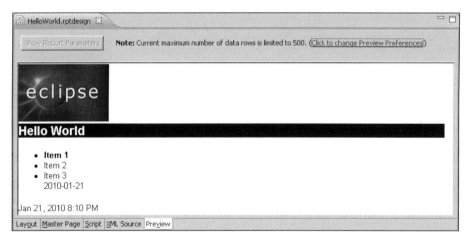

We will notice two different date formats. One is from our VALUE-OF expression. The other is located in an area called the **Master Page**, which we will discuss later.

Of course, with some understanding of HTML there is a lot more we can do with this. The VALUE-OF tag also gives us a lot of flexibility once data becomes part of the picture, which we will see later on. With a little understanding of JavaScript, we can make some really dynamic things happen. With the combination of HTML and JavaScript, we can add some report interactivity.

The **Dynamic Text** component is very similar to the **Text** component using the VALUE-OF tag, except that it uses JavaScript, BIRT report objects, and CLOBS to display its text. For the time being, we needn't go into much detail about this as it will be covered in depth in the *Practical Example – building reports for Bugzilla* chapter. For now we will go through a simple exercise to demonstrate how the **Dynamic Text** component can be used with JavaScript. In the following exercise, we will take a simple phrase and, using the JavaScript function to convert to upper case, we will display the text in all caps. A discussion on JavaScript and JavaScript programming is outside the scope of this book. For this exercise, one needn't know JavaScript; one just needs to understand that we are taking a string and converting it to uppercase.

1. Open the HelloWorld.rptdesign from the Classic_Cars_BIRT_Reports project.

2. From the **Palette**, drag a Dynamic Text object to the **Report Design** pane, just below the **Hello World** label or the **Text** object from the previous exercise.

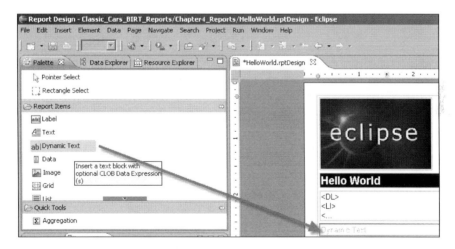

3. The **Expression Builder** will pop up.

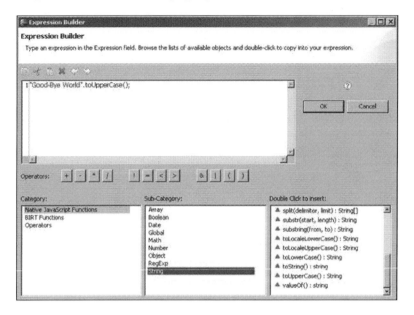

4. We will notice this looks different than the **Edit Text Item** dialog from the previous exercise. The **Expression Builder** is a dialog that will be used a lot in BIRT. It is used to edit small, short JavaScript expressions that will usually return a single value. When we cover scripting in more depth, we will discuss the differences between the **Expression Editor** and the **Script Editor Pane** used in the Report Designer. Type in the following text, including the quotes: "Good-Bye World".

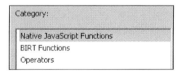

5. At the bottom of the **Expression Editor**, we will notice three different list boxes. These are used as a quick reference for JavaScript objects and methods that can be used in an expression. Put a period at the end of the "Good-Bye World" text. Then, under the **Category** list box at the bottom of the **Expression Editor**, choose **Native JavaScript Functions**.

6. A whole list of items will appear under the **Sub-Category** listbox. These are types of objects and methods we can work with. As "Good-Bye World" is a text string, select the **String** item.

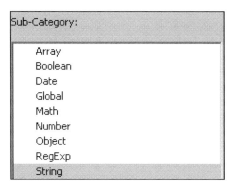

7. Now we have a list of methods we can use with the string "Good-Bye World". Make sure the cursor is after the period that was added after the "Good-Bye World" text. In the third list box, find and double-click on the `toUpperCase() : String` item. When we do that, we will notice that the method will get added to the place where the cursor is located.

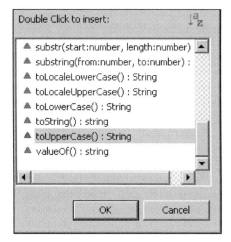

8. Click **OK**.

9. Preview the report.

In the finished report, the string "Good-Bye World" now reads **GOOD-BYE WORLD**. This is a useful component when one needs to perform operations on data values, perform calculations, and do a few other things that would require dynamic, calculation-driven text. There are properties of components that can do similar things such as Maps and Highlights that can perform dynamic text substitutions, enumerate data values, and change formatting of text based on certain conditions. We will discuss these elements in depth later in the book.

Grid

The Grid component is used to visually arrange components in a BIRT report in a particular layout.

BIRT is not a pixel perfect report design environment. In terms of visual arrangement of elements on a page, BIRT is very similar to static HTML. As such, the way to arrange elements in BIRT reports is to use elements such as the Grid, the Table, and the List. The Table and List components are similar to Grids, except that they are bound to data. In the example used in *Chapter 2, Installing BIRT*, we already saw an example of a Table component. We will cover these two components in more detail in the next chapter when we learn about data interaction.

In the following exercise, we are going to take a grid component and use it to change the arrangement of the elements we already have in our existing Hello World report. While this won't be the prettiest visual layout, it will effectively demonstrate how to interact with the Grid while designing reports and how it affects report layout.

1. Open the `HelloWorld.rptdesign` from the `Classic_Cars_BIRT_Reports` project.

2. From the **Palette**, drag a `Grid` object to the **Report Design** pane, just below the **Hello World** label or the **Text** object from the previous exercise.

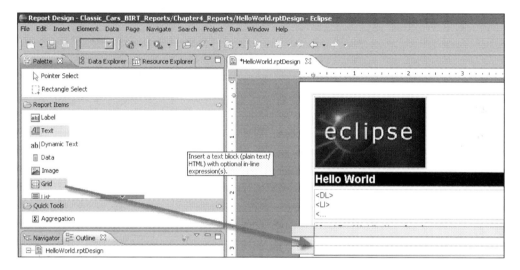

3. In the **Insert Grid** dialog, set the **Number of columns** and **Number of rows** to **2** and click **OK**.

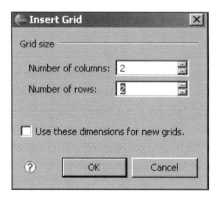

4. Now, in the **Report Designer** pane, click on the Eclipse Image component and drag it to the cell in the first column and first row.

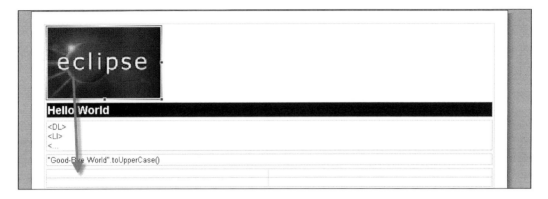

5. To change things a little, open the **Outline** tab. We are going to look at manipulating elements using the **Outline** view instead of using the **Report Designer**. When we expand the Body item, we can see the Label, the Text element, the Dynamic Text element, and the Grid.

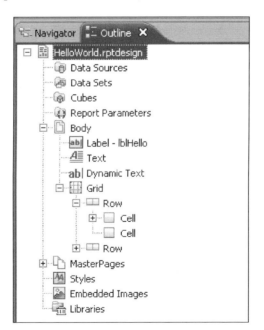

6. Expand the Grid; we should see two row items.

7. Expand the first row, and we should see two cells. The first cell will have the option to expand. This is because we have the Eclipse Image in that cell.

8. In the **Outline**, select the `Label`, and drag it onto the second `Cell` object under the first `Row`. We can see that the `Cell` object gets the `Label` element added under it, making the `Label` the lowest item in the hierarchy. It will also move the `Label` with the "Hello World" text in the **Report Design** pane into the second column, first row cell.

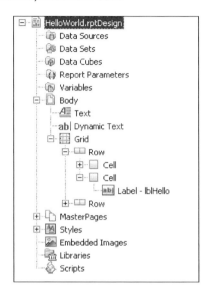

9. Collapse the first row item.

10. Right-click on the second row item. A dialog with the option to insert a new row above or below the current row appears. In our case, it really doesn't matter which one we pick as the current row is empty. Go ahead and select **Insert Row Below**. A new row gets added and we can see a new row appear in the **Report Designer**.

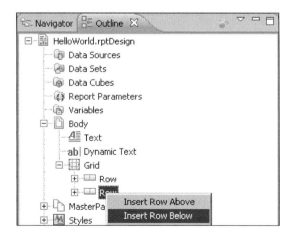

11. In the **Report Designer**, move the mouse to the Grid until a little tab pops up that says **Grid**. When it does, click on that tab.

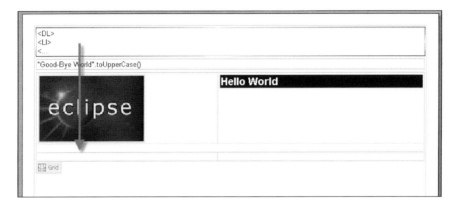

12. In the **Report Designer** pane, this is usually the way we will need to get the option to select an entire container component such as a Table, Grid, or List.

13. We want to combine the cells in the second row into a single cell. Move the mouse cursor into the cell in the first column, second row. Now click and hold the mouse button. Drag the mouse cursor over to the second column, second row and release the mouse button. This has selected both the first and second column cells in the second row.

14. Right-click on the selected cells and choose **Merge Cells**.

15. In the **Report Designer**, select the Text component, and drag it over to the newly merged cell.

16. Using the **Outline** view, drag the **Dynamic Text** component to the cell in the first column, third row. Take care to observe how the different objects are now placed in the **Outline**. The hierarchy of components is now set.

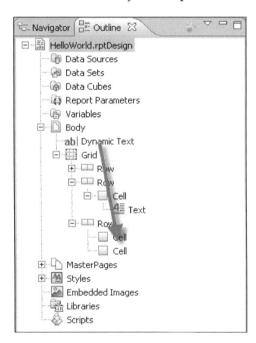

17. The finished outline will look like the following:

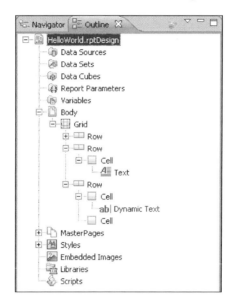

18. Preview the report. With the finished report, we can see how the visual arrangement of the report elements has changed from the previous report previews.

While this is not the prettiest report in the world, it helps one get an idea of how to work with the visual elements in the BIRT palette.

Aggregation

BIRT 2.5 now has a really nice Aggregation visual component.

In the previous versions of BIRT, aggregations were expressions that one would put into the Expression Builder using the Data component. This has changed in newer versions of BIRT to use a simple graphical component that gets displayed visually, and adds in a list of aggregations that are available to the user. This subject will be covered in detail in *Chapter 5, Working with Data*.

Summary

This chapter discussed the various visual report elements that one can use to design BIRT reports. The chapter covered how the various panes in the workspace cooperate together to create and manipulate BIRT reports such as using the component Palette to drag report items over to the Report Design pane, selecting elements in the Outline, moving objects in the Outline under other components, and changing their properties in the Property Editor. The chapter also briefly covered some of the more advanced BIRT report development topics such as the Expression Editor, and got an idea of how BIRT stores reports internally (the hierarchy from the Grids exercise). By now, we should feel pretty comfortable with dragging elements around the BIRT workspace, getting access to properties, and working with the Outline view to select components and move them in the BIRT report layout.

If we look at the Palette, we may notice a few components left such as the Table, the List, the Chart, and the Crosstab. This is because these are data bound components that require a data source. While we discussed this briefly in the previous chapter, I will like to discuss this more deeply in the next chapter.

5
Working with Data

The last few chapters have focused on the BIRT working environment and the visual elements used to develop reports, without the data element. This chapter will bridge that gap and focus on the data-specific elements of the BIRT environment, build some example reports using data from the example Classic Models Inc. database, and work with a separate MySQL database.

BIRT data capabilities

As BIRT is a Java-centric reporting environment built on top of Eclipse, many different data tools provide BIRT with its data capabilities. Building on the Eclipse ODA data platform, BIRT can provide data from a wide array of different sources. JDBC can be used to provide connections to many of the popular Relational Database Management Systems out in the market such as Oracle, MySQL, Microsoft SQL Server, and PostgreSQL. Using plain old Java objects, web services, and persistent data objects are just some of the sources that BIRT can connect to.

In addition to the classic client-or server-based reporting capabilities afforded to BIRT through this mechanism, BIRT also offers some extensible data handling capabilities through a number of different mechanisms. The Eclipse Data Tools Project is being leveraged by BIRT for its XML Data Source handling. The Eclipse Open Data Access Framework (a.k.a. **ODA** framework) allows developers to build custom drivers for data connections that JDBC doesn't actually provide connectors for. The Classic Cars sample database was built using ODA. For the Java-centric developers who are looking for more flexibility or have specific needs in mind, BIRT's extensible event handling model allows Java programmers to write scripted Data Sources where the data is populated either through Java code or JavaScript code at runtime.

Most of these are topics that are beyond the scope of this book. In this chapter, we are going to focus primarily on using the Classic Cars example database and configuring BIRT to use a JDBC database connection to MySQL. This will give the reader some familiarity with the basics of how to establish a connection to a database using JDBC drivers. Some familiarity with SQL is assumed; however, the queries used in the exercises and examples will be provided for those who are not familiar with SQL.

In *Chapter 3, The BIRT Environment and First Report*, we looked at a simple employee listing report using the Classic Cars database. To avoid duplicating exercises, we will leverage that report in the following discussions in order to demonstrate the remaining data centric components of BIRT, and to illustrate how to get data from data containers into reports.

Understanding the data components of BIRT

BIRT's data connection capabilities can be broken into two main logical constructs. Well, actually there would be three, but for the purposes of our discussion, we need to think only about two. The first is the Data Source. A **Data Source** is information about physical connections to databases, text files, or some other data source. In the Classic Cars example, the Data Source is the ODA connection information. If we were connecting to a MySQL database, the Data Source would contain information such as the IP address or DNS name of the database server, the database name, and the user name and password we are using to connect to the database. The Data Sources themselves do not usually contain any data that we will display in our report. There are exceptions, but they are few.

The second is the dataset. For our purposes, the dataset will contain a description of the data we want to retrieve such as SQL queries or custom code that will populate the data in a scripted Data Source. At runtime, the dataset will actually contain the data from that is described by the SQL query. This is where it gets confusing. In reality, the dataset description and dataset instance are two separate things, but for the purpose of report development, one needn't be concerned with that just yet.

The way this works is that datasets are dependent on Data Sources. Without a valid Data Source, the dataset has no way to retrieve data. That Data Source can contain information on any number of different Data Sources such as databases, flat text files, XML data files, a special Data Source called a *Scripted Data Source* that lets BIRT know if one is building his/her own Data Source by hand using Java or JavaScript or a custom data driver using the Eclipse ODA framework. The Data Source does the work as it knows how to communicate with the Data Source backend, the dataset tells the Data Source what to retrieve and then stores the results.

There are a couple of other data components in BIRT. The Report Parameter is a way the report developer can interact with the report user. Report Parameters serve as both an input mechanism and a variable for BIRT reports. Let's say we have a report that returns information about an employee such as their first name, last name, department, and a history of performance reviews used in an HR system. The report would need some way to know which employee we want information on. A report parameter would provide that mechanism. The report developer would create a report parameter to get the Employee ID from the user, and would pass that Employee ID to the dataset to request the relevant information. Report Parameters can also be used as a means to allow the user to control the logic and layout of BIRT reports.

We will be discussing Cubes a little later in the book. But to give you a heads up, a **Cube** is a way of grouping data in a way that allows report consumers to "cut" and "slice" data. This is similar to a Pivot Table in Microsoft Excel, where one can take columns of data, and group them along a Y axis and an X axis, the summary data of the grouping would form the middle cells.

The Data Source

As mentioned in the preceding section, the Data Source is a conduit to our data. Data Sources are the developer's way to specify where data is located, how to get access to that data, and provide a mechanism to retrieve that data from a data location. Out of the box, BIRT provides six different Data Source types:

- The Classic Cars sample database
- DTP XML Data Source
- Flat File Data Source
- Scripted Data Source
- JDBC driver
- Web Services Data Source

We have already seen the Classic Cars Sample database with the Employee Example in Chapter 3. This Data Source is not meant to be a production Data Source, and a report environment would not use in a real world development shop. It is provided as an example Data Source, used as a teaching aid and to demonstrate how an ODA Data Source would function in BIRT. It is also a common Data Source that all BIRT users have access to, so it is useful as a common talking point while explaining features of BIRT and while discussing issues with reports. When using this Data Source, we provide no information as it is all self contained in the Classic Cars Data Source itself. We will use this Data Source in a number of examples throughout this book.

XML Data Source

The second data Source is the **DTP (Data Tools Project)** XML Data Source. The XML Data Source is a driver that allows developers to use XML files as a Data Source.

Let's say we have an XML file containing some entries with employee information. We want to use this XML data file as a Data Source for a report. The XML file looks like the following:

```xml
<?xml version="1.0" encoding="UTF-8"?>
<Employees xmlns:xsi="http://www.w3.org/2001/XMLSchema-instance">
  <Employee>
    <firstName>John</firstName>
    <lastName>Ward</lastName>
    <jobTitle>Developer</jobTitle>
  </Employee>
  <Employee>
  <firstName>Bunson</firstName>
  <lastName>Honeydew</lastName>
  <jobTitle>Professor</jobTitle>
  </Employee>
  <Employee>
  <firstName>Bert</firstName>
  <lastName></lastName>
  <jobTitle>Fuzzy Muppet</jobTitle>
  </Employee>
  <Employee>
  <firstName>Ernie</firstName>
  <lastName></lastName>
  <jobTitle>Sidekick</jobTitle>
  </Employee>
</Employees>
```

The XML file is saved as `EmployeeData.xml`. In order to use this, we need to set up a Data Source. We will follow these steps to achieve this:

1. Create a new report project called `BIRT Book Chapter 5` examples.

2. Create a new report called `EmployeeReportCH5.rptDesign`. Use the blank template.

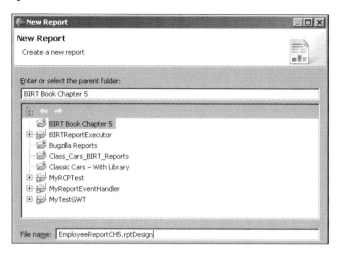

3. Under the **Data Explorer** pane, right- click on **Data Sources** and select **New Data Source**.

4. Under the **Data Source Type** window, select **XML Data Source.** For the **Data Source Name**, type `dsXMLEmployee`.

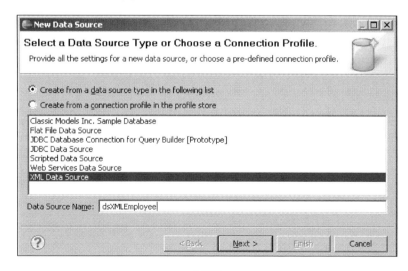

5. Under the location dialog, select the location where the XML file resides. If available, select a DTD file to verify the schema of the XML file. In our case, the XML file resides under the same workspace location as the Classic Cars examples. Once selected, one can test the file by clicking on **Test Connection** or you can just click **Finish**.

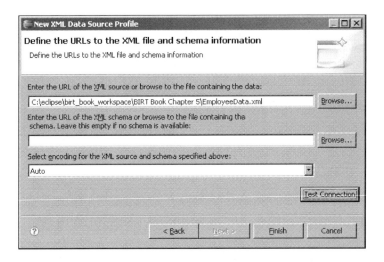

Now we have a Data Source containing employee information. We will work with this a little more when we start working with datasets. For now, we can hold on to this Data Source for use in a later example.

Flat file data adapter

The next type of Data Source we will look at is the Flat File data adapter. The flat file data adapter is pretty much exactly like one would expect—it is an adapter that provides connections to flat data files such as comma separated text files and other delimited text file types. A limitation with this adapter is that there is no way to explicitly use a particular type of delimiter. We are stuck with commas, pipes, tabs, and spaces. This should cover most of the kinds of flat files we will come across.

In the following exercise, we will cover creating a connection to a flat text file that contains employee pay information. The format of the text file is fairly simple. The file will be a comma separated text file, with the fields displayed in the following format: First Name | Last Name | Payment Date | Payment Amount

An example of the file could be shown as follows:

```
John,Ward,1/2/2007,500
John,Ward,1/3/2007,600
John,Ward,1/4/2007,900
John,Ward,1/5/2007,400
Bunson,Honeydew,1/1/2007,300
Bunson,Honeydew,1/2/2007,300
Bunson,Honeydew,1/3/2007,200
Bunson,Honeydew,1/4/2007,100
Bert,Unibrow,1/1/2007,230
Ernie,,1/1/2007,275
```

Here, we can see that there is no header row to tell us what the column names are, so it will be up to us in our dataset later on to name those. We save the above information as `paymentInfo.csv`. Now, to create a Data Source based on this file, we follow these steps:

6. Create or open the report named `EmployeeReportCH5.rptDesign`.

7. Under the **Data Source Type** window, select **Flat File Data Source** and name the Data Source `dsFlatFilePayments`.

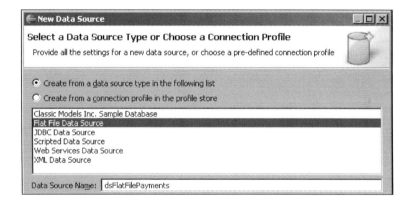

8. Select the folder where the text files will reside. Each CSV text file under this folder will be seen as its own unique table in any dataset we use later on. Specify the character encoding used and the type. In the case of our example, we are setting the **flatfile style** to CSV and **charset** to **UTF-8** encoded file.

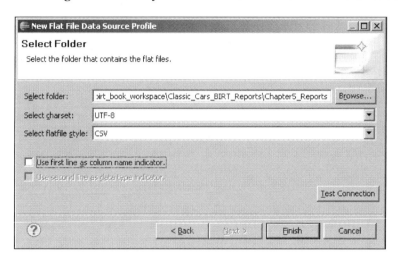

9. Click **Finish**.

Much like the XML Data Source, we will use this a little later when we build the datasets. For now, we have created the Data Source that will be used to retrieve our employees' payment information.

We are going to skip the Scripted Data Source for the time being. This is a special Data Source that is meant as a placeholder for data that gets built manually using BIRT's scripting capabilities, either through Java Event Handlers or through Javascript. We will discuss these more in depth in the later chapters on Scripting.

The JDBC Data Source

The Data Source we are going to look at in detail is the JDBC Data Source. This is the Data Source that one ends up using most often and has the most set of options and facilities for the out of the box Data Source types, which is why I have included it in a separate section. It is used to connect to a RDBMS that has supplied a JDBC driver. Most widely used enterprise RDBMSes such as Oracle, Microsoft SQL Server, MySQL, PostgreSQL, and many others already provide these. Other embedded database platforms such as HSQL and Apache Derby also provide JDBC drivers for accessing data, and in some cases may be the only way to access data stored on those platforms. In fact, the Classic Models database that is supplied with BIRT uses Apache Derby.

One thing to note about JDBC drivers is that the JDBC connecting URL is different for each platform. The JDBC URL for Oracle is not going to be the same for MySQL or Derby. One needs to check documentation for his/her platform. Once one has a basic template, one can set up a basic URL for future projects based on that platform when he/she manages his/her drivers. So, let's go through an example to get acquainted with the JDBC Data Source. In the following example, we are going to work with the Classic Cars database that is provided with BIRT. In the previous example using it, we used a built in ODA Data Source that was based off of the JDBC driver. In this example, we will use the actual JDBC driver for Derby. We follow these steps:

1. Create or open the `EmployeeReportCH5.rptDesign` report.

2. Under the **Data Explorer** tab, right-click on **Data Sources** and select **New Data Source**.

3. Under the list of available drivers, select **JDBC Data Source** and enter `dsSampleDataBase` as the **Data Source Name**.

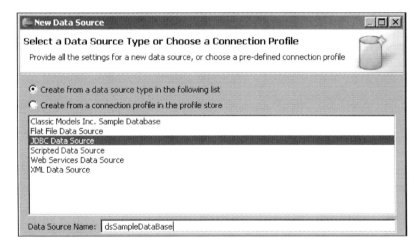

4. The following screen is where all the JDBC connection information appears. From the drop-down list for **Driver Class**, select the `org.eclipse.birt.` `report.data.oda.sampledb.Driver` class. It will automatically fill in our database URL with the appropriate JDBC URL for the sample database.

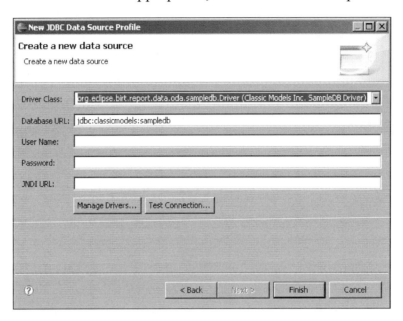

5. Click on **Test Connection** to make sure we are able to connect.

6. Click **Finish**.

This was quite easy to perform on sample database as the JDBC URL template was already filled in for us. Consider we don't have the JDBC URL automatically filled in for us. Let's look at using the Derby JDBC driver that is set up and explore the **Manage Drivers...** dialog a little.

7. We will need to extract the sample database from its archived format in the BIRT plug-ins folder. For this we will need to know where we have BIRT installed. In our case, we have the BIRT Report Designer installed under `C:\birt-all-in-one-2_5_2` and so we need to open the `C:\birt-all-in-one-2_5_2\eclipse\plugins\org.eclipse.birt.report.data.oda.sampledb_2.5.2.v20100205 \db\BirtSample.jar` file in an archive program such as Winzip or Winrar. Don't worry about the extension being `.jar` instead of `.zip`—the file is still a ZIP file.

8. Extract the `BirtSample.jar` file to a known location such as within our workspace or a temporary folder. We have chosen a folder under our Workspace for this, so we will extract the file to `C:\temp\ClassicModelsDataSource\`. This will create a folder called `BirtSample` under that folder. For more information on extracting an archive, we can consult the documentation for our archive program.

9. Create or open the `EmployeeReportCH5.rptDesign` report.

10. Under the **Data Explorer** tab, right-click on **Data Sources** and select **New Data Source**.

11. From the drop-down list, select **JDBC Data Source** and enter the name as `dsDerbySampleDatabase`.

12. Select **org.apache.derby.jdbc.EmbeddedDriver (Apache Derby Embedded Driver)** from the drop-down list for the **Driver Class** option.

13. Under the **Database URL** option, enter the following URL:
`jdbc:derby:<Location where .Jar file was extracted>`.
In our case, we will use the following URL:
`jdbc:derby: C:/temp/ClassicModelsDataSource/BirtSample`.

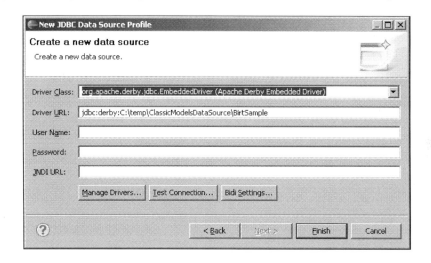

14. Click the **Manage Drivers...** button. This brings up the **Manage JDBC Drivers** window. This is where we will add new JDBC drivers such as an external Oracle, MySQL, or MS SQL Server JDBC driver that is not already in BIRT. We can do so by clicking the **Add...** button and navigating to the location with the driver.

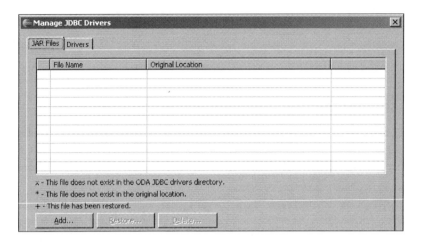

15. Click on the **Drivers** tab.

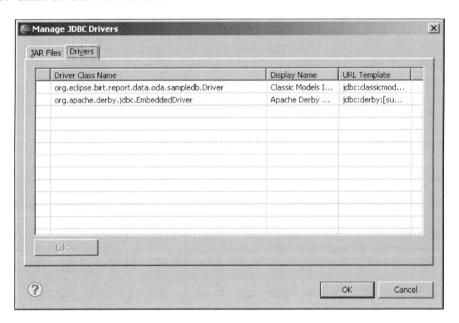

16. This is where we can set the various properties for the JDBC drivers such as the driver name and the default JDBC URL. Select **Derby Embedded** driver and click the **Edit** button. We can see that the default JDBC URL is already filled in. Any time after we have registered a new driver, we can always come here to change the default JDBC URL and driver name.

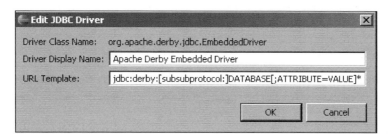

17. Click **OK** to exit the **Edit...** dialog and then the **Manage JDBC driver** dialog.

18. Click **Finish**. The JDBC driver has now been set up.

Datasets

With all the examples discussed in earlier sections completed, we should have four Data Sources in our report. The reason we kept each of these Data Sources is to demonstrate the differences in each while setting up Datasets. As mentioned before, Datasets are basically descriptions of the data one wants to retrieve. Each type of Data Source is going to contain different Dataset types. In the following examples, we are going to create five different datasets, four of which will be based on each of the different Data Sources we have created, whereas one will be a Joined Dataset or a combination of two of the existing Datasets.

First, we are going to build a simple Dataset from the XML Data Source `dsXMLEmployee`. Building the XML Dataset consists of defining columns to be built and then resolving them to XML paths using XPath expressions. This can be a bit tricky if there are namespaces used in the XML file. For our example, namespaces are not used in the XML Data Source.

1. Open `EmployeeReportCH5.rptDesign`.

2. Under the **Data Explorer** tab, right-click on **Data Sets** and select **New Data Set**.

3. Enter the following information:
   - ° **Dataset Name**: dsetXMLEmployee
   - ° **Data Source**: dsXMLEmployee
   - ° **Dataset Type**: **XML Dataset**

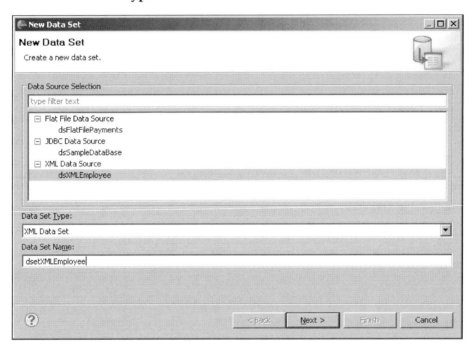

4. On the next screen, make sure that the **Use the XML file defined in Data Source** option is checked and click **Next**.

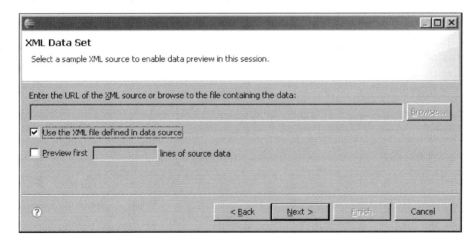

5. On the **Table Mapping** screen, enter /Employees/Employee as the **XPath Expression**. This sets the row mapping or which XML element contains the sequence to act as rows in the report.

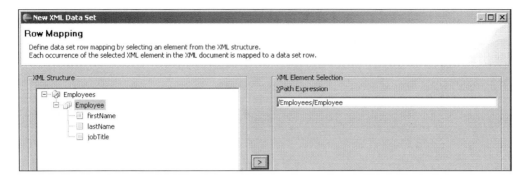

6. On the next screen, click on each of the nodes, then click the > button to create a new field mapping. We can click the preview button to make sure our field mapping works correctly.

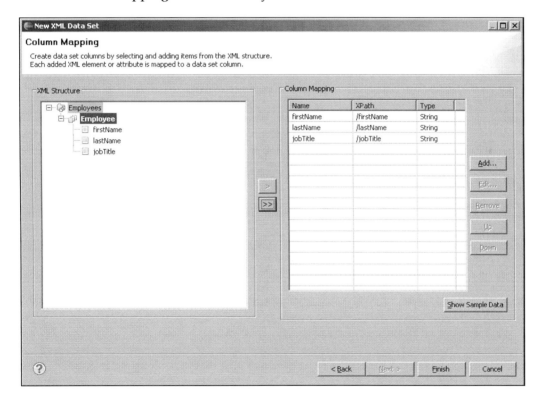

7. Click **Finish**.

The next screen allows us to edit the Dataset after we create it. This allows us to do things such as filter through the data and create additional columns based on computations. Let's take a look at doing that for this dataset. Let's say we want to filter the data returned by this dataset so that only those who have the job title of Developer are displayed. If one is going into this example right from step 7 of the last example, he/she can skip the first few steps.

8. From the **Data Explorer** tab, double-click on dsetXMLEmployee.

9. Go ahead and click on each of the categories on the left-hand side. The ones that are unique to the XML Datasets are the ones we have already seen, the XML Dataset, Table Mapping, and Column Mapping.

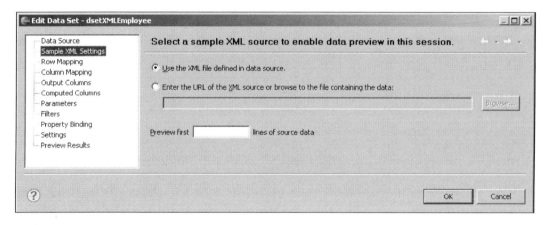

10. Go to the **Filters** category.

11. Click the **New** button and enter the following information:

- ○ **Expression**: `row["jobTitle"].toUpperCase()`
- ○ **Operator**: `Equal To`
- ○ **Value 1**: `"DEVELOPER"`

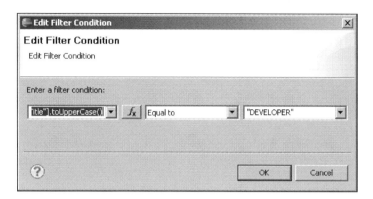

To make expression editing easier, we can use the function button located next to the Expression text box to build our expression using the expression editor. When we do so, we will see an extra category called **Available Data Sets** that was not visible earlier. This category is visible only when working with Datasets or components that are bound to data.

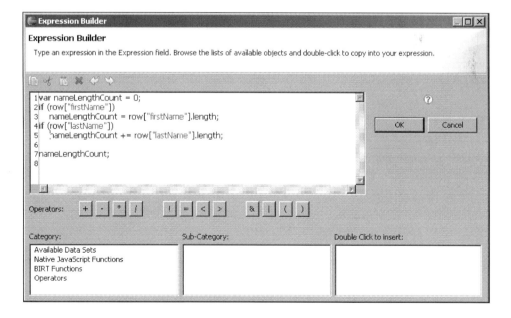

12. Click **OK**.

13. We can now see the filter expression in our list of filters.

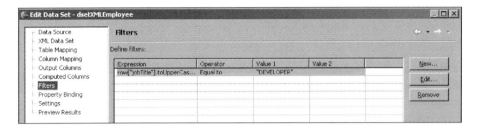

14. Click **Preview Results**. Only a single entry should show up.

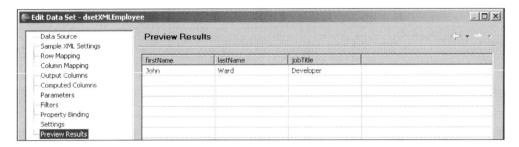

Filters are useful when one is dealing with non-database Datasets, or any Dataset where the backend does not have any sort of filtering capabilities. So now, let's say one wants to add a computed column that will return the number of characters in the first name and the last name. He/she could do this from the **Computed Columns** category under the Dataset Editor. Let's take a look at how to do this.

15. Under the **Data Explorer**, double-click on dsetXMLEmployee.

16. Click on the **Computed Column** category.

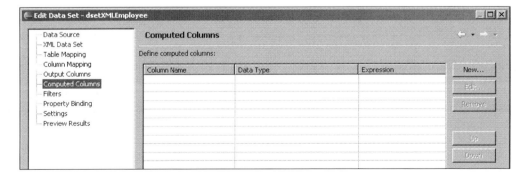

17. Click the **New...** button. Enter the following information:
    ◦ **Column Name**: nameCount
    ◦ **Data Type**: Integer

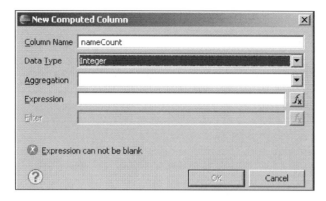

18. Click the function button next to Expression and enter the following expression:

```
var nameLengthCount = 0;
if (row["firstName"])
nameLengthCount = row["firstName"].length;
if (row["lastName"])
nameLengthCount += row["lastName"].length;
nameLengthCount;
```

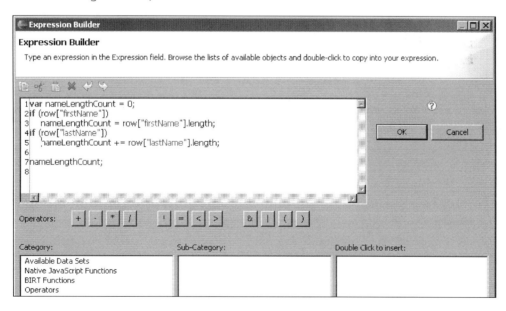

19. Click OK.

20. Go down to the **Preview Results** category. See how the Filter is allowing only those employees with the job title of Developer to be displayed, and now there is an additional column called `nameCount` with the number of letters in each employee's name.

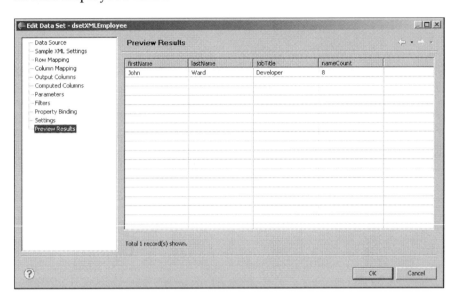

This filter is very simple, but it does demonstrate the Filter and Computed Column functionality. Computed Columns become more useful while dealing with numerical data that we may need to perform aggregation on, or with first name, last name combinations where we may want to display the output as lastname, firstname.

Dataset for flat files

Next, we are going to create a dataset based on the flat file Data Source. This interface will look a little different than the XML Data Source, but the basic idea is still the same. We will define each column's name, data type, and create any filters or computed columns necessary. In this example, we will just be defining the columns.

1. Under the **Data Explorer** tab, right-click on **Data Sets** and select **New Data Set**.

2. Enter the following information:

   ° **Data Set Name**: dsetFlatFilePayments

   ° **Data Source Selection**: dsFlatFilePayments

   ° **Data Set Type**: Flat File Dataset

3. Click **Next**.

4. As the flat file Data Source defined a directory where the data files are located, we need to select the appropriate text file from the **Select file** drop-down list. Choose the `paymentInfo.csv` file created during the Data Source exercise.

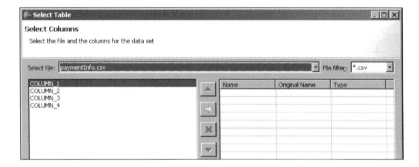

5. There should be four columns, labelled `COLUMN_1`, `COLUMN_2`, `COLUMN_3`, `COLUMN_4` respectively. If we had chosen the option to have a header row during the Data Source creation, these columns would be named whatever the values were in the first line of the text file. For each of the columns, click on it, then click on the right-pointing arrow button.

6. Each of the columns should be in the grid. We can change the values of each of the columns such as original name, name to be used in the dataset, and the data type. Enter the following information for each of the columns:

   ○ Column1: **Name** = firstName **Type** = String

   ○ Column2: **Name** = lastName **Type** = String

   ○ Column3: **Name** = paymentDate **Type** = Date

   ○ Column4: **Name** = paymentAmount **Type** = Float

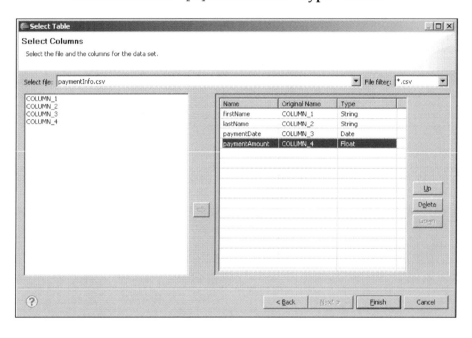

7. Click **Finish**.

Just like with the XML Dataset, once we finish the initial setup, we enter the edit dataset dialog. From here, we can create filters and computed columns in addition to the columns outputted by the data adapter itself. With the XML Dataset, Flat File Dataset, and with the Scripted Dataset, which we will look at later, the ability to create filters inside of BIRT is very useful when there is no backend filtering capability like there would be with a database system using the WHERE clause in an SQL statement.

JDBC Datasets

With the two non-JDBC datasets out of the way, we can now create the dataset for our JDBC Data Sources. Typically, this is where one spends most of his/her report development time; I can tell this from my experience. I have used these types of datasets more than any of the others as so many applications use an RDBMS back-end to store data. In the following example, we are only going to create one dataset because the two JDBC Data Sources we have point to the same set of data. In this dataset, we want to retrieve a listing of `Orders` and `Order Details`, using an SQL statement to join the two tables.

1. In the **Data Explorer** tab, right-click on the **Data Set** option and choose **New Data Set**.

2. Enter the following information:
    ° **Data Set Name**: `dsetOrders`
    ° **Data Source Selection**: `dsDerbySampleDatabase`
    ° **Data Set Type**: `SQL Select Query`

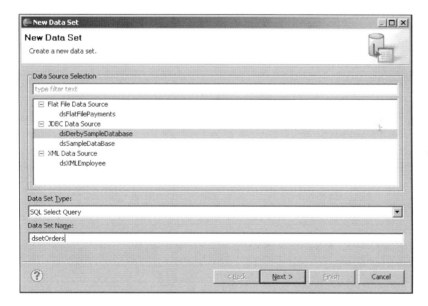

Notice that under the **Dataset Type**, there is an additional option to use an SQL Stored Procedure under Dataset Type. This was not an option with the other dataset. This is applicable to only those Data Sources that are DBMS based. Because our example Derby Database does not have any stored procedures, this doesn't do us any good. We can ignore this and click **Next**.

3. The next screen is the SQL Editor. Here, we can play around with the left-hand tree view to see the available tables and columns in our database. We can either drag tables or columns over to the text editor on the right-hand side, or we can move the cursor someplace in the text editor and double-click on the table or column we want to add. In doing so, we automatically put in the fully-qualified path to that table or column. We can also filter down to see tables in particular schemas in databases where we have access to more than one table. Additionally, we can type in a filter to limit based on table name. A word of caution: in my experience the filtering is case sensitive, that is, "order" is not the same as "ORDER". Put the following information in the Filter data and click **Apply Filter**:

   ° **Schema**: CLASSICMODELS

   ° **Filter**: ORDER

   ° **Type**: Table

4. Use the following SQL query:

```
select
*
from
CLASSICMODELS.ORDERDETAILS,
CLASSICMODELS.ORDERS
where
CLASSICMODELS.ORDERDETAILS.ORDERNUMBER = CLASSICMODELS.ORDERS.
ORDERNUMBER
```

Feel free to experiment with dragging and dropping the columns and tables to get a feel of how the mechanism works.

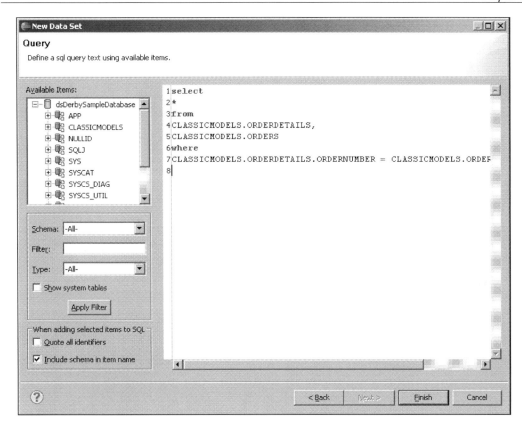

5.   Click **Finish**.

Joined Dataset

The final type of dataset we are going to create is called the Joined Dataset. This is a type of dataset that will combine the results of two existing datasets into one logical dataset. This is a very useful feature when we try to join data from two unrelated Data Sources, such as with a database and a text file, or from two separate databases. In the following example, we will join the `dsetFlatFilePayments` dataset with `dsetXMLEmployee`. To show that there are a few different ways to create datasets, we will also create this one using the **Outline** view instead of the **Data Explorer**.

1.   From the **Outline** view, right-click on **Data Set** and select **New Joined Dataset**.

2. Enter the information as illustrated in the following screenshot:

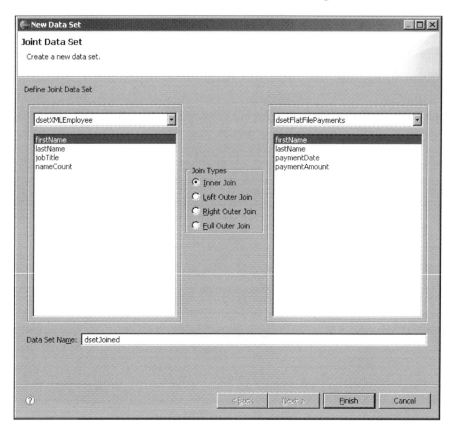

If we apply the filter in dsetXMLEmployee, we will see that only information for John Ward comes back with the payment information. This is because the filter on that dataset, in combination with the Inner Join, is preventing any data from dsetFlatFilePayments from coming back except the information related to John Ward. Feel free to remove this filter to see the full join.

Creating data using the data store

Introduced in BIRT 2.3 is a graphical query designer that is available every time a designer uses a data store. The idea is to provide a visual representation of tables and their relationships for report designers that may not be as fluent in SQL. This also gives developers a chance to quickly create a general SQL statement that can be refined without having to type code. In 2.5, this was expanded to be available from the JDBC Database Connection for Query Builder type of Data Source. Let's now follow these steps and create data:

1. Create a new report titled `dataStoreExample.rptDesign`.

2. Create a new Data Source.

3. Choose the **Create from a connection profile in profile store** option in the **New Data Source** window.

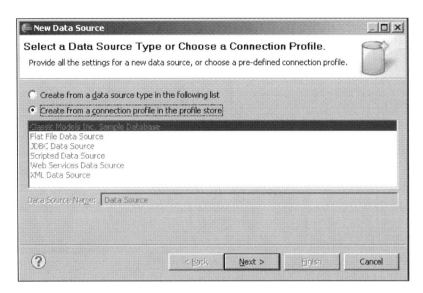

4. In the **Connection Profile** dialog, click the **New...** button.

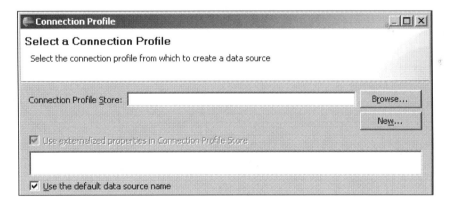

5. On the next screen, we have the option to create a new data profile. This would require us to know the JDBC URL to connect to the database. For this example, just select **BIRT Classic Models Sample Database**. Select a file to store the configuration.

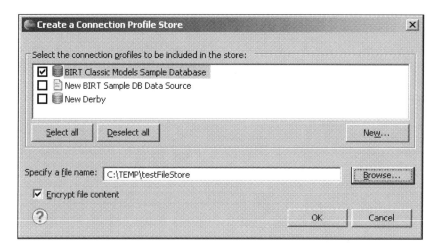

6. We can now use this file any time we want to connect to this database. The information is already filled out in the **Connection Profile** dialog when we return to it. Click on **Next** to continue.

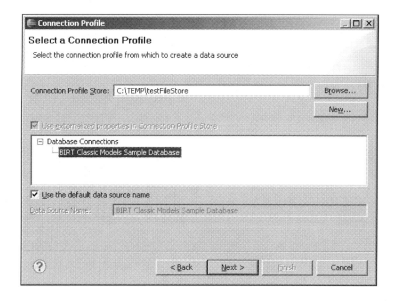

7. On the next dialog, we can set JDBC parameters for this instance of a connection. There is nothing to set for this example, so click on **Finish**.

8. Right-click on the Dataset icon in the **Data Explorer** and choose **New**....

9. In the next dialog, we will notice a new **Data Set Type: SQL Select Query [Query Builder Prototype]**. We can also see the profile information in our Data Source selection. Enter a name for our Dataset.

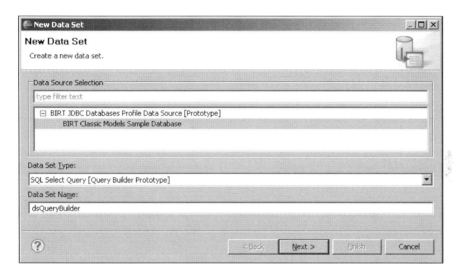

10. We now get a query dialog that is similar to Microsoft Access query builder. To add tables to the dialog, right-click on the middle pane.

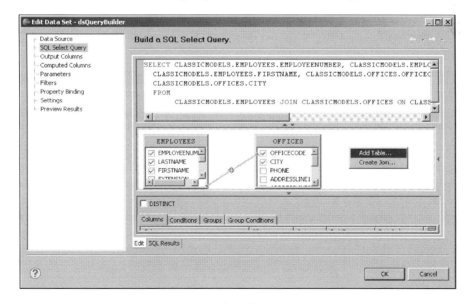

11. Add the EMPLOYEES and OFFICES tables. Select the OFFICECODE field from the EMPLOYEES table and drag it over to the OFFICECODE field in the OFFICES table. This will modify the query to create a join. Then, click on the checkboxes next to EMPLOYEENUMBER, LASTNAME, and FIRSTNAME in the EMPLOYEES table, and OFFICECODE and CITY in the OFFICES table.

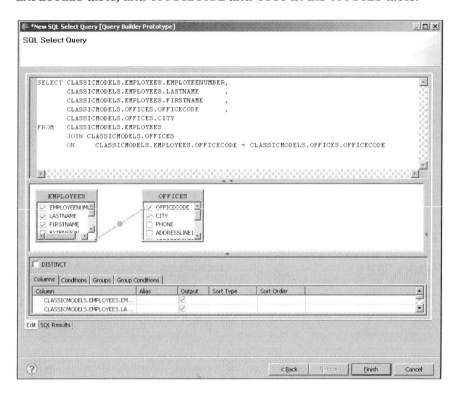

We can now use these datasets in the same manner as we would any of the others.

Tables

In the example Employee Listing report from *Chapter 3, The BIRT Environment and First Report*, we used a visual report element called a Table, even if we didn't know it. The Table is similar to the Grid component we saw in the previous chapter, except that it is data bound. What this means is that the contents of this component are populated by data stored in a data container such as a dataset. In the Employee Listing report, we saw a shortcut method for creating a table. This is very useful when we are building simple listing reports. However, when we need more precise control over our Table, we can also do it manually using the Palette component.

The Table is divided into three logical groups:

- Header, which will contain the name of each report column in the report
- Details, which will actually contain the data returned from the bound dataset
- Footer, which will contain summary or aggregate information about a report

In the following example, we are going to demonstrate two different ways to create tables. First we will build tables using the shortcut drag-and-drop dataset method. Then we will use the second method, which involves manually building a table, binding it to a dataset, and populating the elements of the table.

Creating tables using drag and drop

First we want to get the data from `dsetJoined` and move it over to our Layout view. There are a couple of different ways this can be accomplished. We can drag it over from the **Data Explorer** just like we did in Chapter 3 or we can drag it over from the **Outline** view. If we right-click on the `dsetOrders`, we can also choose the **Insert into Layout** option. The caveat with this is that if there is already any element in the layout, we will have to click on an empty space in the Layout editor for this option to be available.

1. In the **Data Explorer**, under **Data Sets**, right-click on `dsetJoined` and choose **Insert in Layout**.

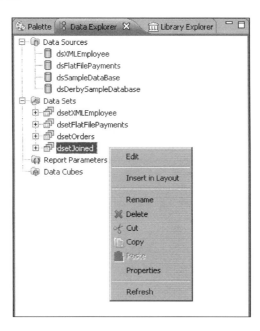

2. From the **Outline**, under the **Body** branch, select **Table**.

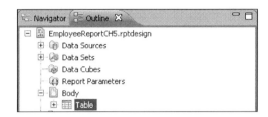

3. Under the **Property Editor**, change the **Name** to tblEmployeePayments.

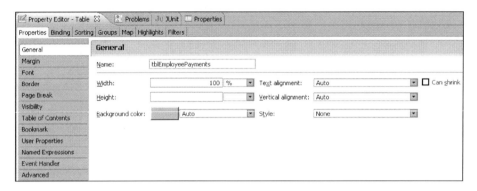

4. In the Layout Editor, find the cells that say dsetFlatFilePayments: firstName and dsetFlatFilePayments. Click on the grey square above these labels to select that entire column. Then right-click, and choose **Delete**. Repeat this for both columns.

5. We need to change each of the column headers contents so that they do not contain dsetXMLEmployee:: or dsetFlatFilePayments. To do this, we can either double-click on each of them or can use the **Property Editor**. To use the **Property Editor**, select the label element either in the **Layout Editor** or, using the **Outline**, select the label under each of the Body, Table, Header, Row, Cell, Label components. Then in the **Property Editor**, scroll down to **Advanced** and select **Content**. Change each label to an appropriate title.

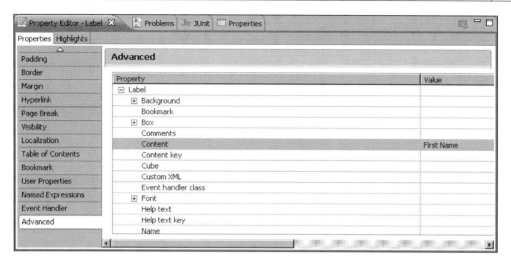

6. From the **Outline** view, select **Body | Table | Header | Row**. In the **Property Editor**, choose the **Font** category and change it to **Bold**.

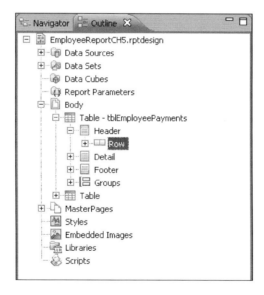

7. In the **Layout Editor**, click on the **Detail** cell under the **Payment Amount** column. Under **Using the Property Editor**, under the **Format Number** category, set the **Format as** property to **Currency**. Check the **Use 1000s separator** checkbox and select the **$** as **Symbol**.

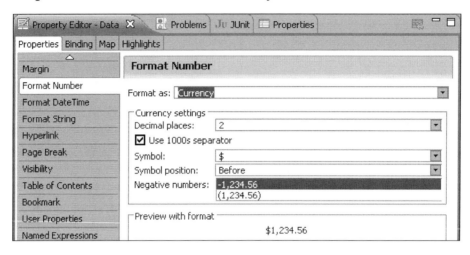

8. We now want to add an aggregation for the **Payment Amount** column. We can drag the **Aggregate** component over from the **Component** palette. Drag the component over to the footer row, in the **Payment Amount** column.

9. Enter the following information:

    ◦ **Column Binding Name**: agrPaymentTotal
    ◦ **Display Name**: **Total Payments**
    ◦ **Data Type**: Float
    ◦ **Function**: SUM
    ◦ **Data Field**: select PaymentAmount from the drop-down list.

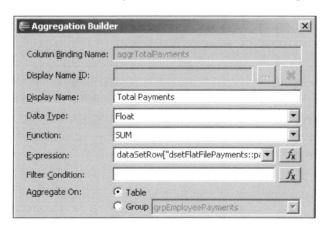

10. Click on the `agrPaymentTotal` component and format it as `Currency`.

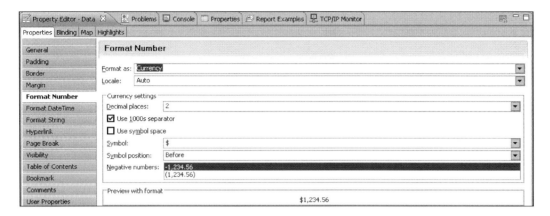

11. Click on **Preview** under the **Layout Editor**.

First Name	Last Name	Job Title	Name Count	Payment Date	Payment Amount
John	Ward	Developer	8	Jan 2, 2007	$500.00
John	Ward	Developer	8	Jan 3, 2007	$600.00
John	Ward	Developer	8	Jan 4, 2007	$900.00
John	Ward	Developer	8	Jan 5, 2007	$400.00
					$2,400.00
Jun 18, 2007 11:11 PM					

So, creating a simple report this way is easy enough, but how would we do so manually. Well, that's exactly what we are going to do next.

Creating tables manually

We want to create a table right below this one with the information from the `dsetOrders`. We will create this one manually as we do not want to display all the information in that dataset, but only certain columns. Because we should be fairly familiar with using the **Component** palette at this point, we are going to create this table directly in the **Layout Editor**.

1. Right-click in the area below the `tblEmployeePayments`, and choose **Insert | Table**.

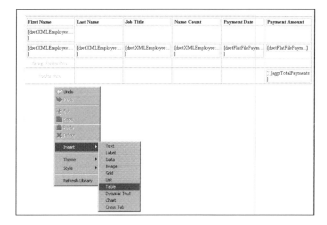

2. For dimensions, use 6 columns, 1 detail row, and use `dsOrders` as the dataset.

3. In the first column of the **Detail** row, right-click, and choose **Insert | Data**.

4. Enter the following information:
   - **Column Binding Name**: `cbOrderNumber`
   - **Display Name**: **Order Number**
   - **Data Type**: `Integer`
   - **Expression**: `row["ORDERNUMBER"]`

Here, we manually created a data element in the detail row. Note the expression. This expression is telling BIRT to use the value or ORDERNUMBER in the current row, as the detail band in a table will cycle through every record returned in a dataset.

5. Click **OK**.

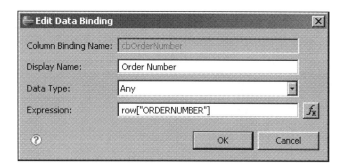

6. Right-click in the first column of the **Header** row, and select **Insert | Label**. For the value, type in **Order Number**.

7. Now that we have seen how to do that manually, here is an easier way. Open up the **Data Explorer** and expand on the dsetOrders node. Drag over the CUSTOMERNUMBER field to the detail rows second column. We can see the header label is automatically created.

8. Repeat for the PRODUCTCODE, PRICEEACH, and QUANTITYORDERED field.

9. Click on the grey square at the top off the last column to select the entire last column. Once done, right-click and select **Insert | Column to the right**.

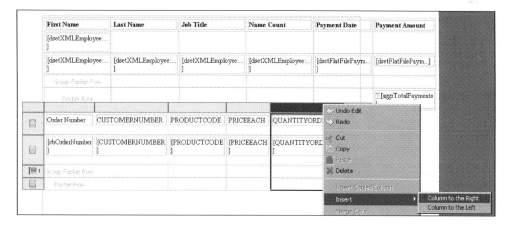

10. Right-click on the new detail cell, and insert a new data element. Use the following information:

    ○ **Display Name: Product Total**

    ○ **Data Type**: Float

    ○ **Expression**: row["PRICEEACH"] * row["QUANTITYORDERED"]

11. Create a label for this column titled **Product Total**.

12. Format both the Product Total detail cell and the PRICEEACH cell as Currency.

13. Save and preview the table.

First Name	Last Name	Job Title	Name Count	Payment Date	Payment Amount
John	Ward	Developer	8	Jan 2, 2007	$500.00
John	Ward	Developer	8	Jan 3, 2007	$600.00
John	Ward	Developer	8	Jan 4, 2007	$900.00
John	Ward	Developer	8	Jan 5, 2007	$400.00
					$2,400.00

Order Number	CUSTOMERNUMBER	PRODUCTCODE	PRICEEACH	QUANTITYORDERED	Product Total
10100	363	S18_1749	$136.00	30	$4,080.00
10100	363	S18_2248	$55.09	50	$2,754.50
10100	363	S18_4409	$75.46	22	$1,660.12
10100	363	S24_3969	$35.29	49	$1,729.21
10101	128	S18_2325	$108.06	25	$2,701.50
10101	128	S18_2795	$167.06	26	$4,343.56
10101	128	S24_1937	$32.53	45	$1,463.85
10101	128	S24_2022	$44.35	46	$2,040.10
10102	181	S18_1342	$95.55	39	$3,726.45
10102	181	S18_1367	$43.13	41	$1,768.33
10103	121	S10_1949	$214.30	26	$5,571.80
10103	121	S10_4962	$119.67	42	$5,026.14
10103	121	S12_1666	$121.64	27	$3,284.28
10103	121	S18_1097	$94.50	35	$3,307.50
10103	121	S18_2432	$58.34	22	$1,283.48
10103	121	S18_2949	$92.19	27	$2,489.13
10103	121	S18_2957	$61.84	35	$2,164.40

Groups

Grouping, much like in an RDBMS, is a mechanism used to group data that falls into a similar category. This can be done with a SQL SELECT statement using the GROUP BY clause or, in BIRT, it can be done by adding a group to a Table or List. We are going to add to expand the above report examples by adding groups.

1. In the **Outline** view, select tblEmployeePayments.

2. In the **Property Editor**, open the Groups tab and click on the **Add...** button.

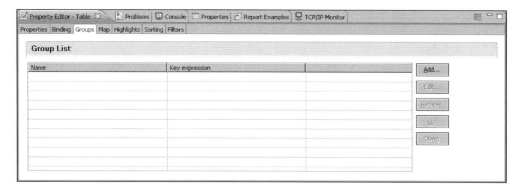

3. Fill in the following information:

   ○ **Name**: grpEmployeePayments

   ○ **Group On**: dsetXMLEmployee::lastName

4. Click **OK**.

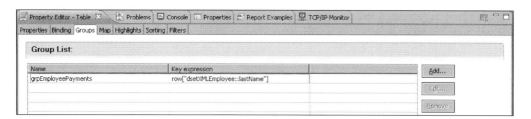

Now, when we preview the report, we can see that it adds an extra header with last names and groups all the like payments together. Of course, this will be better illustrated with the next example, where we modify the `Order` table to display groupings by order number.

5. Add a new group to the table with the Orders.

6. Enter the following information:

   ○ **Name**: grpOrderInfo

   ○ **Group On**: ORDERNUMBER

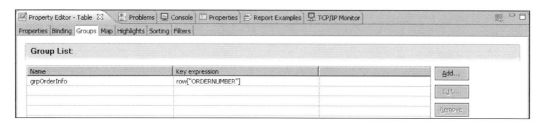

7. Under the **Outline** view, select **Body| Table** (the one with Orders, not the tblEmployeePayments) **| Groups | Table Groups | Header | Row**. Delete the row.

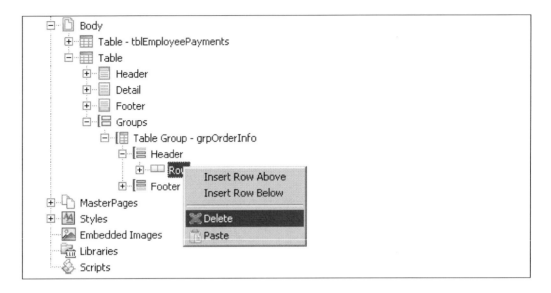

8. In the **Layout Editor**, select the Order Number column. Under the **General** tab, click on the **Suppress duplicates** checkbox.

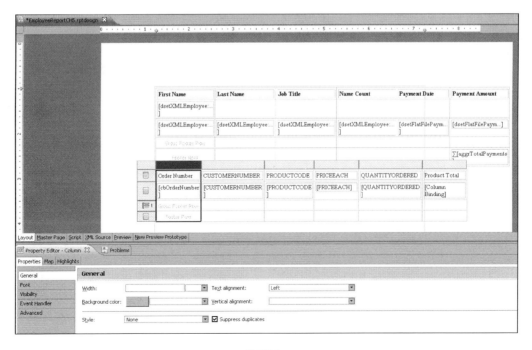

9. Repeat the same thing for the `Customer Number` column.

10. Click **Preview**.

Now, when we click on **Preview**, we can see that the orders are all grouped by the order number and, instead of repeatedly displaying the order number and customer number for each line like in the previous previews, it will now display it only once.

Lists

Lists work in a similar manner to tables, except that they do not have the ability to have multiple columns. This is useful for single column tables, or when using one dataset to drive the results of another during render time, or to create lists of tables based off of a single value. Lists are created the same way as Table, but only support a single column. Lists are typically used for master/detail type reports. We can use the Report Example view to see an example of a report with embedded tables, or use the Master/Detail template.

Aggregations

Aggregations are a way to take data as a whole and apply calculations to them, such as counts or sums of data columns. New to BIRT 2.3+ is the aggregation visual component. In newer versions of BIRT, the developers have broken away from the older, scripting based aggregations. With improvements made in the 2.5 series, it is now possible to do some very powerful and interesting things such as using aggregations in groupings for charts, which wasn't possible in BIRT before. Let's take a look at how to build a simple count aggregation for the employees in our offices.

1. Create a new report titled `employeeGroupCount.rptDesign`.

2. Create a new Data Source off the Classic Models sample database.

3. Create a new dataset called `dsEmployeeOffices` using the following query:

```
select
        EMPLOYEES.EMPLOYEENUMBER,
        OFFICES.OFFICECODE,
        OFFICES.CITY,
        OFFICES.STATE
from
        EMPLOYEES,
        OFFICES
where
OFFICES.OFFICECODE = EMPLOYEES.OFFICECODE
```

4. Right-click on `dsEmployeeOffices` and select **Insert in Layout**.

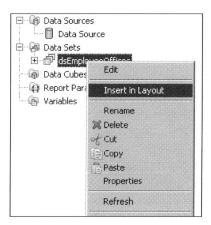

5. Select the table and add a new grouping on the `OfficeCode` column.

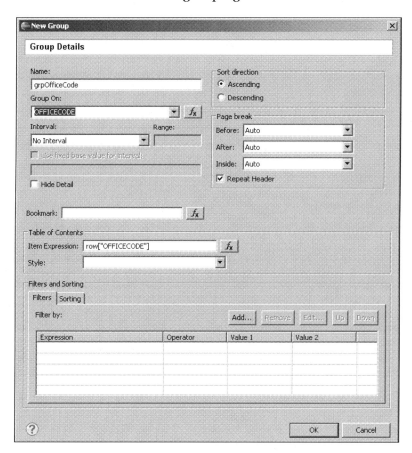

6. Format the table so that the `City`, `State`, and `OfficeCode` are in the `Group` header.

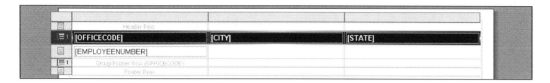

7. Drag an Aggregation component into the Group Footer Row, in the center column. Name the aggregate, change the data type to `Integer`, and set the function to COUNT. For the **Expression**, use **row["EmployeeNumber"]**. Make sure that under **Group** option, the grouping made for the table is selected.

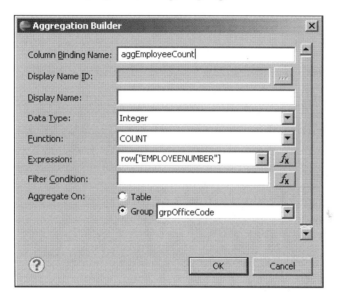

8. Insert a label into the cell to the left of the aggregation and name it `Employee Count`.

9. Run the report. The following example had formatting added to make it easier to read:

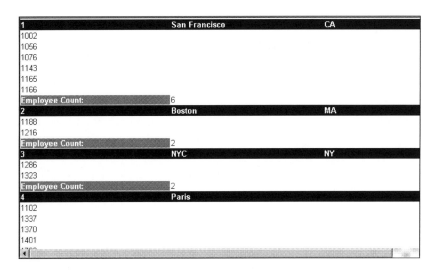

Web service Data Source

The following example is going to look at building a report that uses a Web Service Data Source and dataset to retrieve a weather forecast based on a ZIP code. The reason behind my including this separate from the others is the fact that during the first edition of this book there were no real free web services to utilize as an example. However, these days there are plenty of free web services available to utilize for this purpose. Let's now build a report:

1. Create a new report called WeatherByZipCode.rptdesign.

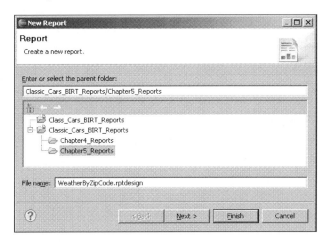

2. Choose the blank template.

3. From the **Data Explorer**, select **Data Source | New Data Source**.

4. From the list of Data Source types, choose **Web Services Data Source**, and set **Data Source Name** as dsWeatherDataSource.

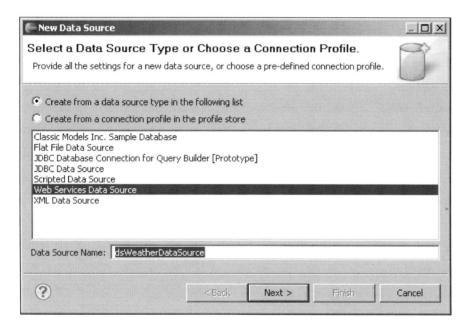

5. As **WSDL URL or Location,** enter the following URL: http://www. webservicex.net/WeatherForecast.asmx?wsdl. We do not need to fill in any of the other information as it will be retrieved from the WSDL file.

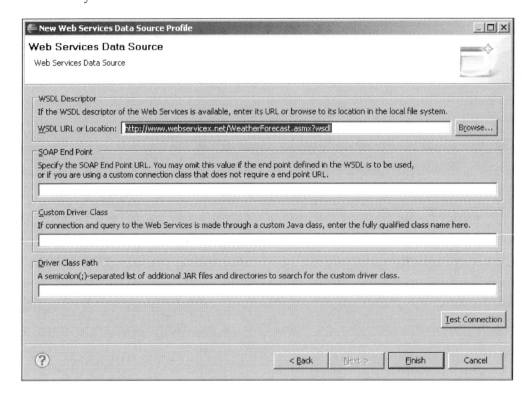

6. Click **Finish**.

7. From the **Data Explorer,** create a new dataset.

8. Call the new dataset as `dsetWeatherByZip`. Click **Next**.

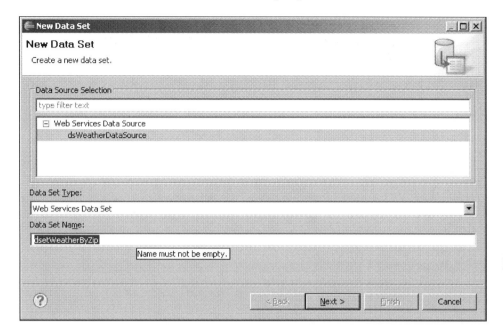

9. From the list of available web services, click down to the `WeatherForcastSoap` and select `GetWeatherByZipCode`.

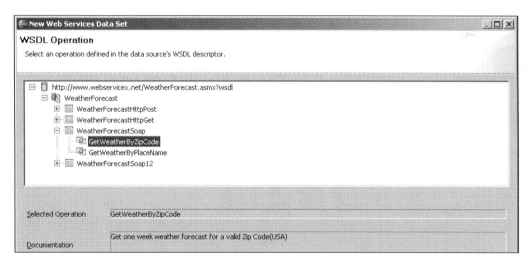

10. Click **Next** for `ZipCode` parameter as it is the only parameter for this web service.

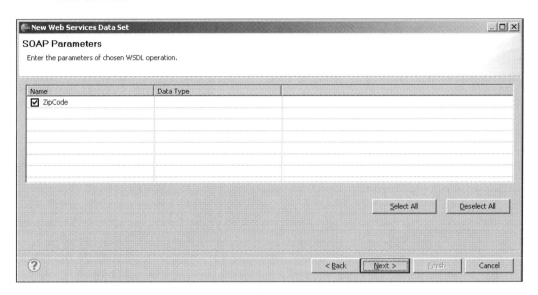

11. The next screen will show a preview of the web service request. If one is familiar with SOAP request formats, he/she can verify that it is correct. Otherwise, click on **Edit Parameter...**.

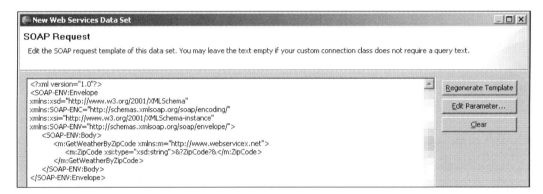

12. Click the **Edit...** button and enter ZIP code as the default parameter. Click **OK**, then click **Next** at the parent window.

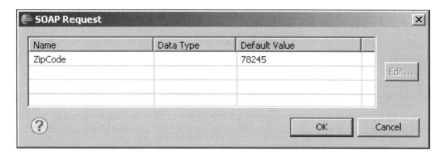

13. For the SOAP response edit dialog, leave all the values as default.

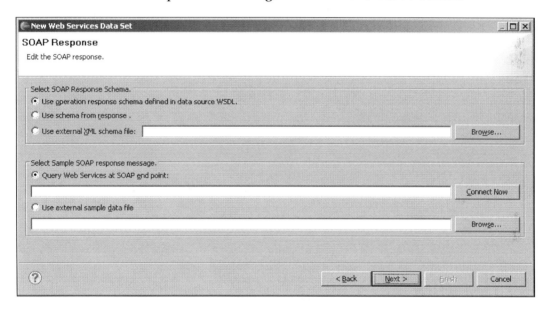

14. The next screen will define an XPATH expression, defining that the rows are in the resulting XML. In this case, we will define a XPATH that points to the result sequence for the weather data. Use the tree view to find the WeatherData node and click on the **>** arrow, which automatically sets the XPATH expression.

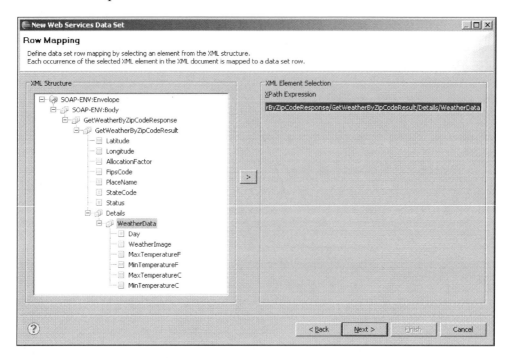

15. On the next screen, we need to define the column mapping for each row. Select the WeatherData node and click on the **>>** arrow. This will add all the child elements as columns for the resulting row.

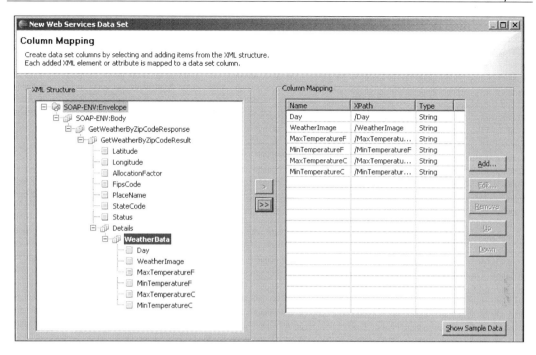

16. Click on **Show Sample Data** to get a preview of the data and verify that the XPATH expressions are retrieving the correct data.

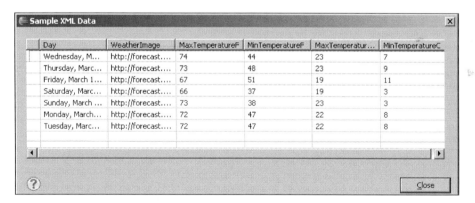

17. Click **Close** on the sample data dialog, and **Finish** in the Dataset wizard.

18. The **Edit Data Set** dialog will look very familiar at this point. One can go back and modify any of the values set in the wizard. Click **OK** in the **Edit Data Set** dialog.

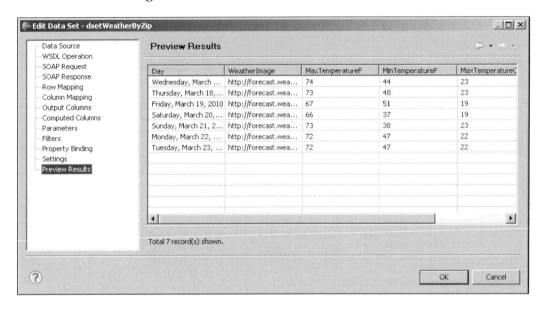

19. Drag the `Weather` dataset over to the **Report Editor**.

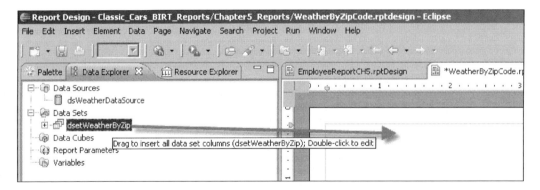

20. At this point, the report is done. However, let's add something extra to it. The `WeatherImage` column points to a URL that will have an icon with the weather conditions. Let's put in a dynamic image item that will reflect this. Delete the `WeatherImage` text item from the second row, second column.

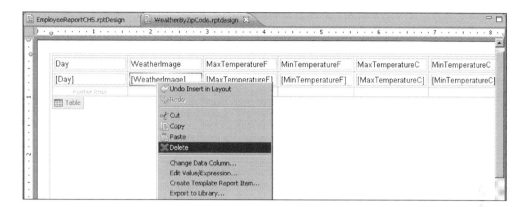

21. Insert a new **Image** item into the empty second column, second row.

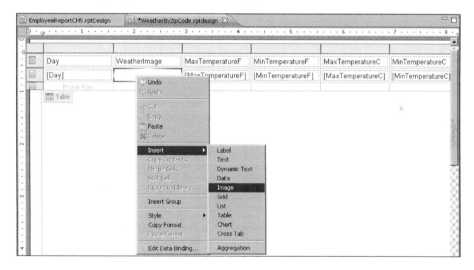

22. In the **Edit Image...** dialog, change the button to the right of the **Enter URI** textbox to **Javascript Syntax**.

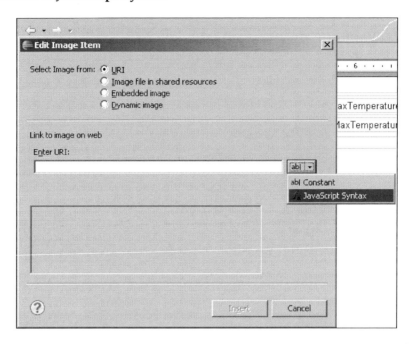

23. As an expression, enter row["WeatherImage"]. We can use the list boxes at the bottom to input this.

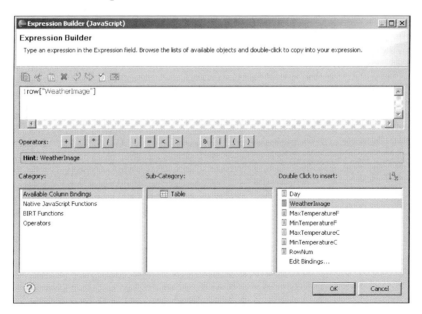

24. Click **OK** and then click the **Insert** button.

25. Save the report and preview it.

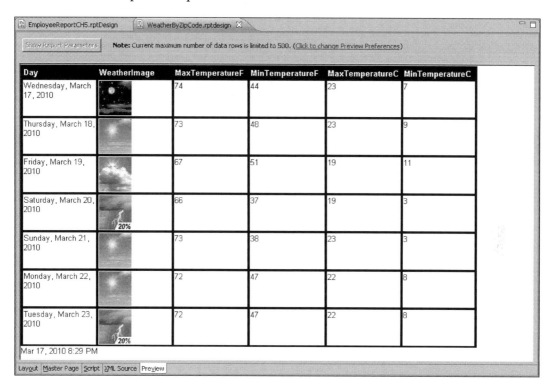

Web service parameters will vary based on the hosting server. It is possible to use Java classes to serve as the web service proxy, if one uses something like Apache Axis. This is a simple example that will get one familiar with the possible uses of this Data Source.

Adding additional data aware components to the palette

As part of an extended social media advertising campaign for BIRT, two extra BIRT visual report items—the Rotated Text component and the DotBar component—have been released for public use. These two components are added in as additional plugins to BIRT, and provide user with the ability to use these components right from the report palette in BIRT reports. This showcases BIRT's ability to be extended in the designer and at runtime.

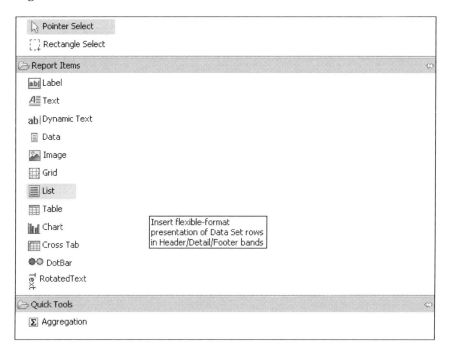

More information on these components, including installation instructions and usage examples, can be found at `http://code.google.com/p/birt-controls-lib/`.

Summary

We covered a lot of ground in this chapter. We explored how to create most of the elements that connect to different Data Sources in a report. and report projects. We saw that BIRT supports different types of data such as XML files, flat text files, and databases. We saw that for each type of Data Source, there are different types of dialogs to describe the data and create datasets. We saw how to bring in the different data bound components. We also explored a few different methods of inserting visual components into a report layout and how to change different properties of components. We saw in detail how to group related data based on the value of columns, how to create a calculated result using some basic expressions, and how to work with the outline, the property editor, and the layout editor.

Hopefully by this point you are getting more comfortable with working in the BIRT environment. This is getting us ready to build some really interesting reports in later chapters. But there are elements that we have not covered but are needed to build fully functional reports. In the next chapter, we are going to learn how to get user input for reports so that they can filter data in a manner they need. We are also going to look at how report parameters are different from Dataset parameters, how they can be linked together, and how report parameters can be used in a data independent way to effect layout of reports. We will also explore the usage of Highlights and Maps.

6
Report Parameters

Up until now, the reports that we have worked with have had one thing in common—they all have been static reports. That means they do not accept any sort of input from the user. Their output depends solely on the data present in a database. While we have demonstrated that a filter can be applied to the data coming back from a data source, we haven't discussed how a report user can specify what details they want to see.

In this chapter, we will look at the different types of parameters that BIRT offers. We will distinguish between parameters that can filter datasets and parameters that can change the look and feel of reports. When we finish reading through this chapter, we will be able to take our reports one step further than the canned reports that we have developed so far, and be able to offer our users the ability to filter down large amounts of data to just the information that is important to them.

Why parameterize reports?

This is a very important question to ask ourselves, and while the answer might seem obvious, it goes a little deeper. Imagine that we are a report developer for a large organization with several different departments. Now we create a report for a department that shows their costs for the fiscal quarter—that's great. Now a second department asks us to create the same report for them. Then a third department asks for a similar report, but they want to be able to see data for both last quarter and this quarter. By this time, we have created three similar reports, each representing the same set of data and running the same queries, only that we have hard coded the department information. Now we have to maintain all three of those reports, and any changes or mistakes we or an analyst find in any of the reports, ultimately we will ultimately have to fix in all three reports.

The solution to this problem is to parameterize our report. In a simple scenario such as this, it becomes obvious that if we created a few parameters such as one for department and a few to handle date ranges, we would then have to maintain only a single report for all the departments and time frames that would be requested. By parameterizing, we are taking a larger number of reports needed to be maintained and verified and reducing it to a more manageable number. This becomes useful as more often than not, report requests remain very similar.

Now, take a step back and let's look at something we haven't addressed up until now. Let's say for each department that runs the report, they want their header to be displayed in the report or their department logo. Now we are looking at something other than data-centric issues and moving into the realm of layout-specific issues. With BIRT, we also have the ability to address these kinds of visual requirements. For example, if the manager from the accounting department wanted alternating row colors, but the other managers did not, we could easily create a report parameter that would ask the report user if they wanted to add alternating row colors. With the logo issue, we can easily create some basic logic that is driven by report parameters to meet these requests. We will look at some examples in this chapter, and explore this more in depth in the chapter on Scripting.

Dataset parameters and report parameters

In BIRT, there is a very important distinction between dataset parameters and report parameters. This distinction can be confusing at first, which is why I want to discuss it now. The difference is one of scope and function. A report parameter has a global scope and can be used in a number of different ways in reports. Report Parameters are user facing variables that prompt the user for input. If you have ever worked with a traditional reporting language, think of report parameters as a global variable, combined with a standard input statement that will fill that variable with a value.

Dataset parameters, on the other hand, are limited in scope to within the dataset that they are declared in. Dataset parameters work more like bind variables in a relational database management system, or a prepared query in a data aware programming model, such as ADO or JDBC. Dataset Parameters are typically linked to Report Parameters to retrieve their values, but that is not always the case. They can be bound to a number of different sources.

This becomes an important concept, especially when working with JDBC datasets. With other types of datasets, Report Parameters will get linked to Filters typically and not to datasets parameters. In the Web Services example from the preceding chapter, we saw that it is possible to use placeholders and dataset parameters with dataset types other than JDBC, but this is mostly used with JDBC SQL datasets and bound parameters. This is something to keep in mind when working in BIRT as the term parameter is used with both Report Parameters and Data Set Parameters, and gets even more confusing when taking into consideration that later versions of BIRT allow users to create Report Parameters directly from the Data Set Parameter dialog. The difference will become clear throughout the chapter.

Getting input from the user

Let's take a look at an example. In the following exercise, we are going to build a very simple query that will let us retrieve all employees that have a particular Employee ID. The user will be prompted to enter an ID number and the report will return the information relevant to that user. Let's work on getting input from the user:

1. Create a new report and call it `Employee-Chapter6.rpDesign`.

2. Create a new data source from the Classic Cars Sample Database.

3. Create a new SQL Statement dataset called `dsetEmployeeInfo` based of the Classic Cars Data Source.

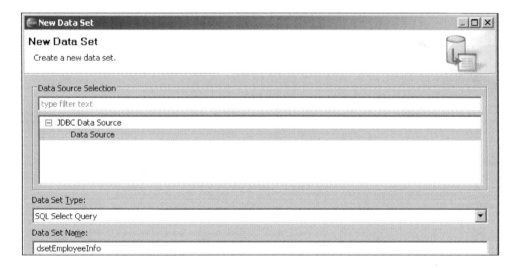

4. Use the following SQL statement as the query. We need to make sure to keep the question mark in the query, as it indicates to BIRT that a dataset parameter needs to be created and used in its place:

```
select
                *
from
                Employees
Where
        EmployeeNumber = ?
```

5. When we click **Finish**, we will be brought to the dataset editor screen. Click on the **Parameters** branch in the tree view on the left-hand side.

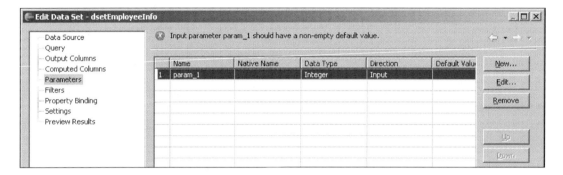

6. We can notice that there is a dataset parameter, `param_1`, created automatically for us. It has already been assigned automatically, the type of the database, so we don't need to change anything. This is a dataset parameter. This parameter is for only within this dataset and its value gets assigned to the ? in the query.

7. We should notice that at the top of the screen there is a red **X** with a comment about a default value. This is because if we do not have a default value in the parameter, BIRT will not have any sort of value in the parameter for report development. Therefore, we need to assign a default value. Select `param_1` and click the **Edit...** button.

8. Change the name to `dsprmEmployeeID`, click on the drop down next to **Default Value**, and set the option to **Constant** and the default value to **1002**. We will notice the drop down that says **Linked to Report Parameter**. Ignore this for now, we will come back to it later. Click **OK**.

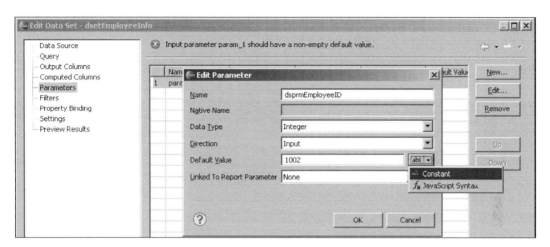

9. Now if we select **Preview Results**, we can see one employee record. Click **OK**.

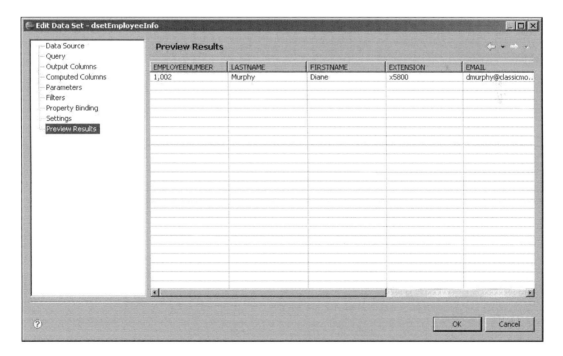

So, we have created a dataset with a parameter and assigned it a default value for us to work with. But we don't have a way to get user input and put that user input into the Data Set Parameter. Don't worry, as we will next create a Report Parameter and will bind it to the dataset for use in our report.

10. From the **Data Explorer**, go to **Report Parameters**, right-click on it, and choose **New Parameter** option from the list.

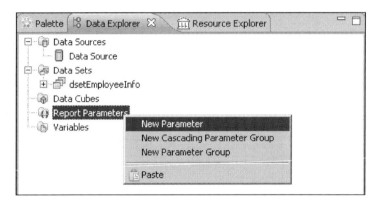

11. On the next screen, enter the properties for the Report Parameter. Here we can set the Report Parameter to be required for report execution. There are several options such as:

   ◦ **Hidden**: This makes sure that the user will not see it in the parameter dialog, although we can still pass values when calling the report with a URL

   ◦ **Is Required**: This makes a value in the parameter mandatory

   ◦ **Do Not Echo**: This is useful for sensitive information.

   Use the following values and check the **Is Required** checkbox.

Field	Value
Name	rprmEmployeeID
Prompt Text	**Enter Employee ID**
Data Type	Integer
Display Type	**Text Box**

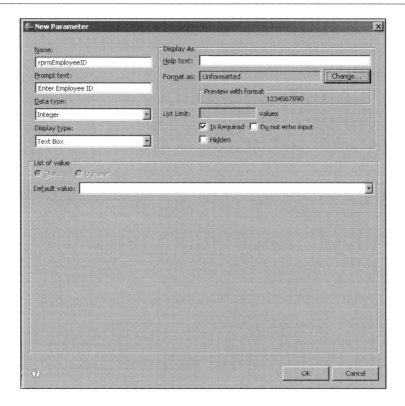

12. The Default value textbox is left blank for the user to fill it. Normally if we filled this in, on the first report run, this value would populate the parameter dialog presented to the user. Click **OK**.

13. At this point, there is no binding between the dataset and the Report Parameter. To create the binding, start off by double-clicking on dsetEmployeeInfo in the **Data Explorer** to open the **Edit Data Set** dialog.

14. Go to the **Parameters** category. Double-click on dsprmEmploeeID, or select it and click on **Edit...** button.

15. There are two different ways by which we can bind the parameter to the dataset at this point. The easiest way is to select rprmEmployeeID from the **Linked to Report Paramter** drop-down box. If we do this now, the default value will blank out. We will now be linked to the report parameter, and the dataset parameter will take on its default value or any value the user enters in the dialog box.

16. Once you are finished, click **OK**.

Here we see the old fashion way, using an Expression to link to the value of the Data Set Parameter to the Report Parameter.

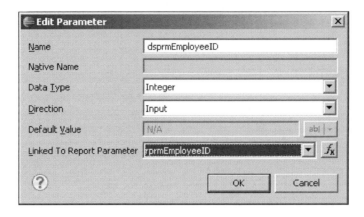

17. Under the Data Explorer, right-click on dsetEmployeeInfo and choose Insert into Layout, or drag-and-drop the dsetEmployeeInfo onto the Report Designers Layout pane.

18. Preview the report.

The first time we preview the report with a Report Parameter, the BIRT Designer will bring up a dialog box asking us to enter the Employee ID. If we put in nothing and click **OK**, we will get prompted that a required parameter is not filled in as rprmEmployeeID was set to required. Enter **1002** for the Employee ID to see the results of report.

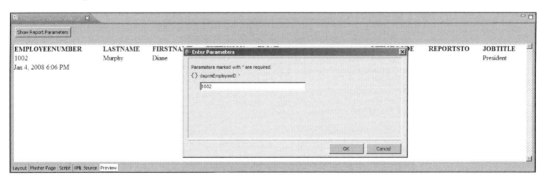

We can change the parameters to see other results after running the preview report by clicking on the **Show Report Parameters** button in the **Preview** pane. The example that we just saw demonstrates that there is a distinct difference between Report Parameters and Data Set Parameters. This will become an important distinction later when we start to use Report Parameters in ways that affect the layout and logic of a report that are separate from data.

Creating parameter binding the easy way

The example in the previous section was a good introduction to using parameters with data. In older versions of BIRT, it was the only way to create the binding between dataset parameters and report parameters. However, there are some tedious steps involved that cause some confusion. Creating parameters as in the previous example, we either need to know what our report parameters are going to be before we put our queries and build them before we create our dataset, or we would need to go back as in steps 13-15 in the previous example. That seems a little counter-intuitive to typical report design. Fortunately there is an easier way to create datasets, report parameters, and bind them in one simple procedure. We might remember the button next to the **Linked To Report Parameter** textbox to which I said we would come back to. In the following example, we will revisit the process of creating a dataset parameter to show how much easier it is to do the linking of Report Parameters and Data Set Parameters in later versions of BIRT. In the next exercise, we will go through the same steps as the previous exercise, except now we are going to use the quick method. Because we are going to use the same query as used earlier, we might want to go ahead and copy the existing one to the clipboard.

1. Under the **Data Explorer** or the **Outline** tab, expand the **Report Parameters** branch, select rprmEmployeeID, and delete it. We can do this by right-clicking and choosing **Delete**, going up to the **Edit** menu item and choosing **Delete**, or just pressing the **Delete** key on the keyboard.

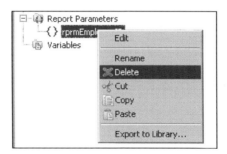

2. Open up the dsetEmployeeInfo dataset from either the **Data Set Explorer** or the **Outline** tab.

3. Under **Parameters**, select `dsprmEmployeeID`, and click the **Remove** button.

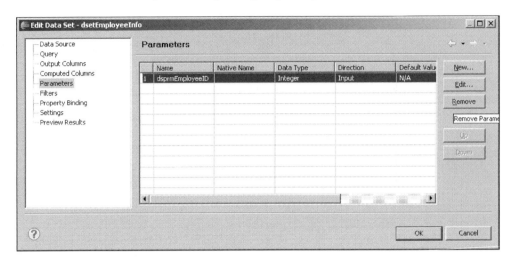

4. Click the **New…** button to create a new Data Set Parameter. At this point, we are basically at Step 6 from the first exercise. We have a new Data Set Parameter with no linking to any sort of values and no default value.

5. From the **New Parameter** dialog, use the same information as did before.

    ° **Name**: `dsprmEmployeeID`

    ° **Data Type**: `Integer`

    ° **Direction**: `Input`

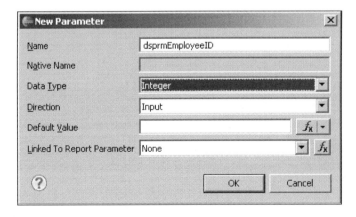

6. Click the **fX** button next to the **Linked to Report Parameter** textbox. This will bring up the Edit dialog for the Report Parameter, with most of the relevant information filled in. Set the **Name** value to `dsprmEmplyoyeeID`, fill in the prompt with what the reader should see when they run the report, and set the **Default value** to **1002**.

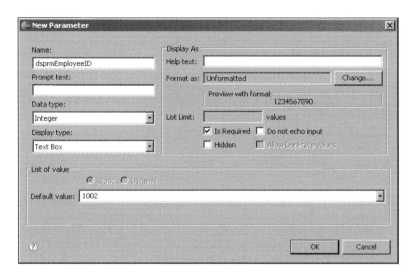

Now, when we click **OK** and go back to the Data Set Edit Dialog, we click on **Preview**. We will see the default value from the link Report Parameter is automatically filtered down to our dataset. Use of this method is preferred as it automatically creates that binding for us and takes out the additional steps of creating the Report Parameter separately from Data Set Parameters.

Dynamic Report Parameters and Filters

We have seen how we can work with database-driven data and report parameters to filter data using parameter binding between Report Parameters and Data Set Parameters. We may ask ourselves, why did we go through the first exercise when the second exercise was so much easier? This is because this concept of binding through expressions is used a lot in BIRT.

Report Parameters may require manual input from a user, but we can also have prepopulated drop-down boxes for Report Parameters that are created at design time or even populated from a database or other dataset. This is useful for cases where the input needs to be exact and it is assumed that the user does not know all of the possible values or exactly what information they are looking for.

While filtering of database data can be achieved through Data Set Parameters and the filtering done on the backend database, other types of datasets such as the XML, Flat File, and Scripted Data Sources do not have that capability. So, how can we filter that data based on user input? The answer is by binding the Report Parameter to a Filter expression. We may recall from the last chapter that we were able to filter an XML Data Set by using a specialized expression to retrieve only those employees who had the job title of DEVELOPER. In this next example, we are going to create a simple Employee listing report using the Employees table and, instead of using a WHERE clause, we are going to use a Filter to limit the returned results. We are also going to bind this Filter to a Report Parameter that will have the possible job titles prepopulated from a database query. Please note, just like with the Report Parameter and Data Set Parameter binding, there is a hard way to do it and an easy way. Let's cover only the easy way:

1. Create a new report titled `EmployeeList-CH6.rptDesign`.

2. Create a new Data Source from the Classic Cars Sample Database.

3. Create a new Report Parameter and call it `rprmEmployeeJobTitle`. Set the **Data type** to `String`, and change the **Display type** to **Combo Box**.

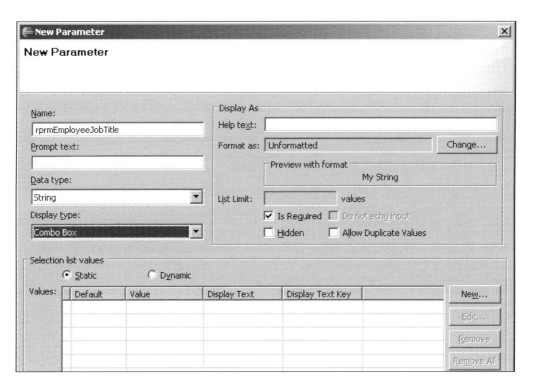

4. Notice that the dialog box changes. We can set the **Selection list values** option to either **Static** or **Dynamic**. Setting the option to **Static** implies that we need to input these values ourselves at design time, whereas setting to **Dynamic** implies the values will be generated based on the results of a dataset. The advantage to this is that we can have a back-end database someplace that we can simply insert values into and they will autopopulate this list. So, it can be populated from an existing table in our database. The disadvantage is that we need a database, which can go offline, and we need to maintain it. Therefore, the wiser option is to choose **Dynamic**.

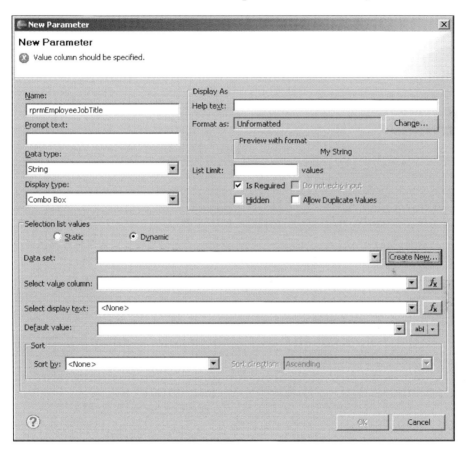

5. Here are all the options we can set for dynamic generation. If we already have a dataset, we can base the dynamic generation off of that. In this example, we will create a new, dedicated dataset strictly for populating our parameters. Go ahead and click the **Create New** button.

6. Name the dataset as `dsEmployeeJobTitles` and use the following SQL statement.

    ```
    select distinct CLASSICMODELS.EMPLOYEES.JOBTITLE from
    CLASSICMODELS.EMPLOYEES
    ```

7. Click **Finish** in the **SQL Editor**.

8   Click **OK** and exit out of the **Edit Data Set** dialog. We will now be back at the **New Parameter** dialog with the dataset already filled in to our new dataset. From the two drop-down boxes, chose **JOBTITLE** for both the value and the display text. Why are there two—the reason is for normalized databases. We can choose an ID for the value and a string to be displayed to the user. For example, if we were choosing a status code for defect tracking, we would have things such as Fixed, New, and In Process as possible status values for an issue, and these would have ID numbers such as 1, 2, and 3. We don't expect the user to know the ID codes, so we would display the names instead. The following is a screenshot of the dialog with the values filled in and the dataset created:

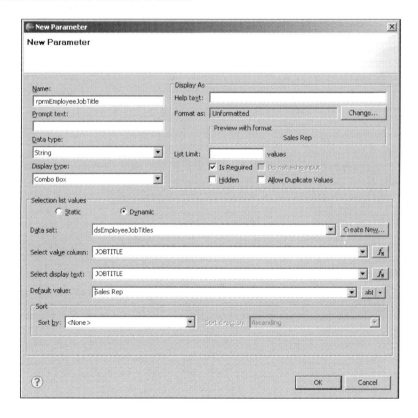

9. As the **Default value**, use **Sales Rep**.

10. Click **OK**.

11. From the **Data Set Explorer**, create a new dataset called dsEmployeeList. Use the following SQL Statement:

```
select
                        *
from
        CLASSICMODELS.EMPLOYEES
```

12. In the **Edit Data Set** dialog, select the **Filters** category. Create a new Filter.

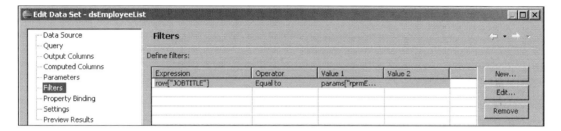

13. Under **Expression**, select **JOBTITLE** from the drop-down list.

14. Under **Value 1**, select **<Build expression...>** from the drop-down list.

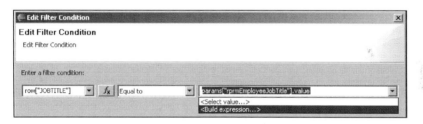

15. In the Expression Editor, under **Category**, select **Report Parameters**, under **Sub-Category** select **All**, and then select the Report Parameter as `rprmEmployeeJobTitle`. Double-click it until it appears in the textbox. Once there, click **OK**.

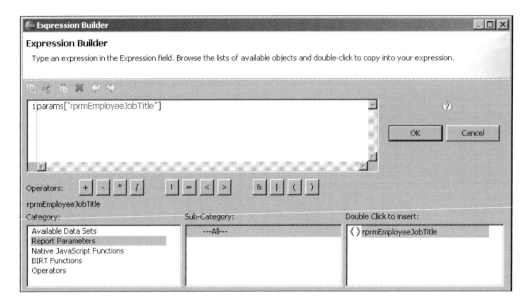

16. Drag-and-Drop the `dsEmployeeList` from either the **Data Explorer** or from the **Outline**.

17. Preview the report.

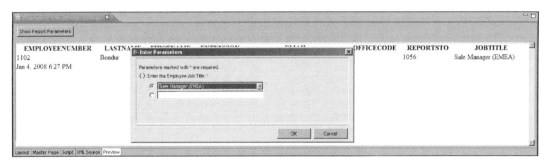

Now, when we bring up the **Show Report Parameters** dialog, we have a drop down with all the possible jobs for the employees. When we select one and click **OK**, it will filter down to employees with that job.

The example that we just discussed used a database dataset instead of one of the static ones. In the case of a database, we usually want to use a dataset parameter instead of a Filter. Using a WHERE clause and a dataset parameter will always outperform a Filter as the data is being filtered on the end of the DBMS. The DBMS is much more efficient at filtering data than BIRT would be. If we pulled a large dataset, BIRT would have to retrieve that entire dataset and apply the filter to it, wasting network bandwidth and processing time. Filters are useful in cases where we don't have a database to work with, such as a text file data source, or XML data source. In those cases, there is no DBMS to process a where clause and we have no choice but to use a Filter. But in either case, we have seen how the user can influence the data that gets returned as the earlier example will apply to the scripted data source, the flat file data source, and the XML data source.

Cascading parameters

In some cases, it is desirable to have the user select a high level category in order to limit the number of parameter choices a user sees. For example, let's say we were looking at a report where a user needed to look at products. In the case of a large company, there could be thousands of possible products or product codes. It is better to filter based on a product line to find the actual products one is looking for. Using the Classic Cars example, we have many different types of car models such as the 1969 Harley Davidson Ultimate Chopper, Dodge Charger, and 1948 Porsche 356-A Roadster. If we want to limit what is displayed, we limit our parameter display by product lines such as Classic Cars, Motorcycles, or Vintage Cars. Once a user has selected one of these, they would see only the vehicles under the corresponding product lines. These are called **cascading parameters**.

Let's look at an example. In this report, we are going to modify the Employee-Chapter6.rptDesign report we created earlier to allow for a drop-down parameter list that allows a user to select a manager and list the employees who are under the manager, and then select an employee and get the report for that employee.

1. Open Employee-Chapter6.rptDesign.
2. Save the report as Employee-Cascading-Chapter6.rptDesign.
3. From the **Data Explorer** delete the Report Parameter dsprmEmployeeID.

4. Create a new dataset called `dsEmployeeManager` and enter the following query:

```
SELECT
        employeenumber,
        lastname || ', ' || firstname employeeName,
        (SELECT
                lastname || ', ' || firstname
        FROM
                EMPLOYEES managerEmployees
        WHERE
                employeenumber = currentemployee.REPORTSTO
        ) managerName
FROM
        EMPLOYEES currentemployee
union all
SELECT
        employeenumber,
        lastname || ', ' || firstname employeeName,
        'All' managerName
FROM
        EMPLOYEES currentemployee
```

5. In the **Data Explorer**, right-click on **Report Parameters** and choose **New Cascading Parameter**.

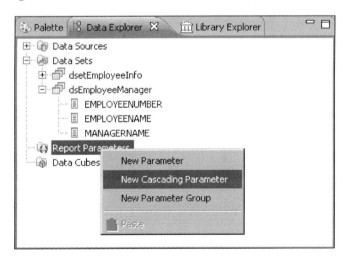

6. Enter `rcprmEmployeeManagers` as the parameter name.

7. Select the **Single Data Set** option.

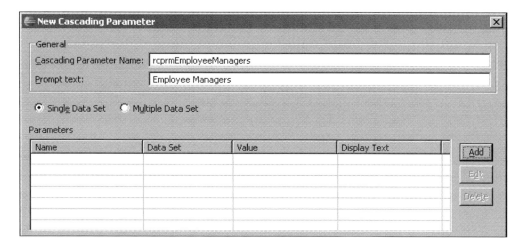

8. Click the **Add** button.

9. Enter the following information in the dialog window:

10. Click **OK**.

11. Now, click **Add** again, and enter the information for the Employee:

12. We can enter the **Prompt text** along with the default values for each of these rows, just like we would enter regular parameters.

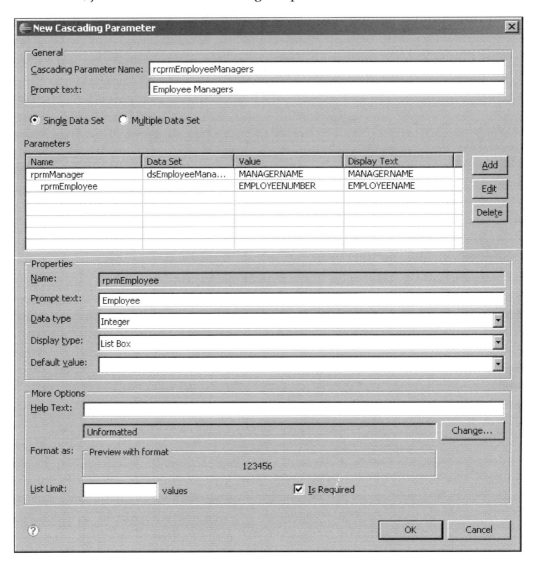

13. Click **OK**. Under the **Data Explorer**, select dsEmployeeInfo and double-click to open the Data Set Editor.

14. In the parameters, select dsprmEmployeeID, and click the **Edit** button.

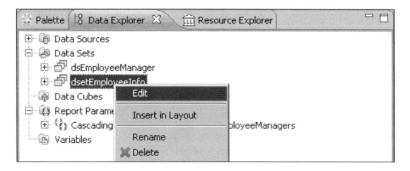

15. In the **Edit parameter** window, set the **Linked to Report Parameter** option to rprmEmployee.

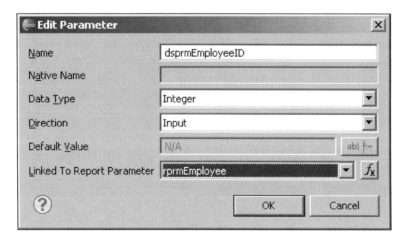

16. Save the report and preview it.

Now, when we run the report, we will have two new parameters. When we select the Manager drop down, the second list will get smaller. So, if we select **All**, then all of the employees will appear in the second drop-down list. Change the Manager drop-down option to something else and the list of employees changes.

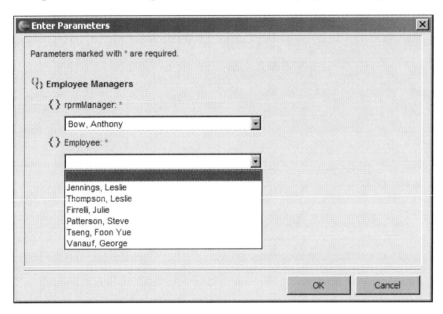

Parameter grouping and reports with multiple parameters

While we won't cover this in detail, I would like to discuss it briefly. With reports, one can create multiple report parameters and bind them to a single dataset or to multiple datasets. Just because a parameter has already been bound once does not mean it cannot be bound again. When we create a report parameter, that parameter becomes a global variable for our report that can be used anywhere in the report. We can also use multiple parameters in a single dataset, both as prepared parameters for queries and filters. For example, let's say we have a query that pulls all orders for a particular market and for a date range. In this query, we would have three parameters—one for the market, and two for the start date and end date. Each of these can be set to a data set parameter and a report parameter.

So, what happens when we start to have more parameters and need to manage them? The simple answer is that we can create a parameter group, and associate multiple parameters with that group. Therefore, in the example that we discussed in the earlier section , we can create a date range parameter group, and associate the "Start Date" and "End Date" parameters with it. This is as simple as dragging and dropping existing parameters in the **Data Explorer** or **Outline** tab, or creating new parameters inside of an existing parameter group.

Setting default parameter values

One of the most commonly asked questions over the past few years in the newsgroups have been "How can I set a date parameter to default to the current date?"

Before BIRT 2.5, this was not an easy task to accomplish. However, new to BIRT 2.5 is the ability to set a date parameter's default value via script. Let's go about it:

1. Create a new report called `defaultParameterValueReport.rptdesign`.

2. Create the Classic Cars Sample Database Data Source.

3. Create a dataset called `dsOrderRange`, with the help of following query:

```
select
       *
from
       CLASSICMODELS.ORDERS
where
       CLASSICMODELS.ORDERS.ORDERDATE between ? and ?
```

4. Link the two dataset parameters to report parameters called `prmStartDate` and `prmEndDate`. Make sure the two dateset parameters and two report parameters are of type `Date`.

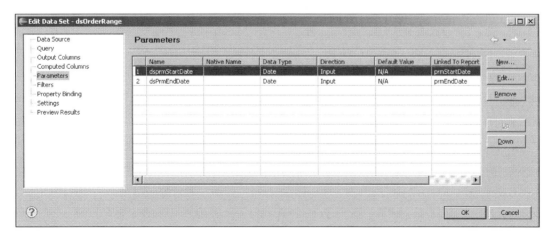

5. Open the editor for `prmStartDate`. In the drop-down box next to **Default value**, select **Javascript Syntax** and continue.

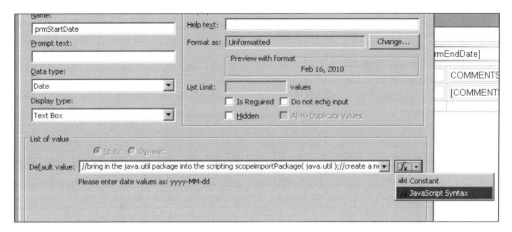

6. Use the following script in the expression builder. Don't worry about what this means, just understand that it will set the start date to 20 days before the current date.

```
//bring in the java.util package into the scripting scope
importPackage( java.util );

//create a new GregorianCalendar object
var cal = new java.util.GregorianCalendar();

//set the date to now
cal.setTime(new Date());

//substract 20 days
cal.add(Calendar.DAY_OF_MONTH, -20);

//return the start date
cal.getTime();
```

7. Do the same for the `prmEndDate` and set the expression to the following:
   `new Date();`

8. Insert the dataset into the report.

9. Create a grid of three columns and a row above the dataset table. In the first column, create a label and set the text to **Orders Between:**.

10. From the **Data Explorer** or the **Outline** view, drag `prmStartDate` to Column 2.

11. From the **Data Explorer** or the **Outline** view, drag `prmEndDate` to Column 3.

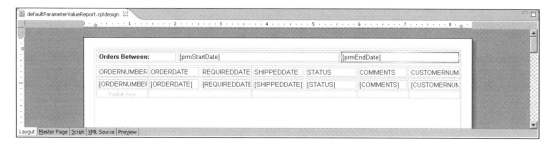

12. Run the report.

Initially, we won't see any date in the report. This is because the data in the Classic Cars Database is from 2005, so there is no date in range. But we can see from the **Orders Between** header that the date range has start date set to 20 days before the current date whereas the end date is the current date. We can change these at run time.

Summary

In this chapter, we have seen how to interact with report users to help them retrieve specific information. Hopefully the distinct difference between Report Parameters and Data Set Parameters has been made clear. In later chapters, we will look at other ways Report Parameters can be used and this concept is going to be used more in depth when we start looking at scripting and changing visual components and properties. We have taken a look at how values can be bound to properties, which is going to be more important as we look at different report types and capabilities.

7
Report Projects and Libraries

Up until now, all the reports we have built have been very simple reports. However, we have seen that each of these reports use very similar components between them such as the data sources to the Classic Cars database and the datasets that pull employee information. These are common elements between the reports we have built. In most project-based development environments, there is a way to share common elements between components, and BIRT is no exception to this.

Also, in the previous chapters we worked with a single project. This chapter will help us create a more structured reporting project and work with libraries to share the common report elements between reports. In most report development shops that I have come across, this is a great way to structure report development and can save developers lots of time, especially when more complex report components get developed. By grouping reports in projects and reusing elements in libraries, common elements such as headers, data sources, and queries can be reused with a minimal amount of development effort.

Report projects

Earlier in the book, we created a report project that contains the examples we have built so far. But the concept of what a report project is and how to work with them is has not yet been thoroughly covered.

A report project in Eclipse is simply a high-level container that will be used to store all files in a given project. In Eclipse, projects are simply folders, either contained inside of a workspace or linked to an external file system folder or directory outside of the workspace. What differentiates projects from regular folders is a special file inside this folder that defines various properties for the project and which is usually named `project name.project`. For our general purpose report development, we don't really need to know anything else about this file; simply knowing that projects are just folders that contain all the files related to our project is enough.

Project types are defined when we first create our project. In earlier versions of BIRT, there was only a Report Project type. In newer versions of BIRT, there are many different types of projects that are BIRT related. We have been working on a Report Project throughout this book. For the remainder of the book, we will continue using the BIRT Report Project; just keep in mind that there are other report project types as well. There is also the BIRT ODA Designer Plug-in and the BIRT ODA Runtime Plug-in projects, for building our own custom BIRT Open Data drivers for the BIRT Designer and BIRT Runtimes respectively. The following screenshot shows the project types that come with BIRT 2.5:

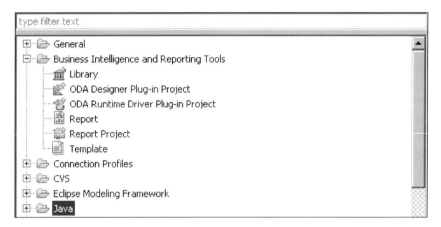

Creating new Report Projects

Creating projects in BIRT is no different from creating projects of other types in Eclipse, such as Java projects.

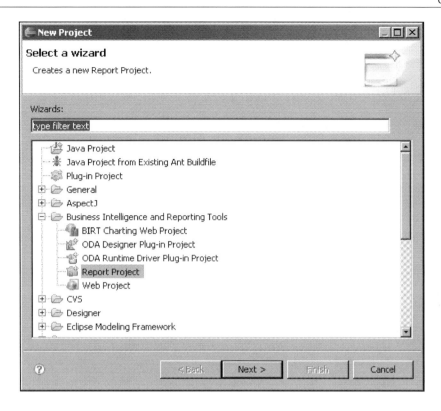

In this screenshot we can see the **New Project** wizard with the different types of BIRT Projects available. This will vary based on the plugins we have installed. In this screenshot, I have a plugin for BIRT Web Projects and Charting web projects from earlier versions of BIRT.

As we have seen previously, report project creation is simple. The general steps to create a Report Project were illustrated in *Chapter 3, The BIRT Environment and First Report*. Therefore, I will touch only a few points as there are a few different ways to create projects in Eclipse.

Project creation is possible from the **File** menu and from the **Navigator**.

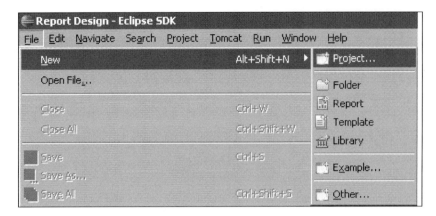

In the preceding screenshot, we can see the **New** option of the **File** menu, with the **Project...** option highlighted.

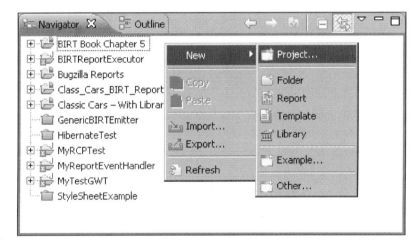

In this screenshot we can see the **New** menu in the **Navigator**, accessed using the right-click context menu. Creating report projects from the **Navigator** is essentially the same as with the **File** menu, with the only difference being that when we create a project in the **File** menu, we will go to **File | New | Project...** instead of right-clicking in the **Navigator** pane. If we are not in the BIRT perspective, we will have different options available under the **New** menu, as seen in the following screenshot when the Java perspective is open.

As we can see, in the Java perspective, the new Report, Template, and Library
options for BIRT are also available. It is advisable to create new projects and reports
from the BIRT perspective, however, as most of the workbench sections, such as the
Palette, do not open by default.

Importing and exporting Report Projects

Because BIRT Report Projects are simply a collection of report design files, the
importing and exporting options available in Eclipse are not entirely useful.
However, there are a few options that can be used for backup and restoration
purposes. The following examples will look at exporting a project to an archive
file and restoring it with the **Import** option.

Let's say that we need to archive the Classic Cars project that we have been building in the book. We will want to archive this as a ZIP file to `C:\Temp\ClassicCars.zip`. In order to do this, we need to right-click on the `Project` directory or the report file we want to archive and select the appropriate option. So, in this case we will use the `Class_Cars_BIRT_Reports` project. We will then specify the archive file(s) to include in the archive.

1. From the **Navigator** pane, right-click on the `Class_Cars_BIRT_Reports` project and select the **Export...** option. You can also select the `Class_Cars_BIRT_Reports` project and, under the **File** menu, select the **Export...** option.

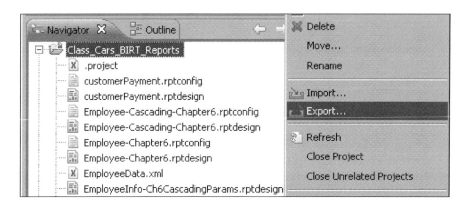

2. Under the **General** option, select **Archive File**.

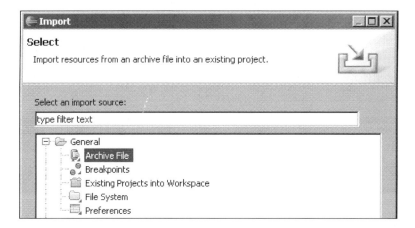

3. From the **Archive File** editor, make sure the `Class_Cars_BIRT_Reports` project is checked. Make sure the files we want archived are also checked.

4. In the **To archive file** textbox, enter the path. This can be done by using the **Browse** button or by manually entering the path. In my case, I will enter `C:\Temp\ClassicCars.zip`.

5. Make sure the **Save in zip format** and **Create directory structure for files** options are selected. This will make sure that the directory structure is identical for the entire project when we extract the archive. If the **Create only selected directories** option is selected, only the files with a checkmark next to them will be selected, and this example shows a complete export. The `.zip` format is supported across multiple platforms, so I usually suggest this over `.tar`.

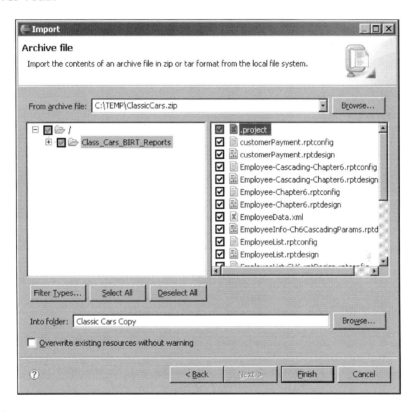

6. Click **Finish**.

Now you have made an exported archive of the project. Let's say that we received this archive and wanted to work with these report files. We would need to import the project into our Eclipse workspace. Fortunately, the process for doing so is very similar to exporting.

7. Right-click on the **Navigator** and create a new Report Project called **Classic Cars Copy**.

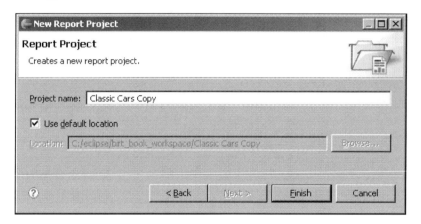

8. From the **File** menu or by right-clicking in the **Navigator**, select the **Import...** option.

9. From the **General** branch of the tree view, select **Archive File**.

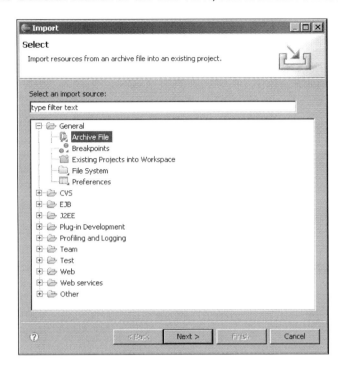

10. In the dialog, enter `C:\Temp\ClassicCars.zip` as **From archive file**. We can also use the **Browse** button to find the archive file.

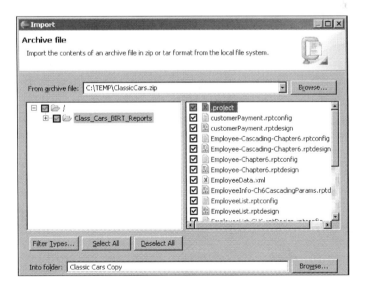

11. From the **Into folder** textbox, make sure the **Classic Cars Copy** project is selected.

12. In the case of this archive, I want to deselect the / directory and the Class_Cars_BIRT_Reports folder. I just want to select the files that are under the Class_Cars_BIRT_Reports folder. This is due to the archive option that created the folder structure. So, I will deselect both folders and manually select the files under the file listbox.

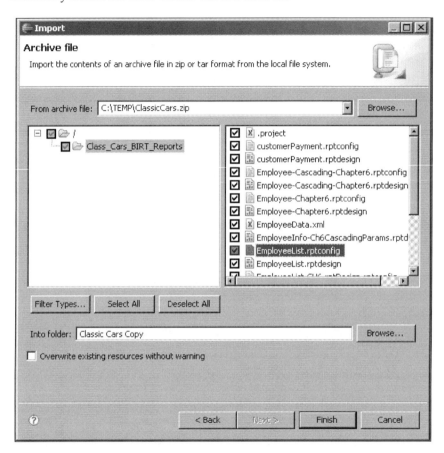

13. Click **Finish**.

We also have the option to choose to import **Existing Projects into Workspace** and choose archive file, but this will use the exact same project name. For this example, we already have a project titled Classic_Cars_BIRT_Reports, so this import would fail if we do not delete the project. I won't show this here; just keep in mind that if we are copying a project or group of projects into a workspace, we can use the **Import Existing Projects into Workspace** option.

Other project options

In terms of reporting, there is very little you will need to do with the vast number of options available for projects in Eclipse. Therefore, if we are working with a lot of projects, we may have other projects open other than the one you are working in, which case we may want to do a mass closing of projects. Eclipse offers a nice option to close all projects unrelated to the selected one.

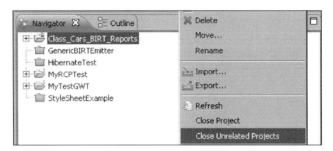

In this screenshot, we can see I have three projects opened — Class_Cars_BIRT_
Reports, MyRCPTest, and MyTestGWT. Because I am only working with the
Class_Cars_BIRT_Reports project, it is the only project I want open. Therefore,
I select it, right-click on it in the **Navigator**, and select **Close Unrelated Projects**.
This will close all but the selected project.

We can also specify that a project is related. Try the following to illustrate.

1. Create three new projects — Project1, Project2, and Project3.
2. Right-click on Project1 and choose **Properties**.

3. Select the **Project References** item.

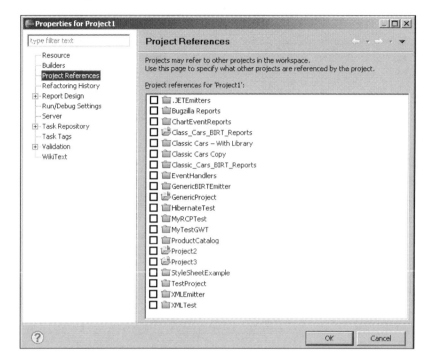

4. Select `Classic_Cars_BIRT_Reports`.

5. Click **OK**.

6. Right-click on `Project1` and select **Close Unrelated Projects**.

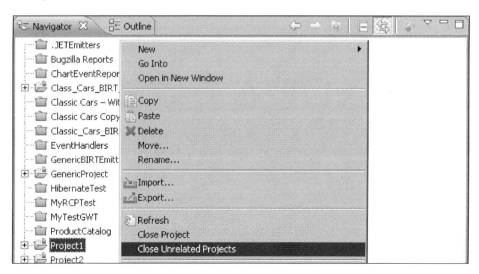

As this example illustrates, once we specify a project is related, it will not close when the **Close Unrelated Projects** option is specified for any project in a relation chain.

If we need to focus a little more on a specific project and closing projects isn't an attractive option, we have the option to **Go Into** a project or folder and only that project's files will be visible in the **Navigator**. In the preceding screenshot, I can right-click on `Class_Cars_BIRT_Reports` and select **Go Into** instead of **Close Unrelated Projects**. This will force the Navigator to display only the files and subfolders that are under the `Classic_Cars_BIRT_Reports` project.

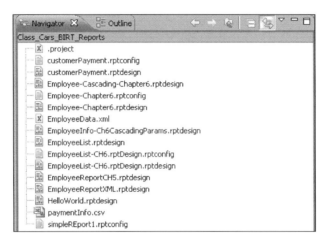

If we look at this screenshot, we can see the `Class_Cars_BIRT_Reports` project when the **Go Into** option has been executed on it. Notice the yellow left arrow is available, whereas the right one is not. The left arrow is the equivalent of a "Go Back" button. The right arrow is the same as the **Go Into** menu option. We also have the folder icon with an up arrow, which gets you directly to the top level workspace.

Let's look at this in an example.

1. Select the `Classic_Cars_BIRT_Reports` project.
2. Right-click and select **Go Into**.

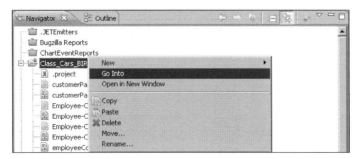

3. Click on the yellow left arrow.

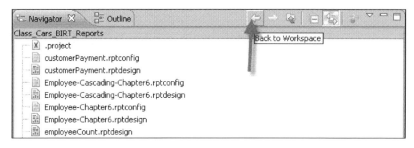

4. Now the right arrow will be available, which allows us to go forward. Click on the yellow-colored right pointing arrow.

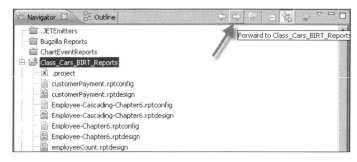

5. Now, click the **Up to Workspace** button.

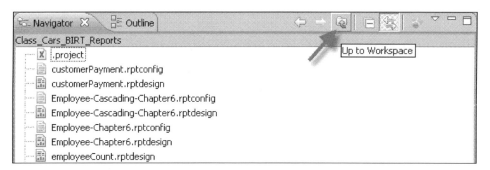

This should demonstrate that these buttons function just like a browser's history buttons, but work with the navigation of the file system within the workspace.

The final option we will look at here is the **Team** option. This is useful when we have a versioning server and we want to submit our files or check out files from it. Eclipse, out of the box, supports only CVS; however, there are plugins available for subversion and other versioning systems as well.

So, let's say we have a CVS server at IP address 192.168.1.103. We want to be able to store out reports in this repository. Let's look at the steps on how to do so.

6. From the **Navigator**, right-click on the project, and select
    Team | Share Project....

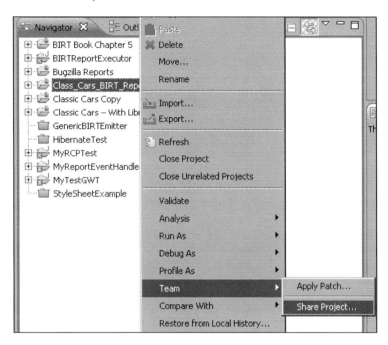

7. From the repository type screen, select **CVS**.

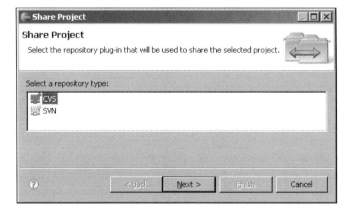

8. Input the necessary information to connect to the repository.

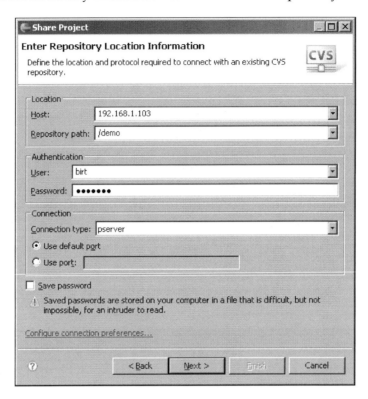

9. Specify a module name or choose to use the Eclipse project name as the repository project name.

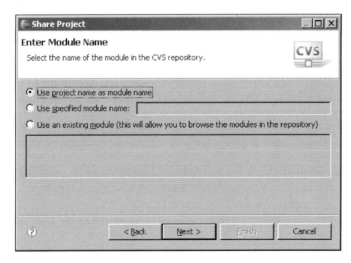

10. Click **Finish**.

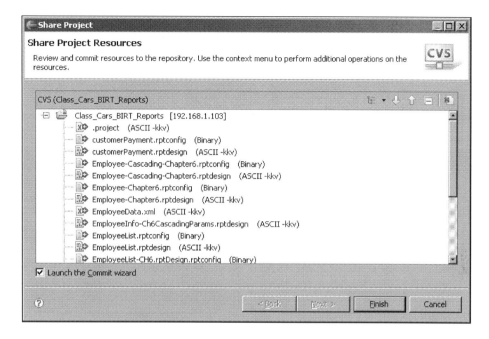

11. We will then be asked to enter a comment for the commit of new files.

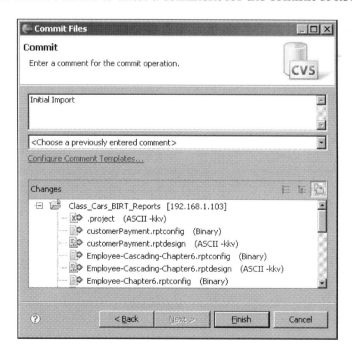

Now, our files have been stored in the repository. In the **Navigator**, a version number and type will appear next to each file. When we edit a file, it will affect only the local copy, and an indicator will appear next to the file indicating that a change has been made. In the following screenshot, the `Hello-World.rptDesign` file has been edited:

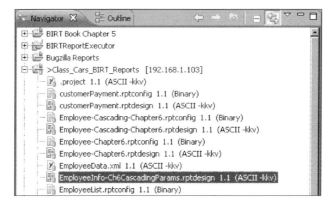

With a project shared, the **Team** menu will change and have additional options. We can synchronize with the repository, which will do a comparison between files to show which files are different in the repository and which ones have been edited locally. We can commit files to the repository and we can update our local files from the repository. We can also disconnect from the repository, which will bring us back to the state where we can edit only our local files and they will not be shared.

It is recommended to use the **Synchronize…**option if we use a repository. From the **Synchronize…** menu, we can see the differences between the local copy of files and the remote versions, see the revision history, and we have more control over the commit and update selections.

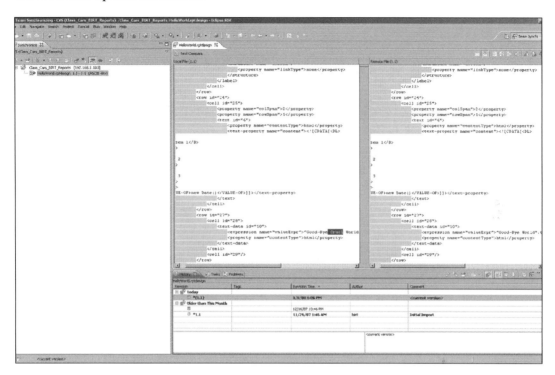

Libraries

Often, report development involves repetitive tasks. Things such as report headers, commonly used datasets and data sources, formatting, and other elements are used in many different reports. This is where libraries come into play. When using libraries, report developers can store commonly used components for later reuse. It is also a useful tool when working in groups.

The concepts of reuse and group development are often overlooked in report development, and this seems to be all but entirely ignored with BIRT. However, if we have worked in a report development group, it is an all too often needed functionality. When I was working in a large report development group, the data that got pulled was often the same, if not similar, to previous report requests, with modification to visual layouts, or modified parameters. Another scenario that was common was to develop reports only to find out that someone had done the same report several months ago. With BIRT's report libraries, these kinds of common tasks can be stored in a central report library and made accessible to other developers to reuse and share their components. This is even useful in single developer situations to avoid having to rebuild commonly used objects in different reports.

In BIRT, libraries are similar in structure and design to a report document. The main difference being that libraries can be referenced inside of report designs and the visual editor for libraries will be different. When there are changes to library elements, these changes will trickle down into the report designs that are using them. The only exception is with chart elements in versions of BIRT prior to 2.2.

Creating a new library

As with report designs, a library can be created using either the **New** option under the **Navigator** or the **File** menu. This is nice as it does not deviate from the expected behavior. In the following example, we are going to create a new Report Project called Classic Cars Library and create a new library using it.

1. From either the **Navigator** or **File** menu, go to **New | Project**. Name the project Classic Cars - With Library.

2. In the **Navigator**, right-click on the new project, and choose **New | Library**. Name the library as ClassicCarsLibrary.rptlibrary.

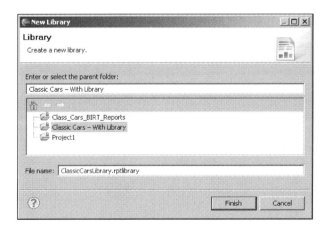

3. When we click on **Finish**, we will get a dialog telling you how to work with the visual designer for a library. Click **OK**.

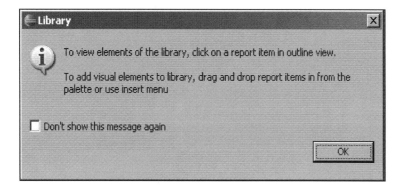

Adding components to a library

Now that we have a library, we need to add a few components to it. With the reports that we have created throughout the book, we have used a consistent data source, the Classic Cars Sample Database. This would make a good candidate for a library item.

Adding a data source to a library

In the following example, we will add a data source to a library.

1. Open the `ClassicCarsLibrary.rptlibrary`, if it is not already opened.
2. Open the **Outline** view.

3. Open the **Palette** view above the **Outline** pane view so that both panes are open at the same time.

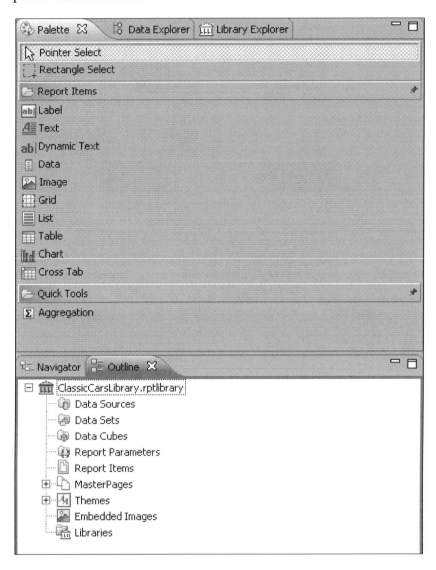

4. Right-click on the **Data Sources** icon under the **Outline** and select **New Data Source**.

5. Select the Classic Models Inc. Samples database and name the datasource `dsClassicCars`. Click **Next**.

6. Click **Finish**.

Now we have a data source in a library. This was easy to do. Most of this should be familiar as it is the same steps to add to a report design.

Adding a visual element to a library

In our reports, we will want to add in simple report headers containing a logo for the Classic Cars Company, a company title line, and a report title line. The report title line will be populated by a report parameter so that the design of the header is consistent, but the title will be dynamic.

1. In the **Outline** view, right-click on the **Report Parameters** icon and select **New Parameter**.

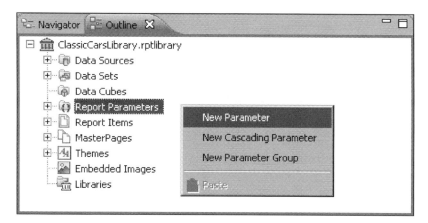

2. Enter the following properties:

   ○ **Name**: rprmReportTitle

   ○ **Prompt text**: **Enter the Reports Title**

   ○ Change the parameter to a hidden parameter by clicking on the **Hidden** checkbox.

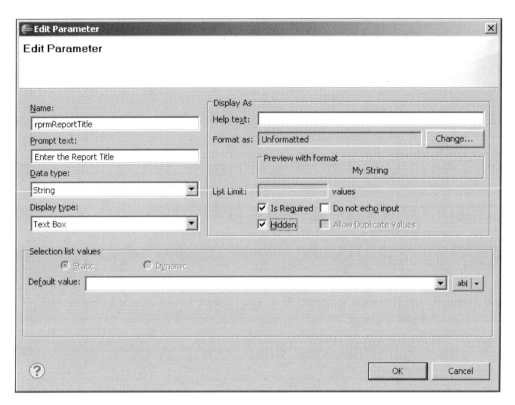

3. Drag a grid item from the **Palette** to the Report Items section under the **Outline**.

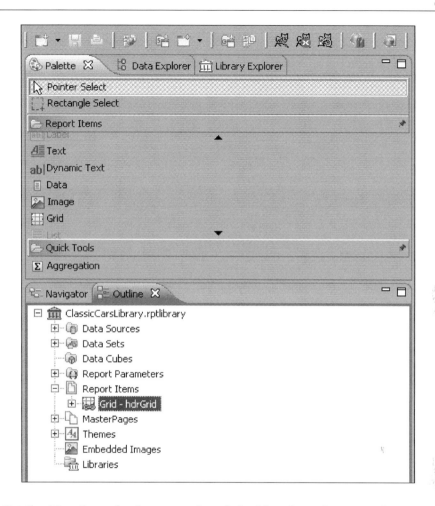

4. Set the **Number of columns** to 2 and the **Number of rows** to 3.

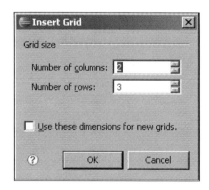

5. In the leftmost columns, select all three rows, right-click on the selection, and choose **Merge Cells**. The **Merge Cells** option is also available from the **Element** menu.

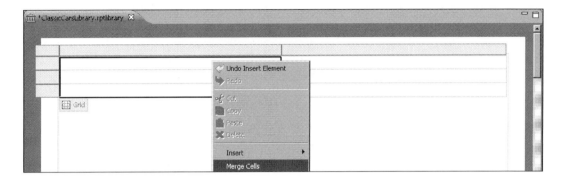

6. Change the name of the grid to `hdrGrid` under the **General** tab of the **Property Editor**.

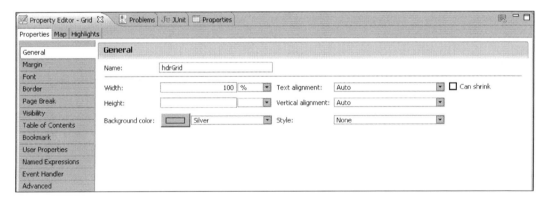

7. Drag an `Image` object from the **Palette** over to the single, large cell.

8. In the dialog that pops up, click on the function button for the URL. Change the type to **Constant** in the drop-down list next to the textbox.

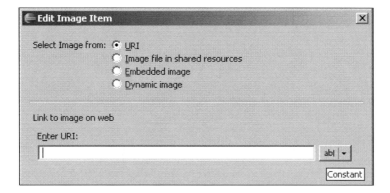

9. Simply borrow the Classic Cars logo from the Eclipse BIRT website. The logo can be obtained from: http://www.eclipse.org/birt/phoenix/ examples/solution/ClassicLogo.jpg.

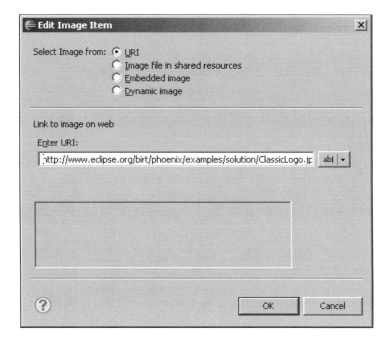

10. Once the image has been added, change the **Name** to `hdrLogo` under the **General** tab of the **Property Editor**.

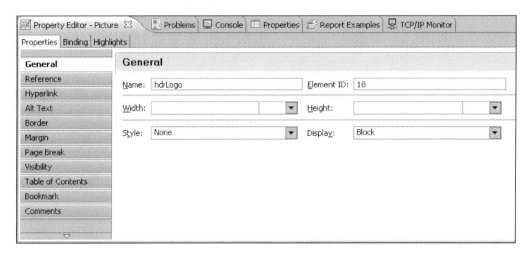

11. Drag the column line over from the center as far as it will go to the left. This will eliminate the empty space in the column containing the image.

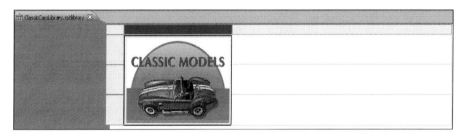

12. Drag a label component over to the second column, first row cell.

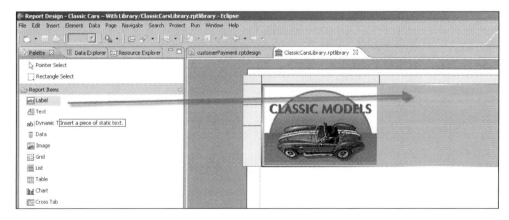

13. For the Text, enter **Classic Cars, Inc.**

14. Set the label name to `hdrHeaderLabel1` under **Properties**.

15. Change the font properties as follows:
    ° **Size: 24 points**
    ° **Weight: Bold**

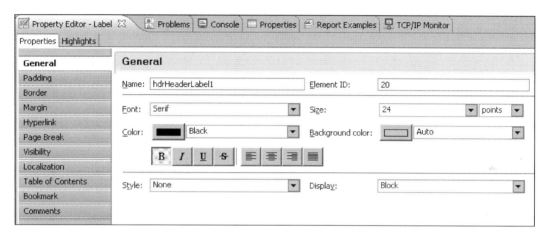

16. Drag a data object to the second row. Set the name to `hdrHeaderLabel2`.

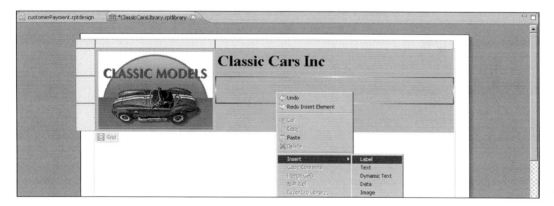

17. Enter the **Expression Editor** for the data component. Navigate to `Report Parameters/All/rprmReportTitle` as the data expression. The final expression should be `params["rprmReportTitle"]` when done.

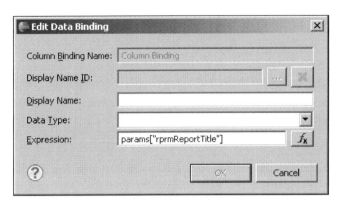

18. Enter the following font parameters:

    ○ **Size: 16 points**

    ○ **Weight: Bold**

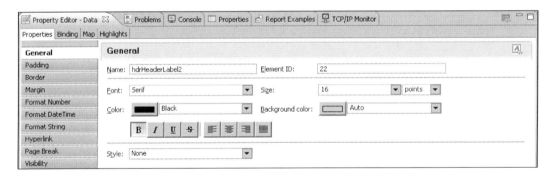

19. Drag a `Text` object over to the third row. Set the name to `hdrHeaderLabel3`.

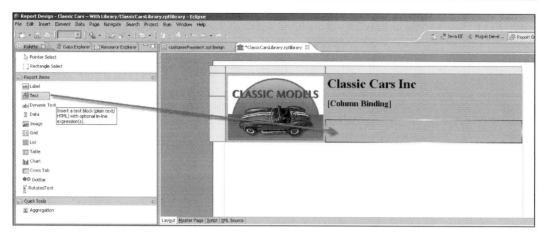

20. Change the value to `<VALUE-OF>new Date()</VALUE-OF>`.

21. Select the grid component and change the **Background color** to **Silver**.

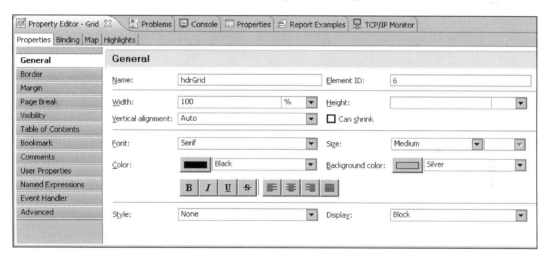

The finished component will look like the following image:

Using components stored in a library

We now have two components stored in a library—a report header and a data source. How do you consume them. Well, that's what we are going to look at next. Using elements in a library is fairly straightforward. We only need to use the library in a report design that is stored in a project, and we are ready to go. We will look at how to do this in the next example.

1. Create a new Report Design under the Classic Cars - With Library report. Call it CustomerOrderForm.rptDesign. Use the blank report template.

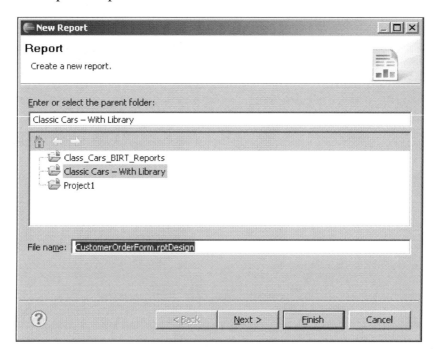

2. Open the **Outline** view for the new report.

3. Open the **Resource Explorer** above the **Outline** view. We should see the library, with a drop hierarchical tree view showing its components.

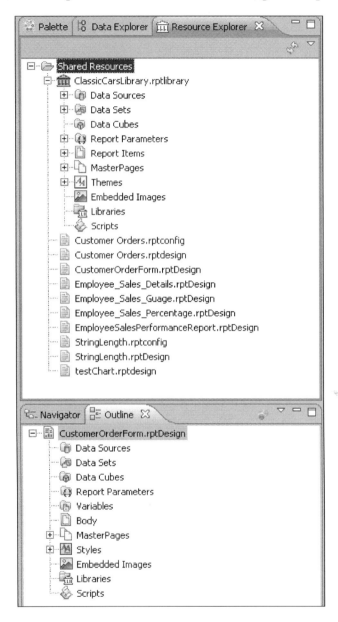

4. Drag the data source from under the **Resource Explorers** data sources to the data sources in the **Outline** view. This will reference the library's data source in the report design.

Take note of the icon in the report outline. The chain in the icon indicates that this report item is linked to a library. This is a different icon from a regular data source icon.

5. Under the **Report Parameters** section of the library, we can either drag-and-drop `rprmReportTitle` to the report or simply right-click on `rprmReportTitle` and choose **Add To Report**.

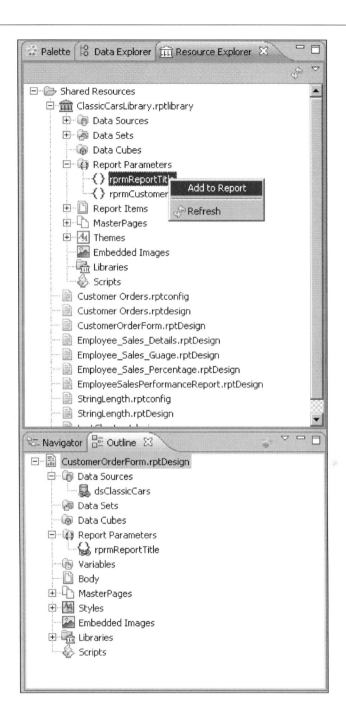

6. Now, under the library, expand the **Report Items** section. Right-click on the hdrGrid object. Select the **Data Sources** icon under the **Outline** tab. We will notice that the option to **Add to Report** is grayed out as the correct target location is not selected in the report design outline. This is one caveat to adding through context menus, which is not an issue with dragging and dropping.

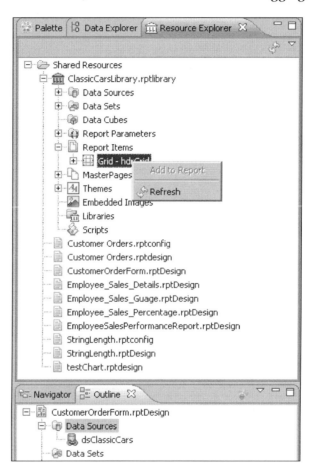

7. Select the **MasterPages** section in the **Outline** tab and then select **Header**.

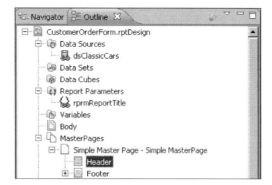

8. Right-click on `hdrGrids` in the libraries and choose **Add to Report**.

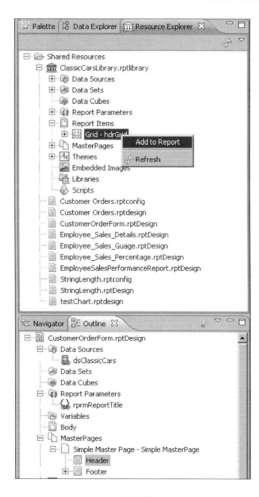

9. In the **Outline** tab, select `rprmReportTitle` under **Report Parameters**, right-click, and choose **Edit**.

10. Enter **Customer Orders Report** in the **Default value** textbox.

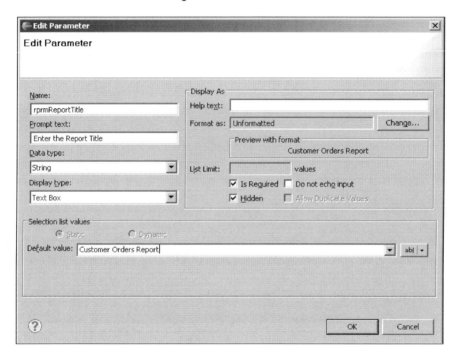

11. Save the report and preview.

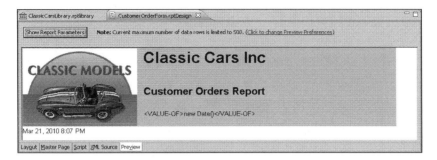

Updating components in the library to update reports

In the previous example, we must have noticed that when we preview the report, date is incorrect. In fact, it is showing us the HTML markup, not an actual date, which isn't right. The problem is that any report that uses this report header will suffer from the same problem. Now, we could fix these in each of the reports themselves; however, the fix would be local to that report only. We would surely like this fix to trickle down to all reports that are using these items. In order for that to happen, we need to edit the library itself.

1. Open `ClassicCarsLibrary`.

2. Under the **Report Items**, select `hdrGrid`. It should become visible in the **Report Design** pane.

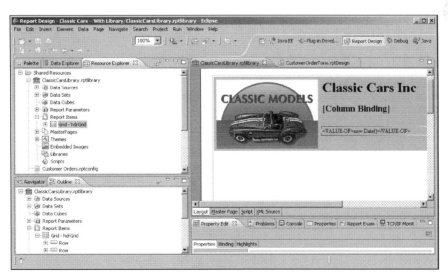

3. Double-click on `hdrHeaderLabel3` in the third row, second column to open the Text Item Editor.

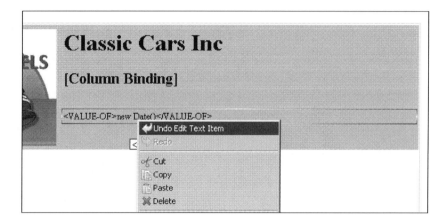

4. Change the value of the mode from **Auto** to **HTML** and click **OK**.

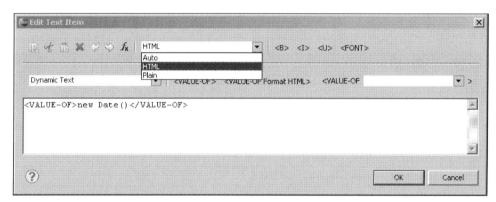

5. Save `ClassicCarsLibrary.rptlibrary`.

6. Open `CustomerOrdersForm.rptDesign`. We will be prompted that the library has been updated and we will be asked whether we want to reload the changes. Choose **OK**.

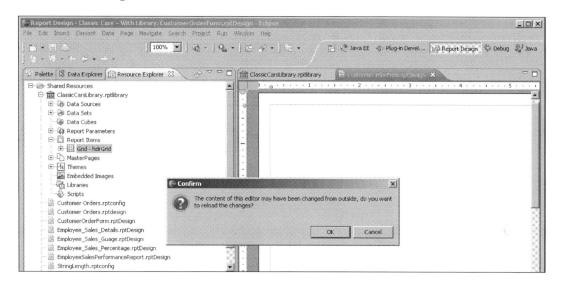

7. Rerun the report. Now that the library has been updated, when we run the report, we can see that the broken items have been fixed and the date gets displayed correctly.

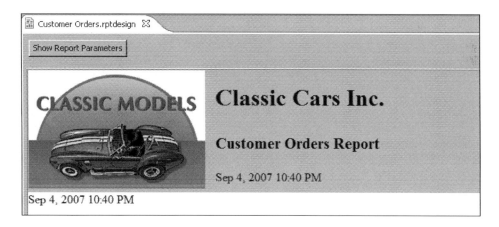

It should be noted that once we change a component in a report such as its text, it then becomes a part of the report and not of the library. This is because technically the components consumed within a report become extensions of components in a library. When we change something, we are changing the extension, not the original; however, unmodified components will still reflect changes. The following example will demonstrate that changes made in the report will take precedence over the original library item.

8. Open the **Master Page** section of the report design.

9. Double-click on the `hdrHeaderLine1` label in the Report Design file.

10. Change the text to read **Classic Cars Incorporated**.

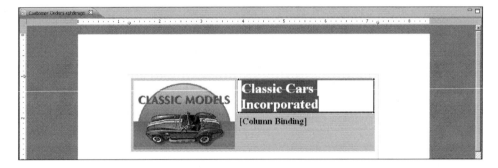

11. Save the report.

12. Open `ClassicCarsLibrary.rptlibrary`.

13. In the **Outline** tab, select **Report Items | hdrGrid** to make the header visible in the Report Designer.

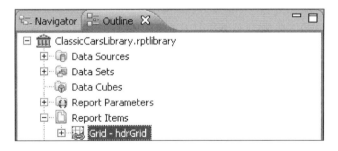

14. Delete the third line with the `<Value-Of>new Date()</Value-Of>` tag. Save the library.

15. In the First line, remove the period from **Classic Cars Inc..**

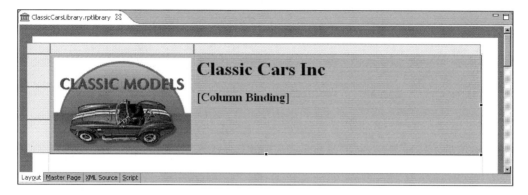

16. Save the library.

17. Run the report.

In the example that we just discussed, the change made in the report will take precedence over the change made in the library, while the deleted line will not be displayed in the report as the change will trickle down. It can be inferred from the following screenshot that the local change to the company title take precedence over the library changes, but the deleted date line shows in both.

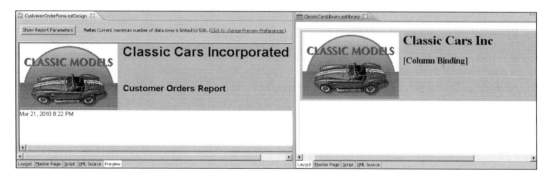

Adding existing components in reports to libraries

So far in this chapter, we have looked at developing and publishing components into a report library from scratch. We then looked at how reports could consume those libraries and link in those components. Next, we looked at editing the libraries and having them trickle down to reports.

So, what happens when we have a report we have developed and there are portions we want to share with others; how do you go about publishing these components to libraries?

Fortunately, there is an easy way to do this. From the context menu, we can right-click on an element and add it to a library.

The next example will show us how to add report components from a report to a library. We will create a basic query to retrieve customer information, which we will use later to combine with a second dataset to have a master/detail type report.

1. Add a dataset called getCustomerInformation to the report.

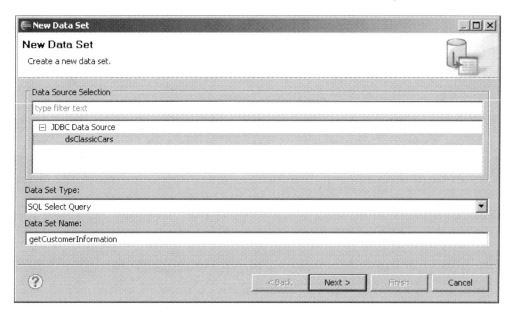

2. Use the following query:

```
select *
from CLASSICMODELS.CUSTOMERS
where CLASSICMODELS.CUSTOMERS.CUSTOMERNUMBER = ?
```

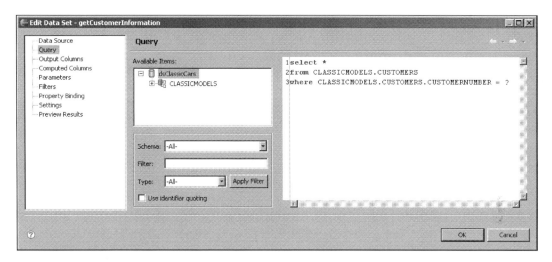

3. Create a report parameter called `rprmCustomerID` and link it to the dataset. Use the default value of 148 to make development a little easier so that we can debug and not have to enter a value each time.

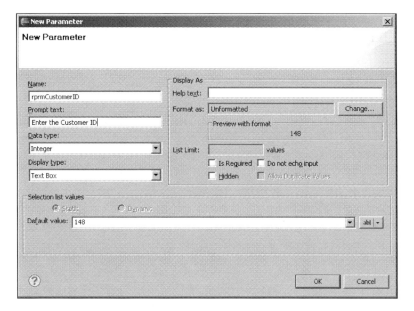

4. Save the report.

5. From the **Outline** or the **Data Explorer** tab, select getCustomerInformation.

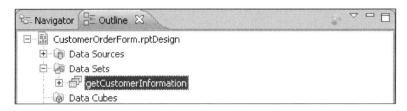

6. Right-click and choose **Export to Library...**.

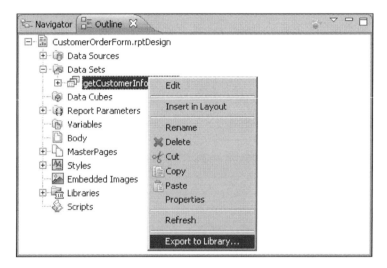

7. Select ClassicCarsLibrary.rptlibrary as the location where we wish to export.

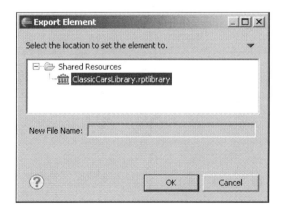

8. Click **OK**.

9. Repeat steps 5 to 8 for `rprmCustomerID`, located under the **Report Parameters** section of the **Outline** or **Data Explorer**.

10. Save the library.

The problem with this method is that the dataset and the report parameter are both two separate instances from the report design files and the report libraries. The way to link them is to delete the instances in the report and consume them using the steps described earlier in this chapter.

1. In the Report Design file, delete both `getCustomerInformation` and `rprmCustomerID`.

2. Add both components from the library back into the report.

 Note: I encountered an issue here and had to close both the library and the report design to accomplish this step.

Master Pages

Master Pages are header and footer sections of reports that appear on each page of a report. For example, if we have a report that prints ten pages in PDF, the Master Page will display on each page in addition to the report detail section as designed in the layout. In the library examples we did in this chapter, we created a header that displays the Classic Models logo, company title, and a report title. If we print a ten page report, that header will display on all ten pages.

Master pages are where report designers will typically set page level settings such as page size, orientation, and margin size.

1. Open `CustomerOrderForm.rptDesign`.

2. From the **Outline**, select **Master Pages**. Drill down to **Simple Master Page**.

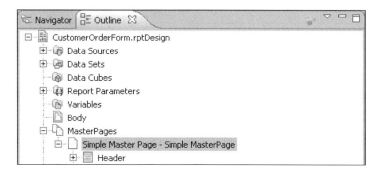

3. Under the **Property Editor**, select **General**. Note that this is where you would set page type, size, and orientation.

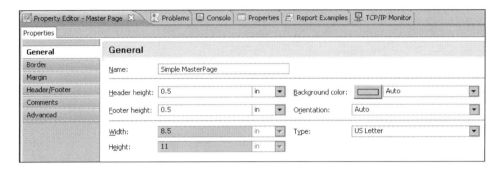

4. Now select **Header/Footer**. This section controls whether a header is shown on the first page and a footer is shown on the last page.

Summary

In this chapter, we looked at the aspects that are available to report projects and at creating a shared development environment using libraries. There are other options such as templates that allow us to create collaborative and consistent report designs across the enterprise. All such concepts will be covered in later chapters.

We have also learned how to create new libraries, new library components, and use those components in report designs. We have also seen how to add components from reports into libraries and how to edit libraries.

We saw some other elements that were new such as the Master Page that is a common header and footer that will get placed on every page of a report in multipage reports.

The next chapter will give detailed information on two themes, the concept of applying a consistent visual design to report designs using styles, and how to apply overall styles in libraries to reports by using themes.

8
Charts, Hyperlinks, and Drilldowns

It has been said that a picture is worth a thousand words. In the world of reporting, we call these pictures as Charts. With the help of charts, one can present a large amount of data with relative ease, in comparison to presenting with the help of huge data outputs. Charts are useful when used with raw data to drive home points such as percentages, or when used with other charts to build dashboards.

BIRT has an exceptional charting engine. BIRT can create a number of different Chart types, including the tried and tested pie chart, bar chart, and line charts. In addition, there are several other chart types that were extras to BIRT's commercial counterpart such as the Meter Chart and Gantt chart.

In the following sections, we are going to look at building a few different charts centered around employee sales performance. First, we will build a pie chart that will illustrate the top employees based on sales. We will then create a gauge chart that will show the progress an employee has made to meet a quota. Finally, we will create a bar chart that will show sales performance for employees across a time period.

Pie chart

In the following exercise, we are going to look at how to build a pie chart. A **pie chart** is a very common report type used in business to display percentages. In this example, we will create a pie chart to show what percentage an employee contributed to the total amount of sales. This will give us a visual representation of who the top employees are in terms of sales.

1. Create a new report titled `Employee_Sales_Percentage.rptDesign`.

2. From the `ClassicCarsLibrary.rptDesign` library, add the `dsClassicCars` data source to the report.

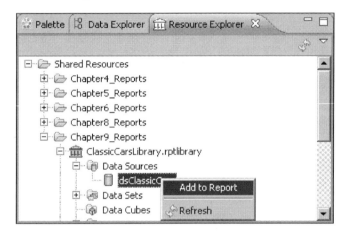

3. Create a new dataset called `totalSales` using the following query:

```
select
    CLASSICMODELS.EMPLOYEES.EMPLOYEENUMBER,
CLASSICMODELS.EMPLOYEES.LASTNAME || ', ' ||     CLASSICMODELS.
EMPLOYEES.FIRSTNAME name,
        sum(CLASSICMODELS.ORDERDETAILS.PRICEEACH) sales
from
        CLASSICMODELS.EMPLOYEES,
        CLASSICMODELS.ORDERS,
        CLASSICMODELS.ORDERDETAILS,
        CLASSICMODELS.CUSTOMERS
where
        CLASSICMODELS.CUSTOMERS.SALESREPEMPLOYEENUMBER =
CLASSICMODELS.EMPLOYEES.EMPLOYEENUMBER
        and CLASSICMODELS.ORDERS.CUSTOMERNUMBER = CLASSICMODELS.
CUSTOMERS.CUSTOMERNUMBER
```

```
        and CLASSICMODELS.ORDERDETAILS.ORDERNUMBER = CLASSICMODELS.
ORDERS.ORDERNUMBER
        and CLASSICMODELS.ORDERS.ORDERDATE between ? and ?
group by
        CLASSICMODELS.EMPLOYEES.EMPLOYEENUMBER,
        CLASSICMODELS.EMPLOYEES.LASTNAME,
    CLASSICMODELS.EMPLOYEES.FIRSTNAME
```

4. Create two report parameters called `startDate` and `endDate` as date types and link them to the two report parameters. Use `2005-01-01` as the `startDate`'s default value, and `2005-05-01` as the `endDate`'s default value.

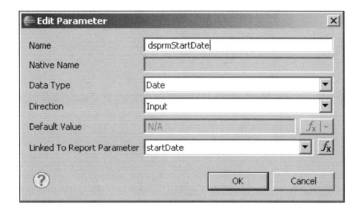

5. Drag a chart component from the **Palette** to the **Report Designer**.

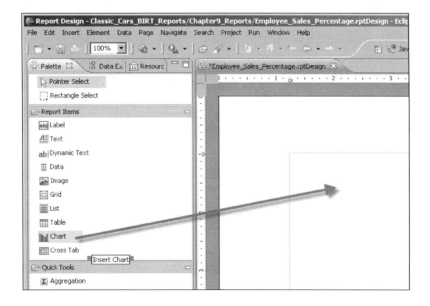

6. In the **Chart** dialog, select **Pie chart**. Change the **Output format** from **SVG** to **PNG**. Typically, I use either PNG or JPEG, as SVG is not a universally supported format. However, SVG does have a distinct advantage over both PNG and JPEG in that SVG images are smaller in size due to the format's vector nature.

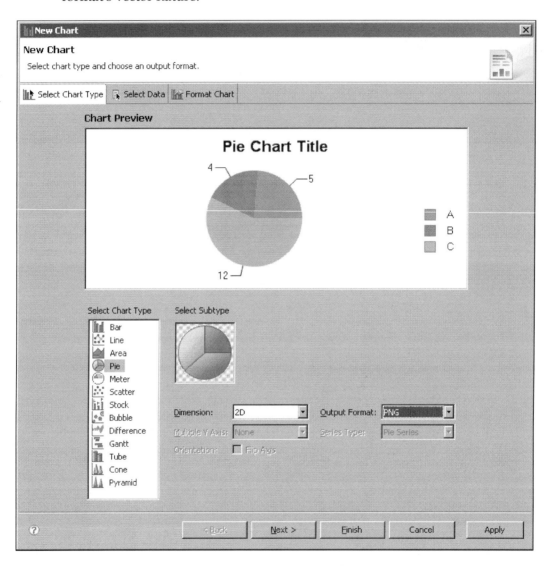

7. Open the **Select Data** tab. Under the **Select Data** section, select **Use Data Set** and choose the totalSales dataset.

8. We can drag the column headers from the dataset to the slice definitions. Drag the SALES column to the **Slice Size Definition** and the NAME column to the **Category Definition**. To make selecting the correct header easier, we can use the **Show data preview** checkbox to see what data is in each column. Without it, the preview box will show only the column names.

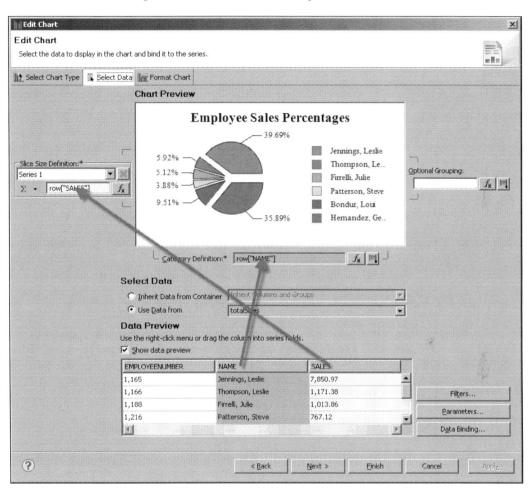

9. Select the **Format Chart** tab. Under the **Title** section, enter **Employee Sales Percentages** as the chart title. In this editor, we change how the chart looks and feels.

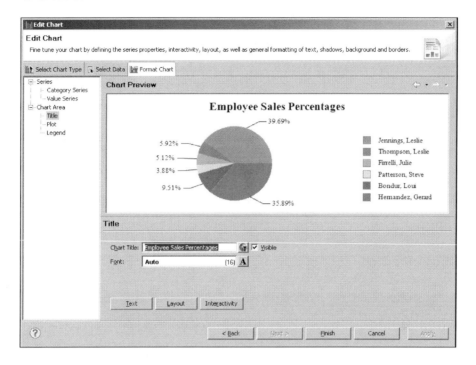

10. Click **Finish**.

11. Resize the chart to take up report page. This can be done by dragging the corner of the chart or by entering the height and width values in the property editor.

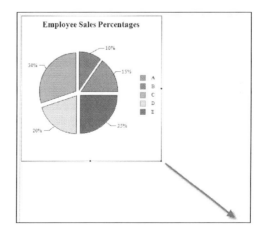

13. The chart will look something like the following screenshot when previewed:

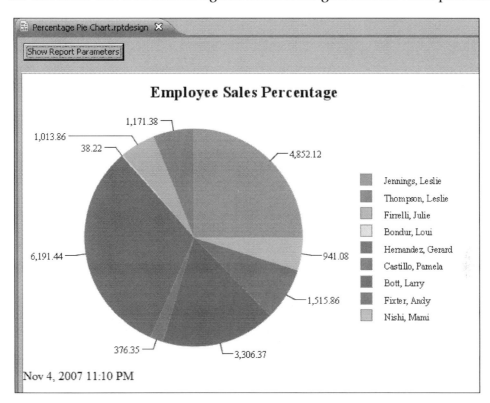

So, we have built a fairly simple report so far. This report is a pie chart with a legend that shows us the employee's color code, with an excerpt that shows us the value of that slice.

Pie chart with explosions

While the pie chart we saw in the preceding section is nice, it would be a little easier to view if the slices were exploded, and if the slices had an outline. Let's take a look at how to modify some of the chart's properties to do this.

1. Double-click on the chart in the report design. This will reopen the chart dialog. Another option is to right-click on the chart and choose **Format Chart...**.

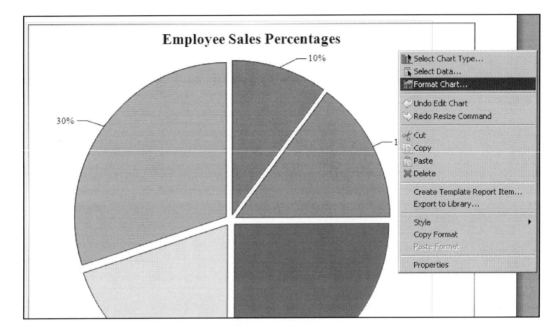

2. Open the **Format Chart...** tab.
3. Open the **Value Series** section.

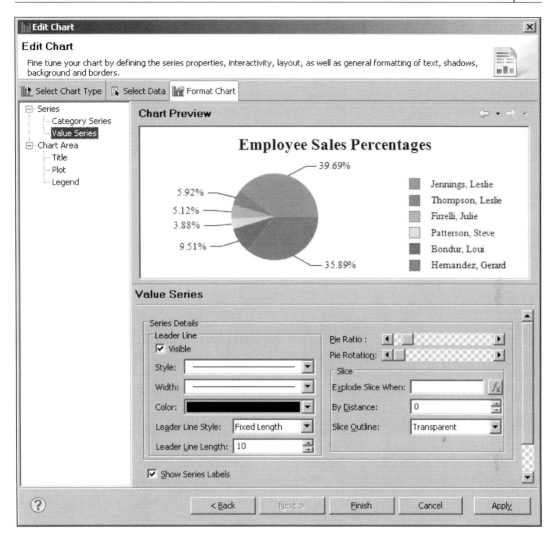

4.   Under the **Slice** section, change the **By Distance** value to **6**.

5. For **Slice Outline,** choose the color black from the palette.

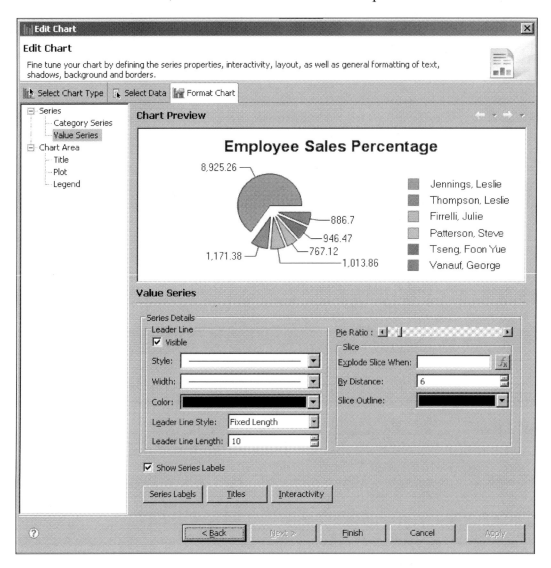

6. Save the chart and preview it. The following screenshot shows what the chart looks like with the explosion and slice outline added.

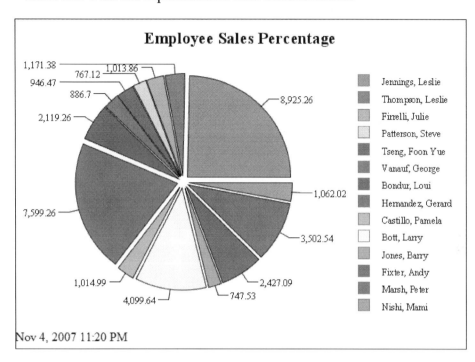

Pie charts—working with percentages

Things are starting to look better. But let's say we want to change the chart to display percentages instead of numbers and add a little interactivity to the chart to display the sales numbers when a section is clicked on.

1. Double-click on the chart to edit it.
2. Select the **Value Series** section.

3. Click on the **Labels** button.

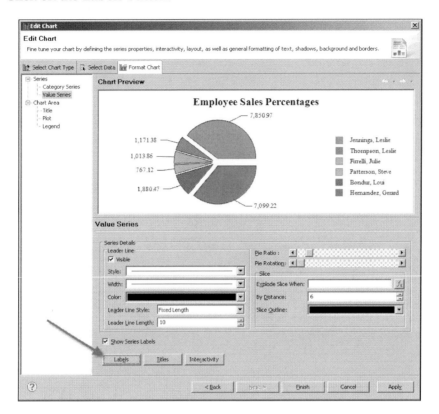

4. Under **Values**, remove the **Value Data** option.

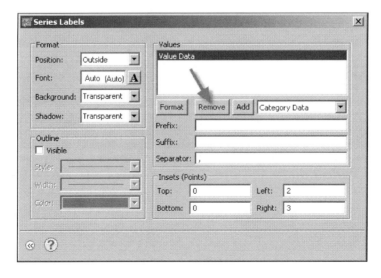

5. Under **Values**, add **Percentile Value Data**.

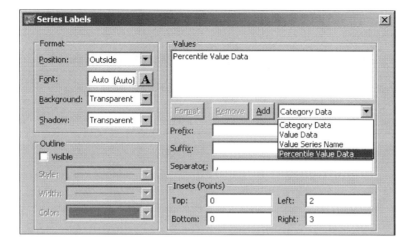

6. Click the **Interactivity** button.

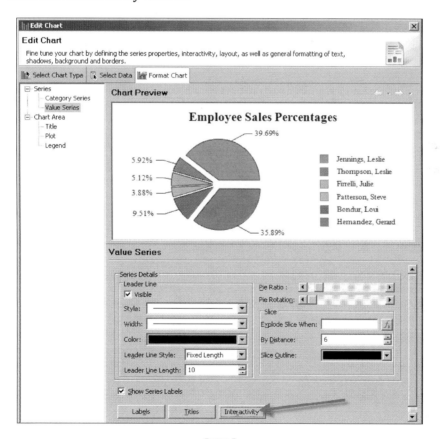

7. Choose **Mouse Click** from the **Event** listbox.

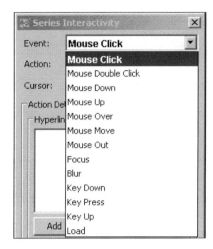

8. From the **Action** listbox, choose **Invoke Script**.

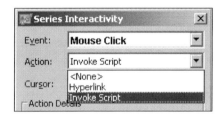

9. Click the **Expression Editor** button.

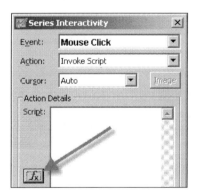

10. Using the editor, click on the **Variables | Chart Data Point | Value Data** option to insert the valueData variable into the editor. Surround it with an alert() method call. It should look like the next screenshot:

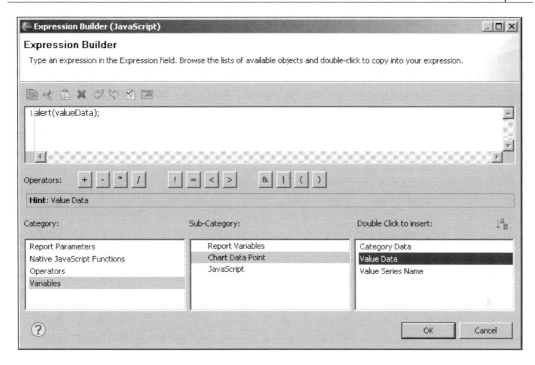

11. Click **OK**. Now click on the **<<** arrows in the **Series Interactivity** window.

12. Click **Finish** in the **Chart Editor**.

When we preview the report, the chart pops up, formatted in the manner we want. If we click on one of the pie slices, an alert window will pop up showing the value for that series.

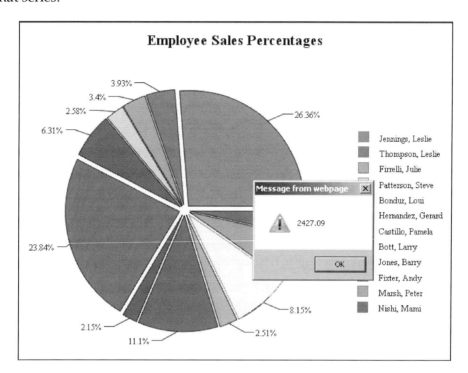

Gauge chart

With the next chart, the guage chart, we will expand on the interactivity a bit and demonstrate how drill-downs work. In addition to viewing the static chart, we want the user to be able to click on the chart and have it pull up an external report with the details for a particular user. This is called a drilldown.

The following meter chart will demonstrate an employees sales vs. a target amount per month, let's say 3000, on a 5000 dollar scale. This will be broken out and grouped monthly in the query statement. When the user clicks on the chart, it will bring them to the detail report we created last chapter for Employee sales.

1. Create a new report titled `Employee_Sales_Guage.rptDesign`.
2. From the library, drag over the `dsClassicCars` data source.

3. Create a new dataset called `employeeSales` using the following query:

```
select
        CLASSICMODELS.EMPLOYEES.EMPLOYEENUMBER,
        CLASSICMODELS.EMPLOYEES.LASTNAME || ', ' || CLASSICMODELS.
EMPLOYEES.FIRSTNAME name,
        sum(CLASSICMODELS.ORDERDETAILS.PRICEEACH) sales,
        rtrim(char(year(CLASSICMODELS.ORDERS.ORDERDATE))) || '-' ||
rtrim(char(month(CLASSICMODELS.ORDERS.ORDERDATE))) orderDate
from
        CLASSICMODELS.EMPLOYEES,
        CLASSICMODELS.CUSTOMERS,
        CLASSICMODELS.ORDERS,
        CLASSICMODELS.ORDERDETAILS
where
        CLASSICMODELS.ORDERS.ORDERNUMBER = CLASSICMODELS.
ORDERDETAILS.ORDERNUMBER
        and CLASSICMODELS.EMPLOYEES.EMPLOYEENUMBER = CLASSICMODELS.
CUSTOMERS.SALESREPEMPLOYEENUMBER
        and CLASSICMODELS.ORDERS.CUSTOMERNUMBER = CLASSICMODELS.
CUSTOMERS.CUSTOMERNUMBER
        and CLASSICMODELS.ORDERS.ORDERDATE between ? and ?
group by
        year(CLASSICMODELS.ORDERS.ORDERDATE),
        month(CLASSICMODELS.ORDERS.ORDERDATE),
        CLASSICMODELS.EMPLOYEES.EMPLOYEENUMBER,
        CLASSICMODELS.EMPLOYEES.LASTNAME,
        CLASSICMODELS.EMPLOYEES.FIRSTNAME
```

4. Link the two dataset parameters to the report parameters, `startDate` and `endDate` respectively.

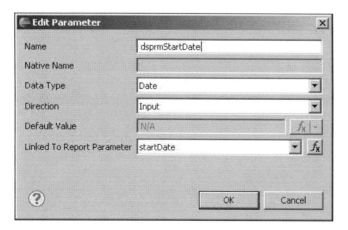

5. Drag the `employeeSales` dataset to the report designer.

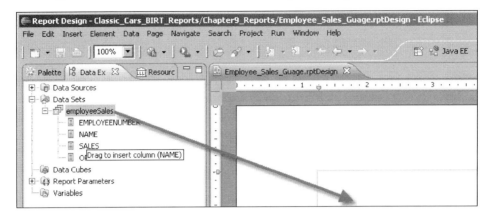

6. Delete the last two columns from the table.

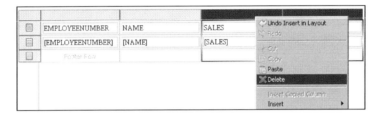

7. Create a group called `GroupByEmployee` in the table and set it to group on the `EMPLOYEENUMBER`.

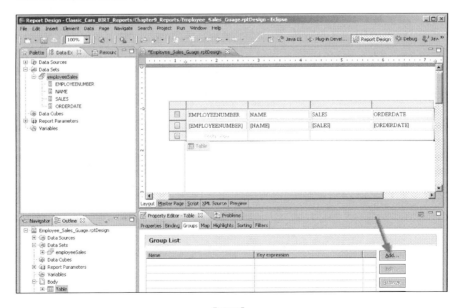

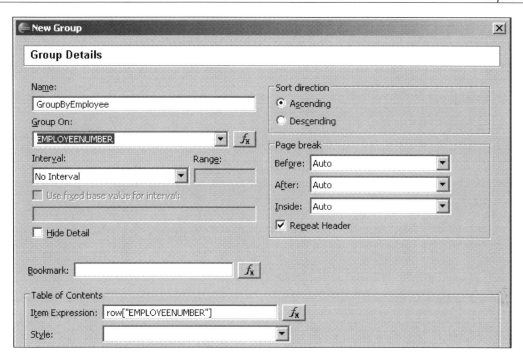

8. Create another group below `GroupByEmployee` and call it `groupByDate`. Set it to group on the `ORDERDATE` field.

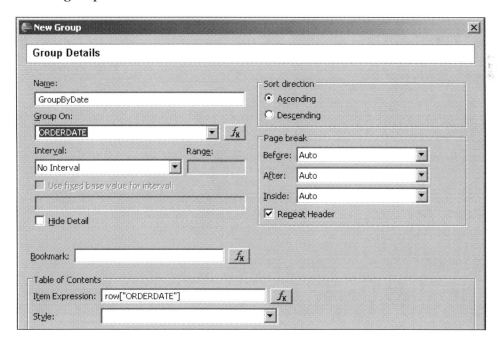

9. Merge all of the cells in the `orderDate` details row into one large cell. Be sure to delete any data items that are still present such as the `NAME` and `EMPLOYEENUMBER` items.

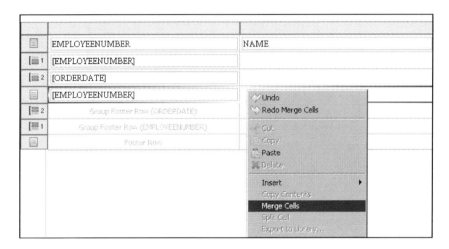

10. In the new large cell, create a chart element.

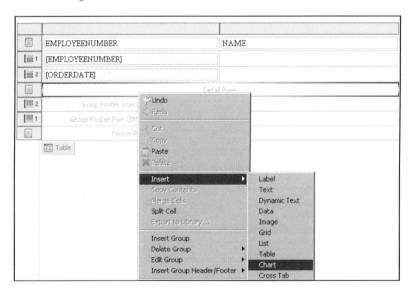

11. Select **Meter** as the type, and select **SuperImpose Meter** as the chart type. If we need to know which type of chart we are picking, hover the mouse over the chart for a second and its description will pop up. Set the **Output Format** to **PNG**.

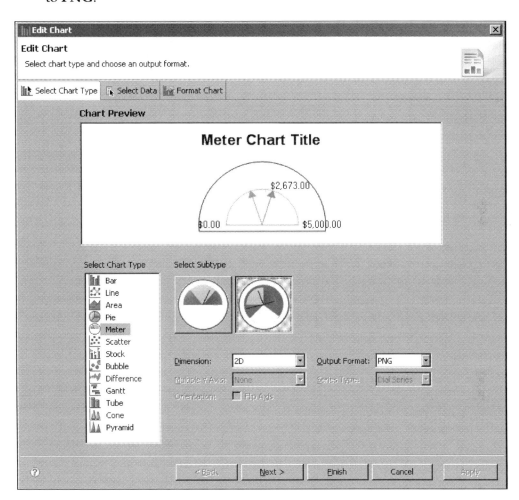

12. In the **Select Data** tab, create another dial by selecting the **Meter Value Definition** drop-down list and selecting **<New Series..>**.

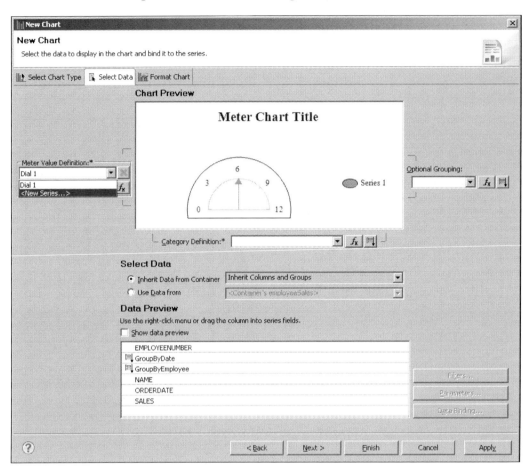

13. For the expression for **Dial 1**, select `row["SALES"]` by either dragging the column over from the **Data Preview** pane or by using the **Expression Editor**.

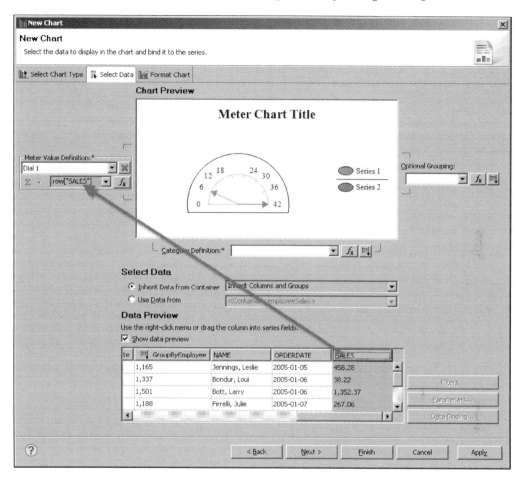

14. The value for **Dial 2** should be set to **3000**.

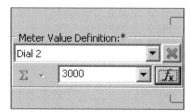

15. As **Category Definition**, use `row["NAME"]` by either dragging the column over from the **Data Preview** section or using the **Expression Editor**.

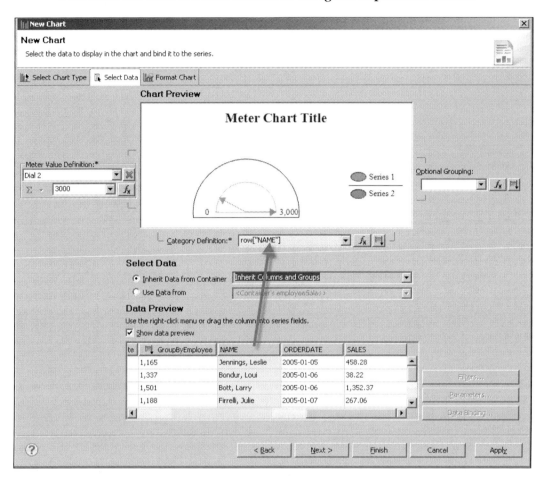

16. In the **Format Chart** tab, under the **Value Series** section, click the **Scale** button.

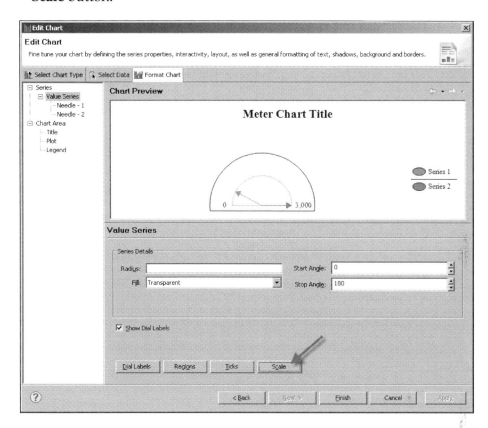

17. Enter **0** for the **Min** value and **5000** for the **Max** value. We have now set up the scale.

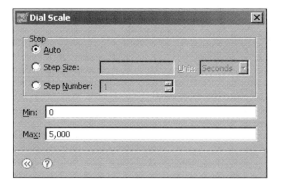

18. On the **Edit Chart** tab, under the **Legend** section, uncheck the **Visible** checkbox.

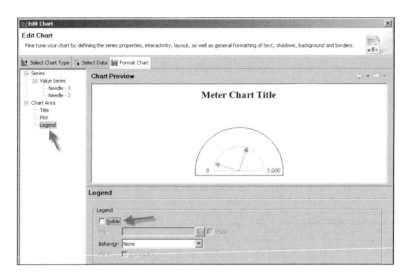

19. Select **Chart Area**.

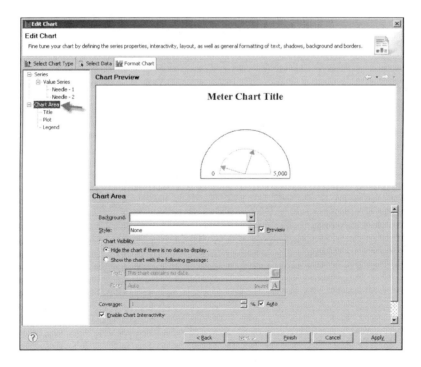

20. Click the **Interactivity** button.

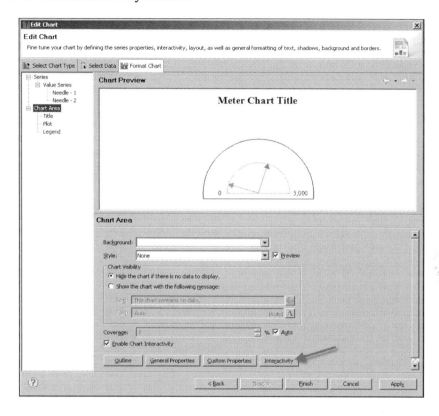

21. Select **Mouse Click** from the **Event** listbox and select **Hyperlink** from the **Action** listbox.

22. Click the **Add** Button.

23. In the **Name** field, insert **NewHyperlink**.

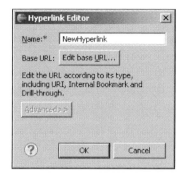

24. Click the **Edit Base URL...** button.

25. Select **Drill-through** as the hyperlink type.

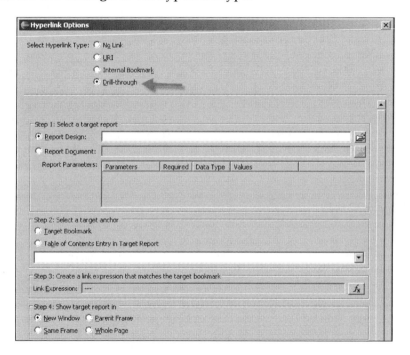

26. For the **Report Design**, navigate and select the report Employee Sales Details Report.rptDesign. This report was created in the preceding chapter.

27. Select the `startDate` and `endDate` parameters under the **Parameters** drop down, which selects the parameters in the target report. Under **Values**, enter `params["startDate"].value` and `params["endDate"].value`, or whatever names that have been used used for the current report's `startDate` and `endDate` parameters.

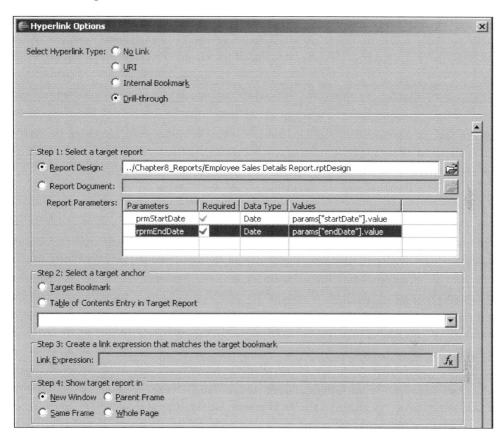

28. Under **Step 2**, select **Target Bookmark**. From the drop-down list, select `row["EmployeeNumber"]`.

29. Under **Step 4**, select **New Window**.

30. We can skip **Step 5** as we are sticking to our default output format, which is HTML. We could have the target report open in any format that we have an emitter registered for. Emitters are plugins for BIRT that produce output in different formats such as HTML, PDF, Microsoft Excel, or Microsoft Word.

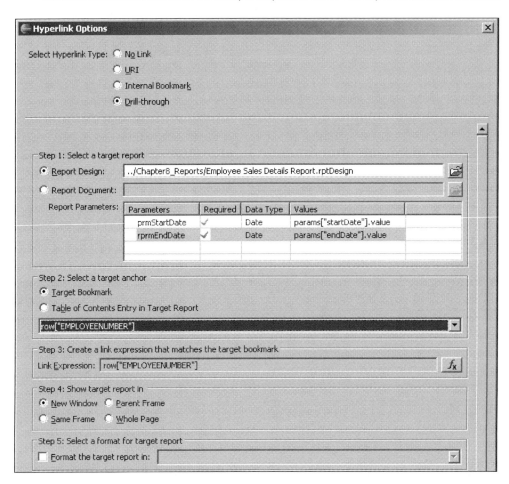

31. Click **OK** to exit the dialog and save the report.

32. Delete the table header.

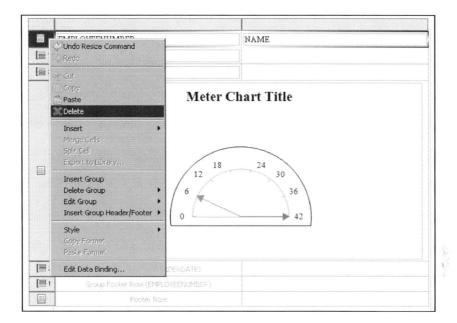

33. Delete the EMPLOYEENUMBER data element.

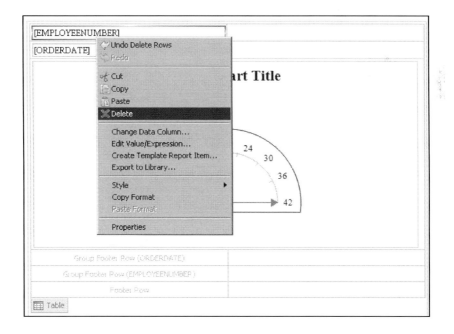

34. Drag the EMPLOYEENUMBER column from the **Data Explorer**, next to the OrderDate report item.

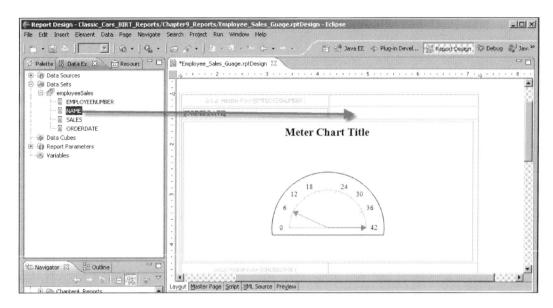

35. Now run the report. When we click on any of the charts, a detailed report will open and the control will automatically jump to the employees section, as specified in the Bookmark in the target report.

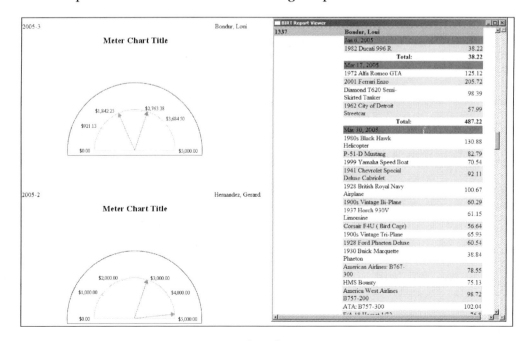

Of course, this example can be heavily modified to simplify things. The charts could be consolidated into single chart, with more needles for each month instead of separate charts for each month, by moving the chart into the `EmployeeNumber` group's header or footer row and adding a group by date in the chart editors dialog under the **Select Data** tab. It is also possible to make the needles interactive and to filter down to a specific user and date range by modifying the bookmarks in the target report, but I will leave that up to the reader to discover. The following is a modified version of the the report that has created different series in the chart itself for the date groupings.

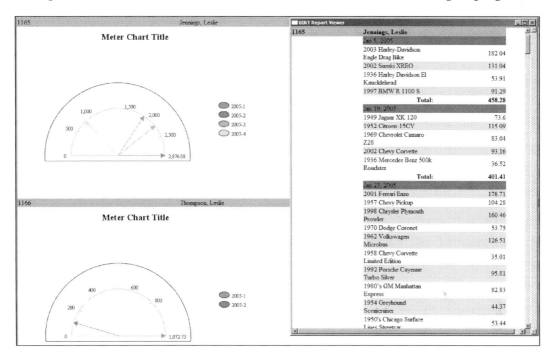

Bar chart

In the earlier section, we saw some of the power that charting can have with reports, by adding both the graphical representation of data and the interactivity for users to see the details of that data in a separate report. We also saw how to pass data through to the target report by using the expression. In this report, the hyperlink will take us to an internal bookmark, which means it will jump us to a location inside the same report containing the details for our report. We will also look at aggregating values inside the chart so that we can provide a simple query that just retrieves the necessary details and lets BIRT handle the tricky stuff for us.

1. Create a new report called `EmployeeSalesPerformanceReport.rptDesign`.

2. Use the `dsClassicCars` data source in the library.

3. Create a new dataset called `employeeSales`, using the following query:

```
select
        CLASSICMODELS.EMPLOYEES.EMPLOYEENUMBER,
        CLASSICMODELS.EMPLOYEES.LASTNAME || ', ' || CLASSICMODELS.
EMPLOYEES.FIRSTNAME name,
        CLASSICMODELS.ORDERDETAILS.PRICEEACH,
        CLASSICMODELS.ORDERS.ORDERDATE,
        CLASSICMODELS.PRODUCTS.PRODUCTNAME
from
        CLASSICMODELS.EMPLOYEES,
        CLASSICMODELS.CUSTOMERS,
        CLASSICMODELS.ORDERS,
        CLASSICMODELS.ORDERDETAILS,
        CLASSICMODELS.PRODUCTS
where
        CLASSICMODELS.ORDERS.ORDERNUMBER = CLASSICMODELS.
ORDERDETAILS.ORDERNUMBER
        and CLASSICMODELS.EMPLOYEES.EMPLOYEENUMBER = CLASSICMODELS.
CUSTOMERS.SALESREPEMPLOYEENUMBER
        and CLASSICMODELS.ORDERS.CUSTOMERNUMBER = CLASSICMODELS.
CUSTOMERS.CUSTOMERNUMBER
        and CLASSICMODELS.PRODUCTS.PRODUCTCODE = CLASSICMODELS.
ORDERDETAILS.PRODUCTCODE
        and CLASSICMODELS.ORDERS.ORDERDATE between ? and ?
```

4. Map the dataset parameters to report parameters `startDate` and `endDate`.

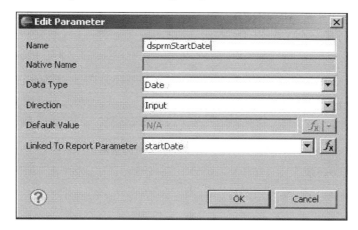

5. Drag a table element over from the palette.

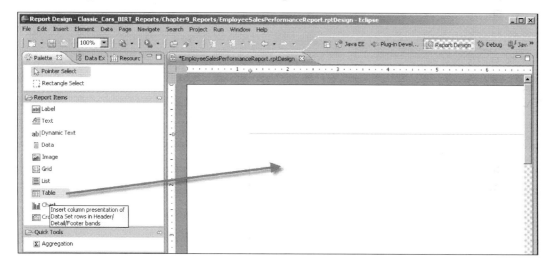

6. Set **Number of columns** to **3** and **Number of details** to **1**, and map the dataset element to the `employeeSales` dataset.

7. In the header row, insert a new row.

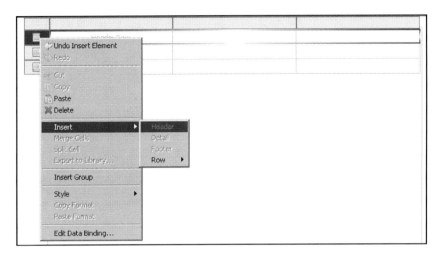

8. In the top most header, merge all the cells into one large cell.

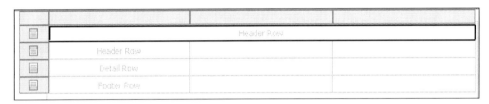

9. Insert a chart element into the large cell.

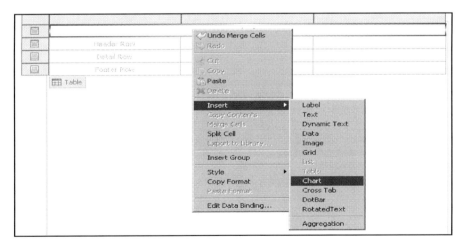

10. Select **Bar** chart as the type.

11. Select the stacked Bar Chart as the subtype.

12. Set the **Output Format** to **PNG**.

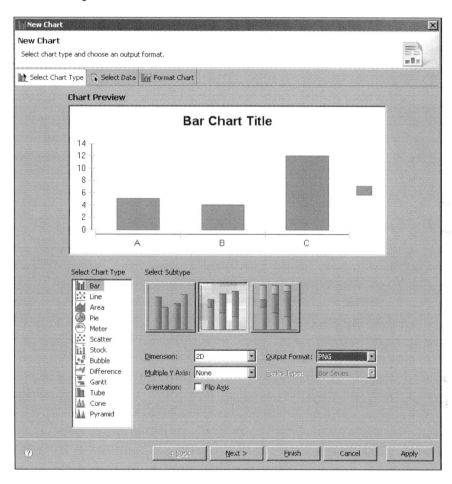

13. Go to the **Select Data** tab.

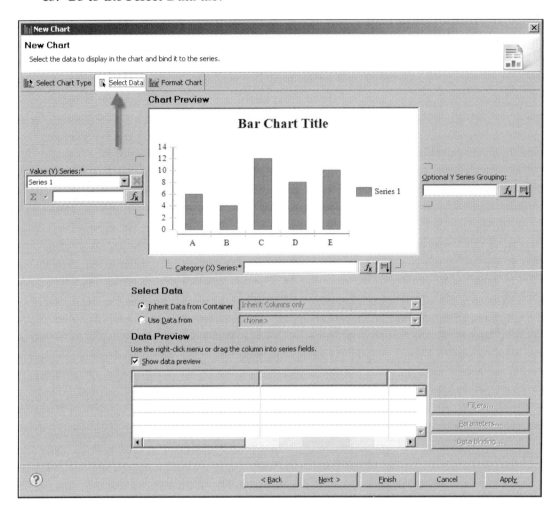

14. For the series value, drag in the PRICEEACH column.

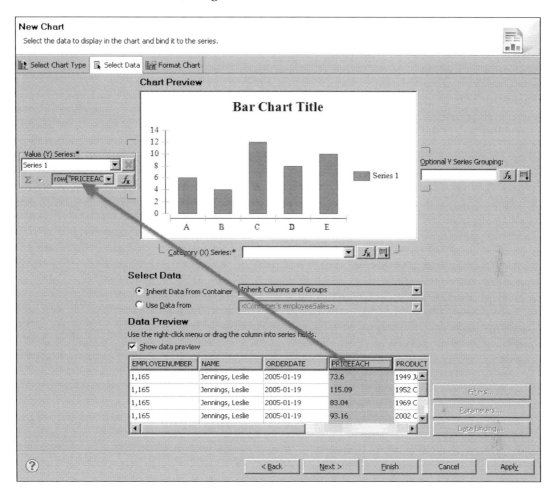

15. For the **Category (x) Series**, use the following expression:

```
(row["ORDERDATE"].getYear() + 1900).toString() + '-' +
(row["ORDERDATE"].getMonth() + 1).toString()
```

This may not make much sense now, but we will explain it further in the next chapter.

1. For the **Optional Y Series Grouping**, drag in the NAME column.

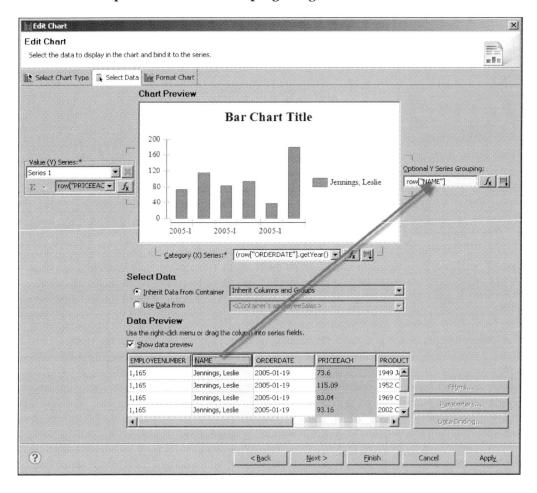

2. In the **Inherit Data From Container** drop-down list, select **Inherit Columns only**. This will set up the chart to ignore any grouping at the table level and let the chart engine do its down grouping.

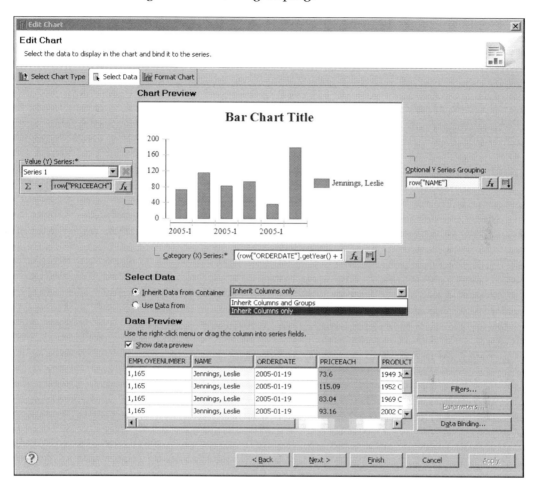

3. Next to the **Category (x) Series** expression editor button, there is a button to edit group and sorting. Click that button.

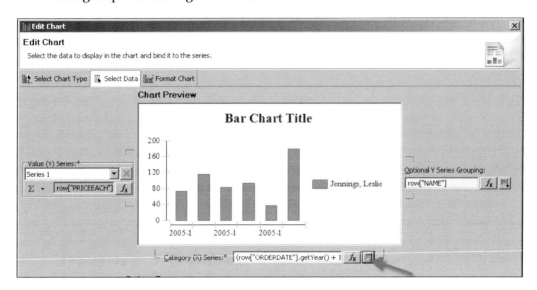

4. Select **Ascending** from the **Data Sorting** drop down.
5. In the **Grouping** checkbox, check the **Enable** option.

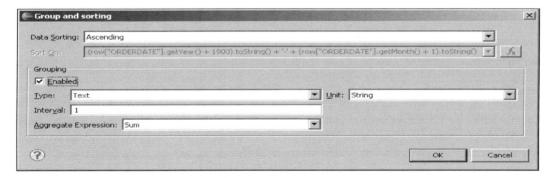

6. Keep the other values at their defaults and click **OK**.
7. Click **Finish** and save the report.
8. Select the table, and create a group on EMPLOYEENUMBER.

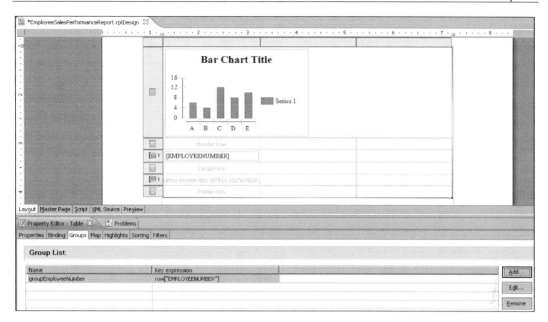

9. Create a grouping on `OrderDate`.

10. For the detail row, drag over the `PRODUCTNAME` into the second column and `PRICEEACH` into the third column.

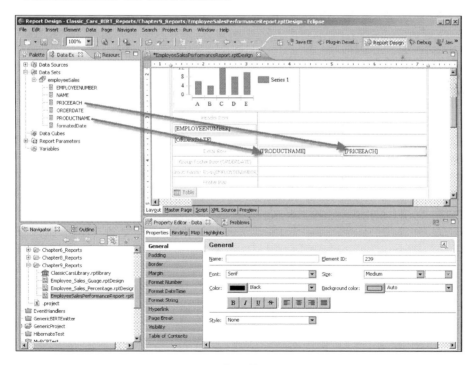

11. From the **Palette**, drag over an **Aggregation** element into the `groupFooter` for the `OrderDate` grouping.

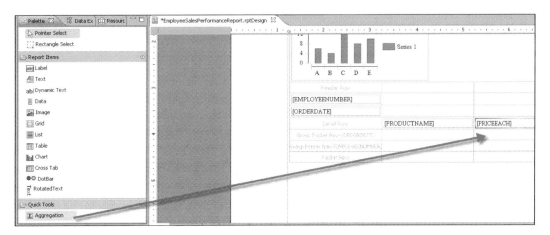

12. Create the aggregation on the `PRICEEACH` field for the `salesDateGroup`.

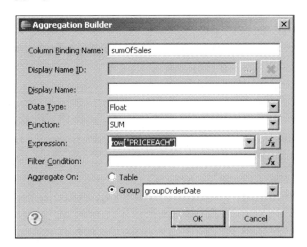

13. Add in any formatting that might spruce up the look of our report.

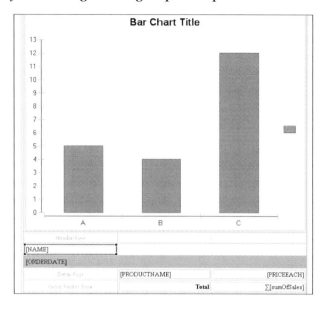

14. Select the `OrderDate` groupings header row. Select the **Bookmark** tab under the property editor. Use the following expression for the bookmark:

```
row["EMPLOYEENUMBER"] + row["ORDERDATE"]
```

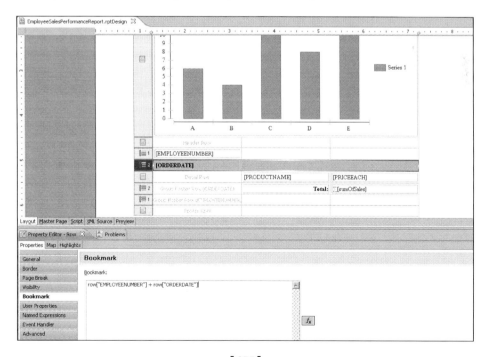

15. Double-click on the chart to enter the Chart Editor.

16. Select the **Format Chart** tab.

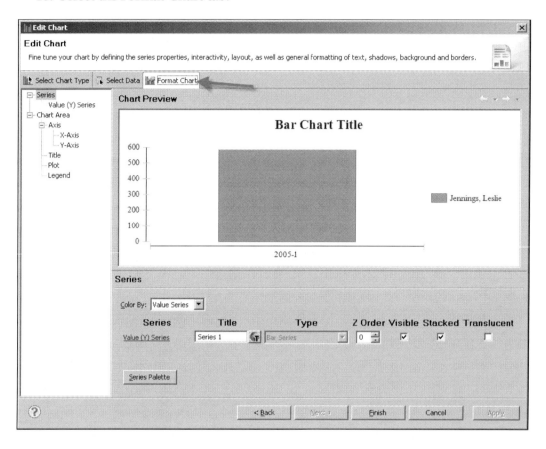

17. In the **Edit Chart** window, select the **Value (Y) Series** section and click the **Interactivity** button.

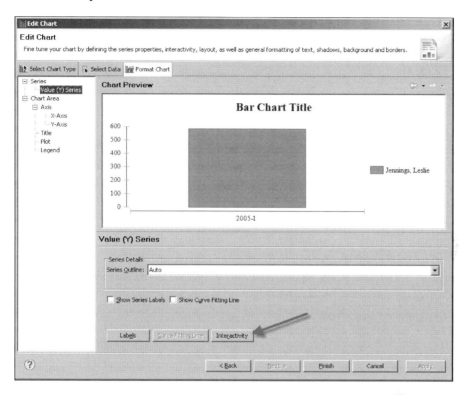

18. In the **Event** drop-down list select **Mouse Click**, whereas in the **Action** listbox select **Hyperlink**.

19. Click the **Add** button.

20. Enter ChartHyperlink for the **Name**.

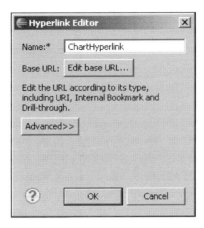

21. Click the **Edit base URL...** button.

22. In the hyperlink dialog box, select **Internal Bookmark** as the type.

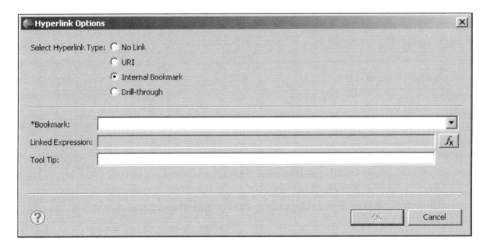

23. Select the following from the drop down:

    row["EMPLOYEENUMBER"] + row["ORDERDATE"]

24. Click **OK** to save the report. Now run it.

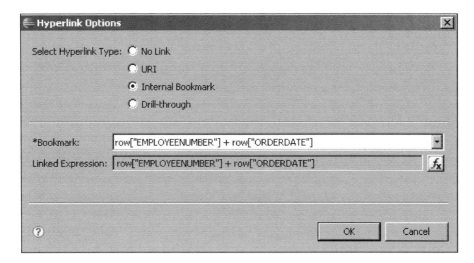

Now, when we click on any of the different colored sections of the bar chart, it will bring us to the details section within our own report.

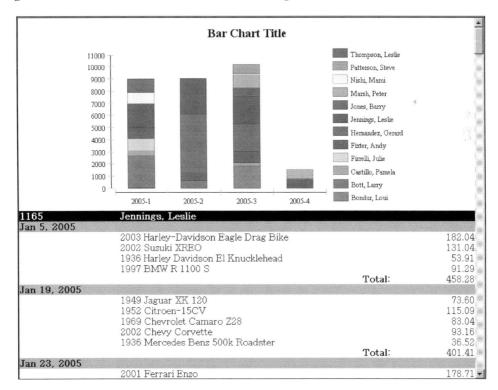

Summary

In this chapter, we have seen how to create several different chart types. We have seen how we can create interactivity within a single report and how to drill down into a separate report using charts and passing through parameters. We have seen how to aggregate data within a chart to serve as a summary for the more detailed data. We have opened the dialog to edit properties of charts and seen how a few of the properties affect the look and feel of charts as well as the behavior.

In the next chapter, we are going to explore the basic of scripting in BIRT reports. Throughout this book we have been using a basic type of script called an expression. We will explore this in following chapters and expand into event handling as well.

9
Scripting and Event Handling

We have come a long way since we started this book. We have seen all the different aspects of the BIRT Report Development environment. We have seen how to drag-and-drop reports with the Palette and the Report Designer, how to work with the outline and the navigator, and how to set properties or each of the report components.

We have seen how BIRT can link to data sources through JDBC drivers and how to build dataset through those connections. We have seen how to format reports using properties and styles.

Now we are going to look at the aspect of BIRT that makes it really powerful—scripting. Scripting is a complex topic, but once we understand it, we will be able to make BIRT do some really amazing things such as:

- Modifying data as it comes through
- Building data sources off of Java objects
- Building reports from the ground up

BIRT utilizes the Mozilla Rhino Engine to handle its scripting capabilities. What this means is that inside of BIRT reports, Report designers have full access to all primitive types, object, methods, and libraries accessible to JavaScript. As an added bonus, report developers even have full access to all Java classes that are in the classpath. In the BIRT Report Designer, this means one have full access to all the Java objects in the Eclipse environment. One can even use custom Java objects in his/her report to handle certain aspects of processing.

In the following sections, we are going to look at the two different types of scripting that BIRT has to offer—expressions and event handling. We are going to look at how to access different types of BIRT properties using expressions. We will then look at how to handle report generation events using BIRT's implementation of the Rhino engine and how to handle those same events using Java objects. Although a prior knowledge of Java or JavaScript is not necessary, it will greatly enhance the understanding of the topics covered in this chapter. But to follow along effectively, the reader should understand:

- Variables
    - Types
    - Creation
    - Assignment

- Operators
    - Arithmetic
    - Logical
    - Comparison

- Functions

- Objects
    - Properties
    - Methods

Types of Scripting

In BIRT, there are two different types of scripting—expressions and event handling. **Expressions** are simple bits of script, usually ranging from 1 to less than 10 lines of code, returning a single value for use in a BIRT report. **Event Handling** scripts are usually a bit larger than expressions, and are meant to accomplish some sort of task such as retrieve a row from a dataset, manipulate some data before it is sent to output, or handle preparations for rendering. It is recommended that the reader learn more about JavaScript to assist with their report development.

Expressions

Expressions make up a bulk of the scripting used in BIRT. In fact, we have used Expressions multiple times already in this book. Expressions are usually single line statements that return a single result. Tasks such as retrieving a value from a row and outputing it in a data element, retrieving parameter values, and the Highlight expressions used in the last chapter are all examples of Expressions. Any time we use the Expression editor in BIRT, we are working with Expressions.

Let's take a look at the most commonly used Expression—the Data element. Open up the Customer Orders report that we've used in the last chapter. Here we have a finished report with numerous Expressions used throughout. Let's take a look at what one of these Expressions look like.

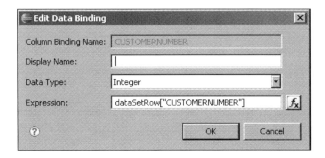

This preceding screenshot shows us a very simple expression that retrieves the value of the CUSTOMERNUMBER column from the current row. It is taken from the Data element in the Orders detail table. dataSetRow is an array that represents the current row in the detail band. The screenshot illustrates that a single value is returned with a simple line of code.

Let's take a look at another more complicated example. Look at step 14 of the Bar Chart example from last chapter. There, we have an expression that looks like:

```
(row["ORDERDATE"].getYear() + 1900).toString() + '-' +
(row["ORDERDATE"].getMonth() + 1).toString()
```

This Expression retrieves the ORDERDATE value from the current row using the row array, and in two separate parts—one part will retrieve the year and another will retrieve the month using the standard Javascript functions getYear and getMonth. In BIRT, getYear will return the number of years since the epoch, which is 1900. So, in order to get the actual number of years, we need to add 1900 to the result. Therefore, for the year 2007, the result from getYear will return 107, so adding 1900 will return 2007. The situation arises with getMonth; it will return the month from a zero offset. So, January will return 0, February will return 1, and so on, requiring us to add 1 to get the correct month.

As we want to return a string, and the results returned by `getYear()` and `getMonth()` are integer or number values, we use the `Javascript toString()` method to convert these numbers to strings. Finally, we need to concatenate the converted strings and the separating character to get the final result. This Expression, although doing many different things such as retrieving portions of a date value, adding offsets, converting numbers to strings, and then concatenating strings together, returns only a single result.

So, let's get our hands on this. In the following example, we are going to add a line number to the order detail table.

1. Open the Customer Orders report. How to create this report can be read from the *Styles, Themes, and Templates* chapter, which is available at free download on Packt site.

2. Insert a column to the left of the `OrderNumber` column.

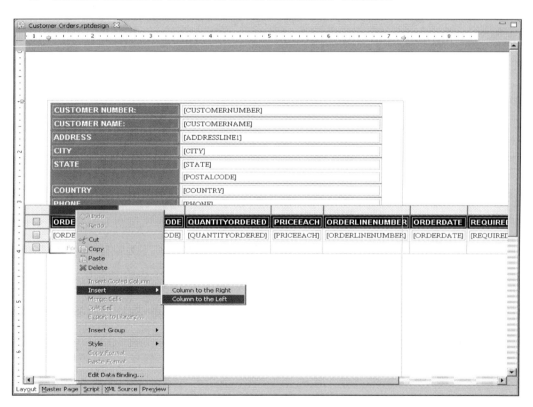

3. Insert a Data element in the cell for the details band:

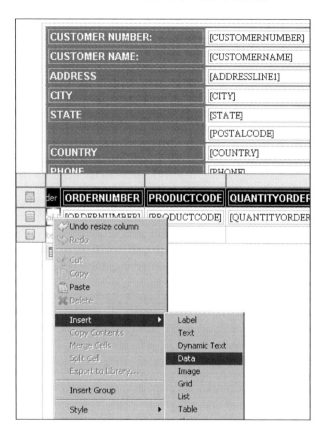

4. In the **Expression** field, enter the following expression:

```
row.__rownum + 1
```

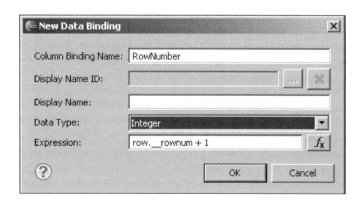

5. Click **OK** to preview the report.

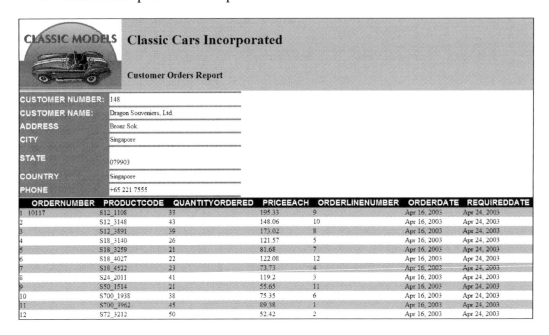

There is now a column with the current line number for the report. While not exactly the most attractive addition, the expression works. We have seen expressions such as these throughout the book. In the Customer Orders report, the Report Title is pulled from the `rprmReportTitle` parameter using the `params["rprmReportTitle"]` expression. We use the same row number expression in the highlight example in the Customer Orders report as well.

As we saw with the Bar Chart example, expressions are simply JavaScript. Expressions also have access to JavaScript methods, operators, and objects. In the line number example we just saw, we used the addition operator, and in the Bar Chart example, we used the `toString()`, `getMonth()`, and `getYear()` methods. All assignment, math, comparison, and logical operators available in JavaScript are included. Let's look at the following example that shows the JavaScript string methods being used to return the length of a string:

1. Create a new report called `String Length.rptDesign`.

2. Drop a Data element anywhere on the Report Design.

3. Use the following Expression.

    ```
    "This is a test".length
    ```

4. Click **OK** and preview the report.

A simple report with the number 14 should be displayed. The above expression can also be replaced with the following expression.

```
var testString = "This is a test";

testString.length;
```

In the example, we are breaking from the one line expression and using multiple lines and a variable. The key is that the last line is returning a single value. All sorts of computations can take place, as long a single value is returned. Now consider we change the expression to the following:

```
var testString = "This is a test";
var splitString = testString.split(" ");

splitString[3].toUpperCase();
```

The report will now return only the word TEST. Again, while multiple things are being done in this expression such as the assignment of the string, splitting the string, and converting the element 3 to upper case, only a single result is returned.

At the end of *Chapter 6, Report Parameters*, we went through an exercise where we set a default parameter, using expressions in BIRT's new expression-based default parameter value mechanism, to set a range of current date minus 20 days as a start date and current date as the end date. This exercise is an example of using more complex expressions.

```
//bring in the java.util package into the scripting scope
importPackage( java.util );

//create a new GregorianCalendar object
var cal = new java.util.GregorianCalendar();

//set the date to now
cal.setTime(new Date());

//substract 20 days
cal.add(Calendar.DAY_OF_MONTH, -20);

//return the start date
cal.getTime();
```

In this example, we utilized some Java objects that were in the execution environment's classpath. Any Java object in a classpath can be utilized in BIRT expressions, as long as the `importPackage` method is called or it is referenced with the `Packages.path` syntax. For example, we used `importPackage( java.util )` to import the `java.util` package. But we could have omitted that line and just as easily declared the `GregorianCalendar` as:

```
var cal = new java.util.GregorianCalendar();
```

The reason for this is that as the Eclipse environment already has the `java.util` package loaded, so there is no need to explicitly load it with the `importPackage` call. The key to complex expressions are that a single value gets returned, as in the result of the last line of our expression, `cal.getTime()`, which returned a single Date value.

Event Handling

Now if Expressions are simple lines of code that return a single value, how do Event Handlers fit into the scripting world of BIRT? The answer is simple—they do exactly what they claim they do, handle events. What does that mean exactly?

Well, to understand that we need to look at how BIRT reports are generated. BIRT Reports are generated in phases. As explained in the BIRT Report Object Model Scripting Specification at `http://www.eclipse.org/birt/phoenix/ref/ROM_Scripting_SPEC.pdf`, there are five phases in the report generation lifecycle.

- Startup
- Data Transformation
- Factory
- Presentation
- Shutdown

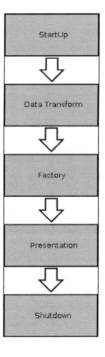

In each one of these phases, particular events are triggered that allow the report developer to override the default behavior of the report generation. This allows us to do all sorts of advanced things with BIRT such as custom filtering of data, dynamically adding or removing BIRT objects to the report, or even building an entire BIRT report through script.

Let's simplify things just slightly. If we look at the dataset element, we can see five different events are associated with it:

- beforeOpen: Executed before opening the dataset for processing
- beforeClose: Executed before closing the dataset
- onFetch: Executed each time a row is retrieved from a data set
- afterOpen: After the dataset is opened
- afterClose: After the dataset is closed

Consider we have two things we need to do with the dataset. First, we need to initialize a counter variable to 0 for the number of rows that are going to be processed. Next, we need to add to the counter each time a row is retrieved. So, these things are important. The order in which these events take place is beforeOpen, afterOpen, onFetch, beforeClose, and afterClose. Therefore, in either beforeOpen or afterOpen, we need to set our variable to 0. Then, in the onFetch event, we need to add 1 to our counter. Let's look at an example of how to do that:

1. Open Customer Orders.rptDesign.
2. First, we need to define the global variable that we will use for our count. In the report designer, open the **Script** tab.

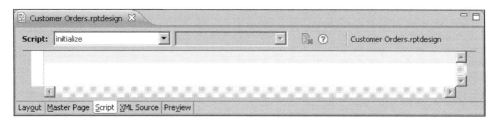

3. Under the **Outline** tab, select the root element, `Customer Orders.`
   `rptDesign`.

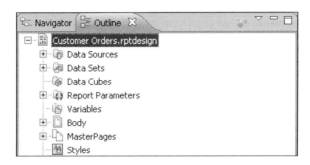

4. In the Event drop down, select `initialize`. Be aware that initialize can be called twice in certain circumstances. If we are doing heavy processing, we can also consider using the `beforeFactory` method. But for our example, we are using initialize.

5. Use the following code to define our global variable:

   `var globalCount;`

   ○ As we are creating `globalCount` in the `initialize` method, it will be global to the entire report.

6. Select the `getCustomerOrders` dataset from the **Outline** tab.

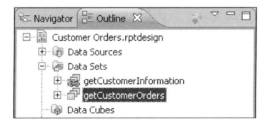

7. From the event drop down, select `beforeOpen`.

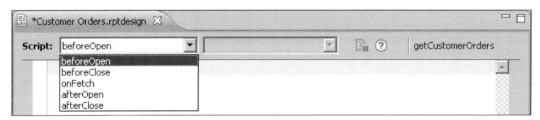

8. Use the following code to initialize the `globalCount` variable:

   ```
   globalCount = 0;
   ```

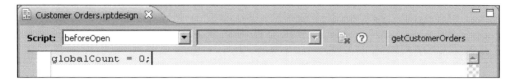

9. From the event drop down, select `onFetch`.

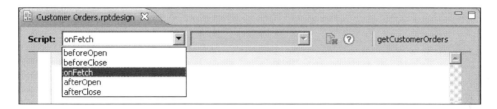

10. Use the following code to increment the counter:

    ```
    globalCount++;
    ```

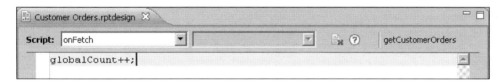

11. Open the report designer's **Layout** tab.

12. Drag a Data element to the bottom of the report design. Use the following expression:

    ```
    globalCount
    ```

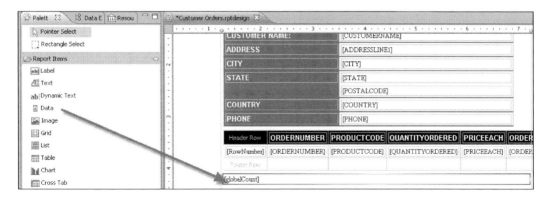

13. Run the report.

Understanding the order of execution is important. The report's `initialize` method will get executed before any of the other methods and declare `globalCount`. Next, the dataset gets generated in the data transform phase calling `BeforeOpen` and initializing `globalCount` to `0`. During each row request, the `globalCount` gets incremented by one. And finally, the value of `globalCount` gets inserted into the data element we dropped into the report design in the factory phase.

Contexts

From any of the report generation phases, we have access to various contexts. For the most part, each of the five phases has its own context. In addition, there are also a few extra contexts—one for the data row and the other for displaying an element.

In BIRT, contexts are used to access objects within the scripting environment. At a high level, one has access to the Report context. The **Report Context** is a mapping in the BIRT scripting environment to the Java object `IReportContext`, inside the `org.eclipse.birt.report.engine.api.script` package. This object allows script developers access to the design object, report parameters, and various other aspects of the report. Many of these objects are shorthanded by other, easier-to-use references such as using the params array to access report parameters. Let's take a look at how to access the report context.

1. Create a new report called `stringLength.rptDesign`.

2. Create a new report parameter called `accessMe` as a string and assign it the default value of **Test Parameter**.

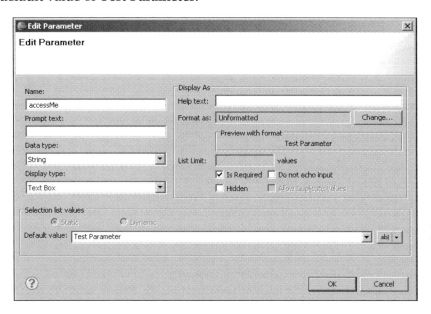

3. Drag a data component over to the report designer, and for the expression, put in `valueFromScript`.

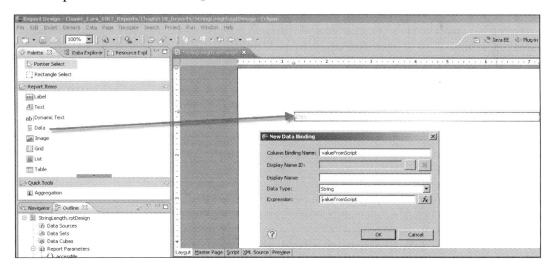

4. In the report designer, open the **Script** tab.

5. Open the **Outline** view.

6. Under the **Outline** tab, select the root element `StringLength.rptDesign`.

7. Open the **Palette** view.

8. When the **Script** tab is open, the **Palette** view changes to allow quick access to different objects and methods in the same way the expression editor does.

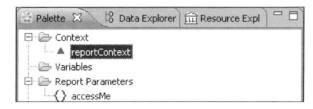

9 In the **Script** editor, under the `initialize` event, put in the following code:

```
valueFromScript = params["accessMe"];
```

10. Take a moment to play around with the Palette. If we double- click on the `reportContext` under the `Context` folder, it will automatically put that into the script editor. Also, when we type, we may notice a drop-down box that allows to see all of the objects and properties associated with the `reportContext` object.

11. Run the report to see it work.

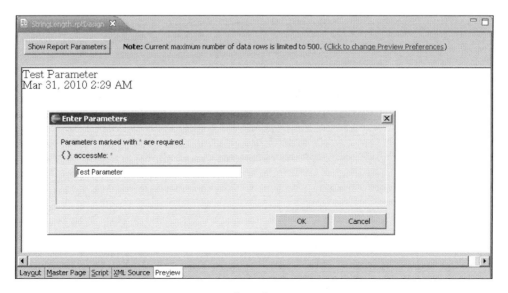

12. After running the report, modify the `initialize` method as follows:

```
valueFromScript = reportContext.getParameterValue("accessMe");
```

13. Run the report.

In the last modification, we didn't use a local context. Instead, we used the global `reportContext` to access the reports parameters and used the report context's `getParameterValue()` method to retrieve the value entered in `accessMe`.

Adding elements to report

Let's now look at using the `reportContext` to add a new element to the report. In order to do this, we need to change only the `initialize` method from the last example with the following code:

```
valueFromScript = reportContext.getParameterValue("accessMe") + "
modified";

//import the needed packages from the Java API
importPackage(Packages.org.eclipse.birt.report.model.api);
importPackage(Packages.org.eclipse.birt.report.model.api.elements);

//using the report context, get the design handle
design = reportContext.getReportRunnable().designHandle;

//get the element factory to create the new label
elementFactory = design.getElementFactory();
dataElement = elementFactory.newLabel("testElement");

//set the text from the valueFromScript variable and add
//to the report designs body
dataElement.setText(valueFromScript);
design.getDesignHandle().getBody().add(dataElement);
```

So, let's take a look at this example. The `valueFromScript` variable is assigned from the report parameter, retrieved from the `reportContext`, similar to the previous example. The next two lines are not really necessary, but illustrate that we will be using objects retrieved from the BIRT API packages. Any time we reference Java objects in code, we should use the `importPackage` method to reference the package containing those objects. For example, if we were to use the `java.util.GregorianCalendar` object, we should use `importPackage(Packages.java.util)`.

The next step is to retrieve the Design Handle from the report context. First, we use the `getReportRunnable`, which is a reference to the open report design. Then we use the `designHandle` reference to get the report design handle.

The next two lines retrieve the report element factory, which is a convenient way to create report design elements from the design handle. It then uses that element factory to create a new Label element called `testElement`. We then set the text of that label to `valueFromScript`.

The last part of the script needs to reference the `getBody` method in order to get a slot in the report to add a new element to. We then add the new element to the report.

Now, where we add elements is important. Recollect the phases from earlier? Well, one cannot add new elements after the factory phase. This means if we look at the Report Root, we can use the earlier code snippet only in the `initialize`, `beforeRender`, and the `beforeFactory` events. The `afterFactory` and `afterRender` events will not work. If we move the code to those elements, then the element will not get added.

If one looks in the `beforeFactory` event, he/she will notice that the context that points to the `IReportDesign` object is available, but it is not available in any of the other events. When working with reports through scripting, remember that objects are not always going to be available, depending on what point of the report creation cycle we are at.

Removing elements from a report

The easiest way to drop elements from reports is to find the element using the Design Handle's `findElement` method. This method will return a reference to a `DesignElementHandle`, referencing the items name used. Let's say we wanted to change the name of the Data element to `dataElementToRemove`, with the test string expression used earlier in this chapter. The following code will search the report design, find the matching element, and remove it from the report. It is run from the report's `initialize` method.

```
reportContext.getReportRunnable().designHandle.getDesignHandle().findE
lement("dataElementToRemove").drop();
```

Adding sorting conditions

In addition to adding report elements, it is also possible to add conditions such as Highlights, Maps, and Sorting conditions. The following example will show how to dynamically add sorting conditions to a report, based on the value of a report parameter checkbox:

1. Create a new report in a BIRT reporting project. Call this new report as `customerPaymentDynamicSort.rptdesign`.

2. Bring in the `dsClassicCars` data source from the library.

3. Create a new dataset using the following query:

```
select
  *
from
  CUSTOMERS,
  PAYMENTS
where
  CUSTOMERS.CUSTOMERNUMBER = PAYMENTS.CUSTOMERNUMBER
and customers.customernumber = ?
```

4. Name the parameter for the dataset as dsprmCustomerID.

5. Under the dialog window for the dataset parameter, create and link to a report parameter called rptprmCustomerID. Set it as a textbox entry.

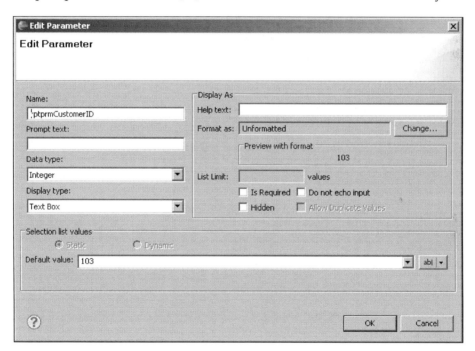

6. Drag-and-drop the newly created dataset over to the report design pane. Delete all columns except for the following:

  ○ Customer Number

  ○ Customer Name

  ○ Payment Date

  ○ Amount

7. Create a new report parameter called `rptprmSortOrder`. Set **Hidden** option checked.

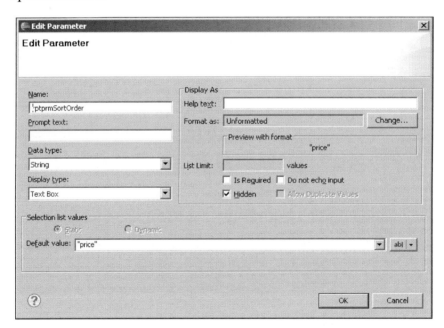

8. Add the following script to the `OnPrepare` event of the table. There are two versions of this script.

One for BIRT 2.3 and above:

```
importPackage(Packages.org.eclipse.birt.report.model.api.
simpleapi);

if ( params["rptprmSortOrder"].value != null )
    if ( params["rptprmSortOrder"].value.length > 0 )
    {
        var sortCondition = SimpleElementFactory.
getInstance().createSortCondition();

        switch (params["rptprmSortOrder"].value)
        {
            case "date" :
                sortCondition.
setKey("row[\"PAYMENTDATE\"]");
                break;
            case "price" :
                sortCondition.setKey("row[\"AMOUNT\"]");
                break;
        }

        sortCondition.setDirection("asc");

        this.addSortCondition(sortCondition);
    }
```

The other for BIRT versions prior to 2.3:

```
//We only want to add this into our code when the value is not
null for the
//parameter sort
if ( params["rptprmSortOrder"].value != null )
{
  //Bring in the BIRT Report Model API and for CONSTANTS
  importPackage( Packages.org.eclipse.birt.report.engine.api.
script.element );

  //Create a dynamic sort condition
  var sortCondition = StructureScriptAPIFactory.
createSortCondition();
  //Based on the value of the sort parameter, set the appropriate
key value for sorting
  switch (params["rptprmSortOrder"].value)
  {
      //Remember that for the key, we need to use the fully
qualified row and field name as a string, not as a value
      case "date" :
          sortCondition.setKey("row[\"PAYMENTDATE\"]");
```

```
            break;
      case "price" :
            sortCondition.setKey("row[\"AMOUNT\"]");
            break;
}

//set condition to ascending order
sortCondition.setDirection("asc");

//Add to the table
this.addSortCondition(sortCondition);
}
```

There are two versions because the scripting packages changed in BIRT 2.3. I am keeping the previous version here as a reference because there are software packages that embedded the older versions of BIRT.

9. In the header row, we need to create hyperlinks that will call this report and pass in parameters to tell which column to sort by. So, save the report as it is, otherwise the parameters will not show up in the drill down dialog. Select the `PaymentDate` column header.

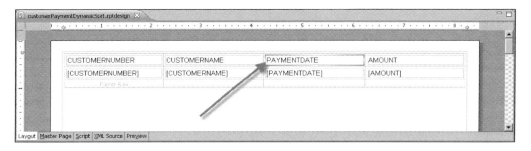

10. In the **Property Editor** window, from the left-hand side menu, select **Hyperlink**.

11. Click the **Edit...** button.

12. Select hyperlink type as **Drill-through**.

13. Link to the `customerPayment.rptdesign` file.

14. Select the `rptprmCustomerID` field and set the value to
    `params["rptprmCustomerID"]`.

15. Select the `rptprmSortOrder` parameter from the **Report Parameters** list and
    set the value to `"date"` with the quotation marks.

16. Set **Show target report in** to the **Same frame** option to open report in the
    same window.

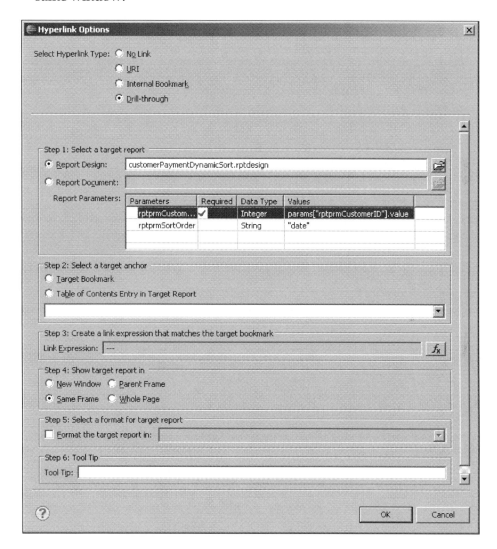

17. Do the same thing for the `Amount` column, except set the value of
    `rptprmSortorder` to `"price"`.

With this done, we can now reorder the report in view time when the user clicks on the date or the amount columns. With a little more logic developed in, we can have the report do both ascending and descending sorts, and even have it refresh the report without having to refresh the viewing page.

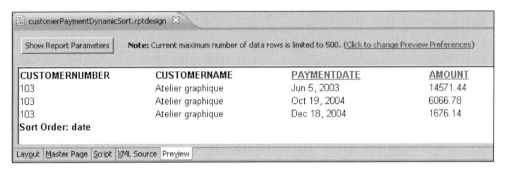

Affecting behavior of report rendering based on condition through script

Sometimes it is preferable to have a single report behave in a particular way based on some environmental factor. Parameters such as Environment Variables, Output Format, and the time of day may affect the way we want a report rendered. In the following example, we are going to use a real life scenario that I encountered when a client wanted a single report to not enable hyperlinks when they rendered to PDF.

1. Create a new report called PDFhyperlink.rptDesign.

2. Insert a label component and set the label to **My Link**.

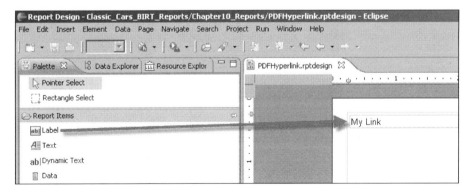

3. In the **Property Editor**, set the Hyperlink to **http://www.eclipse.org/**.

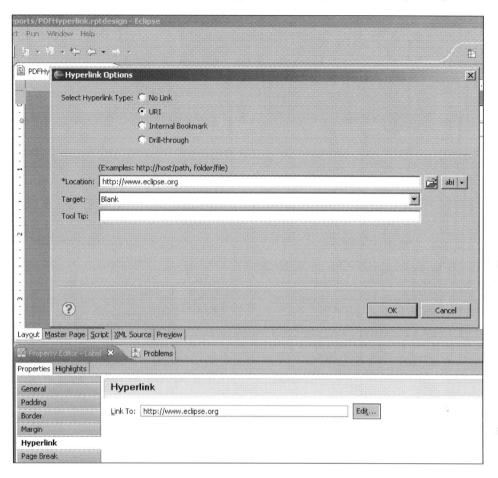

4. With the label component selected, open the **Script Editor**.
5. Set the event to `onRender`.

6. Use the following code for the `onRender` script:

```
if (reportContext.getOutputFormat().equalsIgnoreCase("PDF"))
{
        this.setAction(null);
}
```

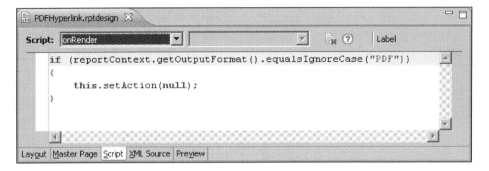

7. Save the report.

If we go to the **Run** menu, and choose **View as HTML**, we will see that the report has a hyperlink which, when clicked, opens the BIRT homepage. If we view as a PDF, that hyperlink will not exist and it will just be a label.

In the example that we just saw, we are affecting only the `onRender` event for output format. This is affecting report generation at the presentation phase. The example uses the report context to determine the output format. If the output format is nothing, the above script will take the labels action property, which is of type `org.eclipse.birt.report.engine.api.iaction`, and set it to nothing or null. This will essentially cancel any actions for this component when the output format is equal to PDF.

Scripted data source

One of the other things we can do with BIRT scripting is create a data source. In the following example, we will create a simple report that will return the numbers 1 through 10 using a scripted data source:

1. Create a new report called `countOneToTen.rptDesign`.

2. Right-click on the **Data Sources** section under the **Data Explorer** and choose **Scripted Data Source** as the type. This type of data source will use pure Java or JavaScript to generate data for a BIRT report.

3. Create a new dataset called `dsCount`.

4. A dialog will pop up for the columns to return. Add one column called `cnt` of the type `Integer`.

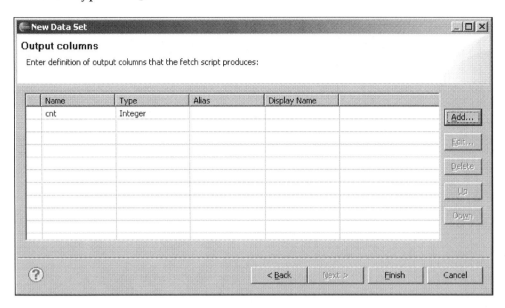

5. The script editor will open once we click **Finish**. In the `Open` event, add the following code:

```
reportContext.setGlobalVariable("currentCount", 0);
```

6. In the `fetch` method, use the following code:

```
var currentCount = reportContext.getGlobalVariable("currentCou
nt");


if (currentCount < 10)
{
        currentCount++;
        row["cnt"] = currentCount;

        reportContext.setGlobalVariable("currentCount",
currentCount);
        return true;
}

return false;
```

7. In the report designer, drag the `dsCount` data source to the Report Designer.

8. Run the report.

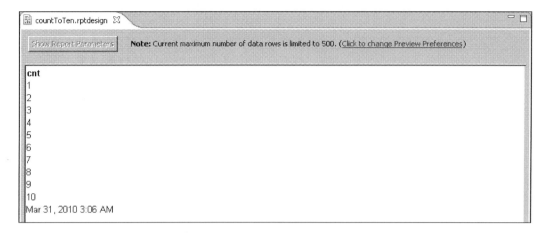

In the example that we just saw, we did a few things in a different but interesting way. First, we created the Scripted Data source. The way this works is that the `fetch` method needs to return `true` when data is returned and `false` when data is not returned. To get data into the returned row into the `cnt` column, we then use the `reportContexts` global variable to keep track of the running count.

Using Java objects as Event Handlers

The last thing we are going to look at in this chapter is using Java objects as Event Handlers instead of JavaScript in the script editor. In order to implement Java-based Event handlers, the designer needs to extend the appropriate Event Handler object. For example, if we are going to implement the last example as a Java object, we would need to extend the `org.eclipse.birt.report.engine.api.script.eventadapter.ScriptedDataSetEventAdapter` class.

Therefore, to do this, let's create a separate Java project in Eclipse. Let's create a class like the following:

```
package com.birtbook.eventHandler;
import org.eclipse.birt.report.engine.api.script.
IUpdatableDataSetRow;
import org.eclipse.birt.report.engine.api.script.ScriptException;
import org.eclipse.birt.report.engine.api.script.eventadapter.
ScriptedDataSetEventAdapter;
import org.eclipse.birt.report.engine.api.script.instance.
IDataSetInstance;
```

```java
public class ScriptedDataSetHandler extends
ScriptedDataSetEventAdapter {
        private int currentCount;

        @Override
        public boolean fetch(IDataSetInstance dataSet,
IUpdatableDataSetRow row) {
                //increment the counter
                currentCount++;

                if (currentCount < 11)
                {
                        //set the rows value
                        try {
                                row.setColumnValue("cnt", currentCount);
                        } catch (ScriptException e) {
                                e.printStackTrace();
                        }

                        return true;
                }

                return false;


        }

        @Override
        public void open(IDataSetInstance dataSet) {
                super.open(dataSet);

                //initialize the count
                currentCount = 0;
        }

}
```

Now, we need to restart Eclipse in order for it to recognize the class in our report design. Then, once we restart Eclipse, we are able to use our class and debug in Eclipse when we run the report. Next, we go into the report design, select my dsCount as the data source, clear all of the script out of the events. Then, under the **Event Handler** tab in the **Property Editor**, we click on the **Browse...** button and select my class. When we run the report, it will use our new class as the event handler.

The benefit to this approach is that it is much easier to debug during development. Plus, we have full access to the Eclipse IDE, code completion, and a much cleaner IDE to develop event handlers with. The drawback is that we would need to deploy the classes with the reports and make sure they are visible in the classpath for our runtime environment.

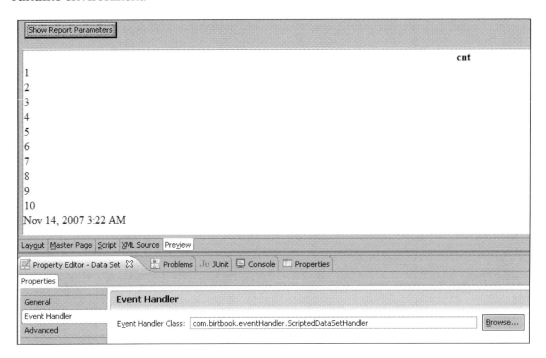

How Chart Event Handling differs from other report items

While Event Handling can be a tricky concept in BIRT, there is something that complicates things even further—charts. Charts use a completely different Event handling mechanism as they are extended item types in BIRT. What this means is that charts are not intrinsic BIRT components. When BIRT executes a Chart, there is a marker saying "Hey, I'm an external component, I need to use the Chart Engine API to execute and Render". Because Charts do not get created until Render time, charts have only an onRender event, with several subevents that internal to the Chart Engine API. This is a little confusing at first. So, let's go through an exercise to illustrate what this means. The following will use BIRT's Chart Event Handler to override the action for a Pie Slice. Pie slices will jump to a corresponding table bookmark for all values except the number 5.

1. Create a new report called `ChartEventOverride.rptDesign`.
2. Add in a Scripted Data Source.
3. Add a scripted dataset. Add in two columns—one called column of type String, and the other called value of type Integer.
4. In the open event for the dataset, use the following code:

```
count = 0;
column = 0;
```

5. For the `fetch` method, use the following code:

```
if (count < 500)
{
        row["column"] = column;
        row["value"] = count;

        count++;

        if (column > 5)
        {
                column = 0;
        }
        else
        {
                column++;
        }

        return true;
}

return false;
```

6. Insert the dataset as a table into the report.

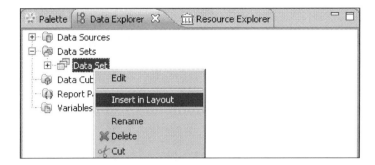

7. Insert a row in to the header above the two column labels and merge the cells.

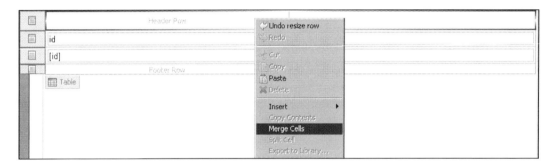

8. Insert a chart into the new header with the merged cells.

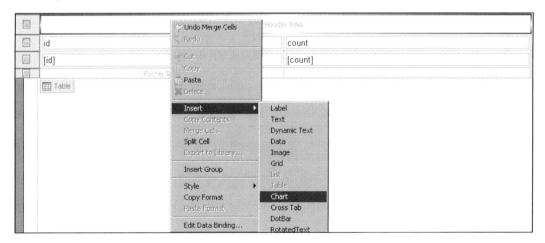

9. Set the type to Pie chart and the output format to PNG.

10. Select **Inherit Data from Container** and set this option to **Inherit Columns only**.

11. For Category Definition, drag over the `id` field. For the value series, drag over the `count` field.

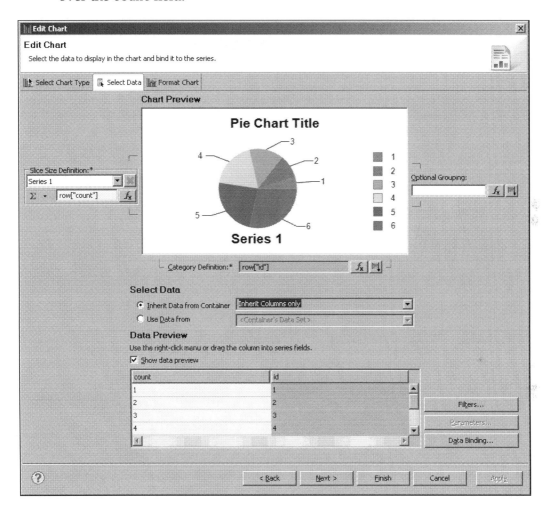

12. Click on the Grouping button next to the Category Series. Set **Grouping** to **Enabled** and set the **Aggregate Expression** to **Sum**.

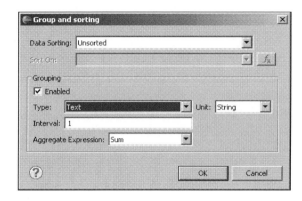

13. Select the **Format Chart** tab. Under the tree view, select **Series | Value Series**. Click on the **Interactivity** button.

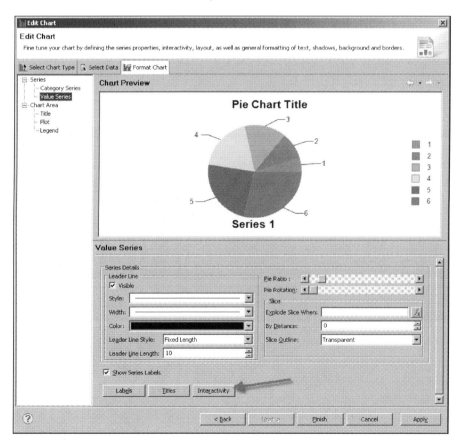

14. For **Event**, choose **mouse click**.

15. For **Action**, choose **Invoke Script**.

16. Click the **Add** button.

17. Put in anything as the name and click on **Edit base URL**.

18. For **Hyperlink**, choose **Internal Bookmark**. From the drop-down list, select `row["column"]`.

19. Save the report.

20. Preview it.

So right now, we have a basic interactive chart. When we click on any of the pie slices, it executes the hyperlink and jumps to the correct section. Let's now override that behavior through the script:

21. Select the Chart. Open the Script editor.

22. Use the following script for the `onRender` event:

```
var oldHandler;
/**
 * Called before drawing each datapoint graphical representation
or marker.
 *
 * @param dph
 *              DataPointHints
 * @param fill
 *              Fill
 * @param icsc
 *              IChartScriptContext
 */

function beforeDrawDataPoint( dph, fill, icsc )
{
//get the value of our currently rendering series
            //dph is of type DataPointHandler in the Chart
            //Engine API
value = dph.getBaseValue();

            //we need to use reflection to get to the data point
implementation
            //normally this isn't necessary, but these values are
            //not exposed. This is complex stuff you don't need
            //to know under normal circumstances. But we need to
            //get access to our current data point so we can
            //override its action behavior
```

```
            dphClass = dph.getClass();
            dataPointInstance = dphClass.getDeclaredField("dp");
            dataPointInstance.setAccessible(true);


            implementation = dataPointInstance.get(dph);

            pieInstance = implementation.eContainer();

            //make sure the object we are working with is a pie
series impl object
            if (pieInstance.getClass().getName().
contains("PieSeriesImpl"))
                {
                    //ok, if our value for the current category
equals X, then we want to do our action
                    if ( value.equals("5"))
                    {
                        //save the old action. if we dont, any
further actions that dont meet the criteria won't
                        //execute. then clear the action so it
wont execute
                        oldHandler = pieInstance.getTriggers().
get(0);
                        pieInstance.getTriggers().clear();
                    }
                    else
                    {
                        //If we cleared the triggers, we need to
re-initialize the action
                        if (pieInstance.getTriggers().size() <
1)
                        {
                            if (oldHandler != null)
                            {
                                pieInstance.getTriggers().
add(oldHandler);
                            }
                        }
                    }
                }
            }
```

23. Save the report and run it. When we run the report, we will notice that the slice for category 5 will no longer jump to the table section as it had its action cleared in the event handler.

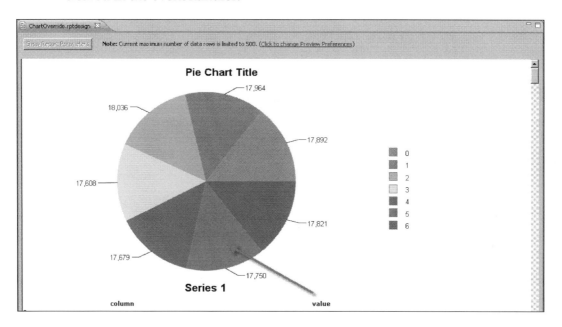

As we can see, chart event handling is much more complex than regular event handling. In the example that we just saw, we had to use Java's reflection mechanism to get access to some properties that are not normally exposed to the end developer in order to change the action of an individual slice. We can also note that there is a submethod called `beforeDrawDataPoint` that we are implementing. This is an internal Chart Engine API event.

Chart events and the bookmark property for interactivity

In the following exercise, we are going to look at building a very complex chart interactivity example using a combination of chart interactivities, which get rendered as client side JavaScript, text elements containing client side JavaScript, and BIRT Event Handlers to replicate a chart several times for an old fashioned image swap. It will be important that we use either PNG or JPEG charts as SVG already has its own mechanisms for doing this.

1. Create a report called `interactiveChartExample.rptDesign`.

2. Create a new Scripted Data Source.

3. Add a new Scripted Data Set, with two columns—one for `ID` and an other called `COUNT`.

4. For the open event on the dataset, use the following script:

    ```
    count = 0;
    id = 0;
    ```

5. For the `fetch` event, use the following code:

    ```
    if (id < 20)
    {
        id++;
        count++;

        row["id"] = id;
        row["count"] = count;
        return true;
    }

    return false;
    ```

6. Insert the dataset into the report.

7. Insert a row above the header row and merge the two cells. This cell will contain our chart.

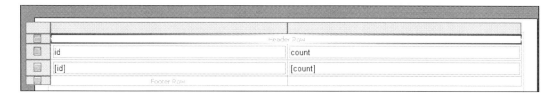

8. Select the detail row. In the **Property Editor**, select the **Bookmark** tab under **Properties**. Use the following bookmark: `row["id"]`.

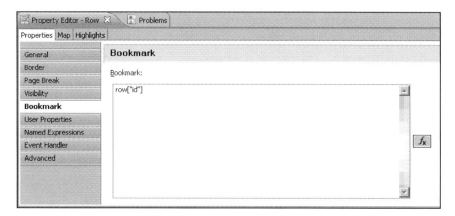

9. In the footer of the table, under the ID cell, insert a text element. Set the text element's type to HTML. It is important to note that we will be putting in some client side JavaScript code, which will be used in cooperation with a Chart Interactivity. These scripts are not the same as BIRT events, even though both are written in JavaScript.

```
<script type="text/javascript">
/**

Javascript for setting up the image swap from all the chart
instances
**/
        //Define a new array, which will contain all references to
chart images
        //with exploded slices
    imageArray = new Array();
```

```
        //the mainImageSrc will be a reference to a chart with no
slices exploded, and
        //will be the default image used when no mouse over exists
        mainImageSrc = document.getElementById("Chart-Main").src;

        //we are expecting 20 chart instances, so iterate through all
        for (x = 0; x < 20; x++)
        {
            //current image will be prefixed by "Chart-", plus the
number
            currentImage = document.getElementById("Chart-" + (x +
1));

            //get the current image, and hide it using standard HTML
style properties
            imageArray[x] = currentImage;
            currentImage.style.display = "none";
        }

        //This function will swap an image, and gets called from a
chart Interactivity
        function swapImage(num)
        {
            //get the main image reference. We will be swapping it out.
don't worry,
            //the actual image is stored in mainImageSrc
            mainImage = document.getElementById("Chart-Main");

            //swap images with the array
            mainImage.src = imageArray[num - 1].src;
        }

        //set back the main, unexploded pie image
        function showMain()
        {
            document.getElementById("Image-Main").src = mainImageSrc;
        }
</script>
```

10. In the footer cell below COUNT, insert another text element, set the type to HTML, and use the following JavaScript. Again, this is client side JavaScript. It creates an HTML tag called tableAnchor. The code will find this div tag and will go up the parent tree to find the TBODY tag, which is inserted when a BIRT table is rendered. This script will highlight a table row when a user hover over an area of the chart.

```
<!-- Dummy tag to get parent nodes -->
<div id="tableAnchor"></div>

<script>
    // Get the table object itself
    var o = document.getElementById("tableAnchor");
    while(o != null){
        if (o.tagName == "TBODY")
            break;
        o = o.parentNode;
    }

    // Add the mouseover event to each of the table rows
    for (var i = 1; i < o.children.length; i++) {
        var ro = o.children[i];
        ro.onmouseover = function(){highlight(this.
id);swapImage(this.id);};
        ro.onmouseout = function(){unhighlight(this.id);};
    }

    // Highlight function is called from mouseove events (see
above)
    // and also from chart mouseover events.
    var g_previousHighlight = "";
    function highlight(category) {
        // Remove previous highlight (if any)
        if (g_previousHighlight > "") {
            var o = document.getElementById(g_previousHighlight);
            o.style.backgroundColor="";

        }

        // Apply new highlight
        var o = document.getElementById(category);
        o.style.backgroundColor="#8080ff";
        g_previousHighlight = category;
    }

    function unhighlight(category) {
        // Remove previous highlight (if any)
        if (g_previousHighlight > "") {
            var o = document.getElementById(g_previousHighlight);
```

```
                        o.style.backgroundColor="";

            }

            // Apply new highlight
            var o = document.getElementById(category);
            o.style.backgroundColor="#FFFFFF";
            g_previousHighlight = category;
        }
    </script>
```

11. The report so far should look like the following:

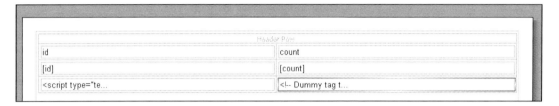

12. Insert a new chart into the top header cell that we created and merged.

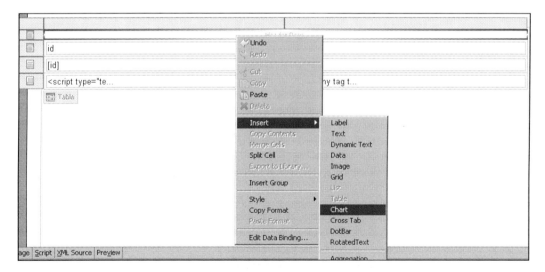

13. Set the type to **Pie Chart**, with an output format of **PNG**.

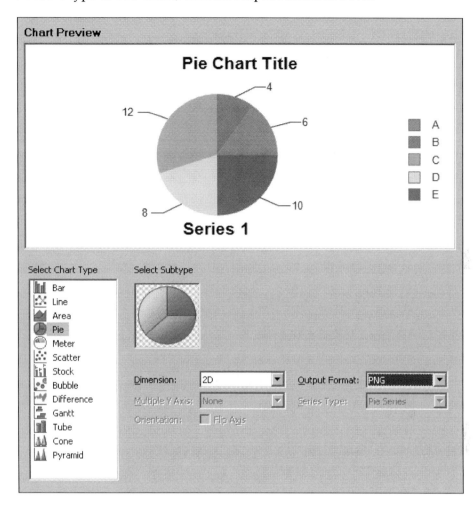

14. In the **Select Data** tab, use `id` as the category definition and `count` as the slice.

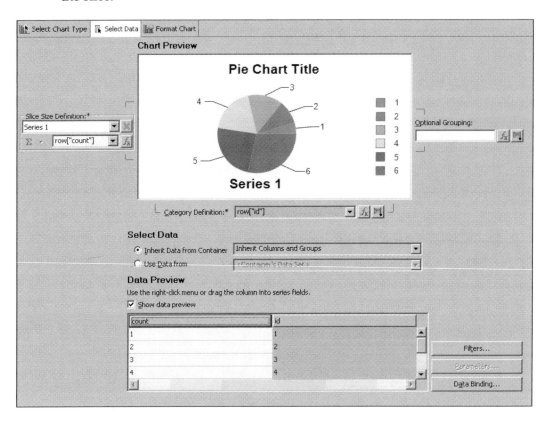

15. In the **Format Chart** tab, under **Series | Value Series**, click the **Interactivity** button. Change the **Event** to `MouseOver`. Set **Action** to `Invoke Script`. Use the below script. Again, it is important to note that we are not using BIRT server side scripts here. These are client side, executed in the user's browser at run time. What this does is add in chart interactivity so that when we mouse over a pie chart slice, it will call the swap image and row highlighting code we defined in the two text elements.

```
swapImage(categoryData);
highlight(categoryData);
```

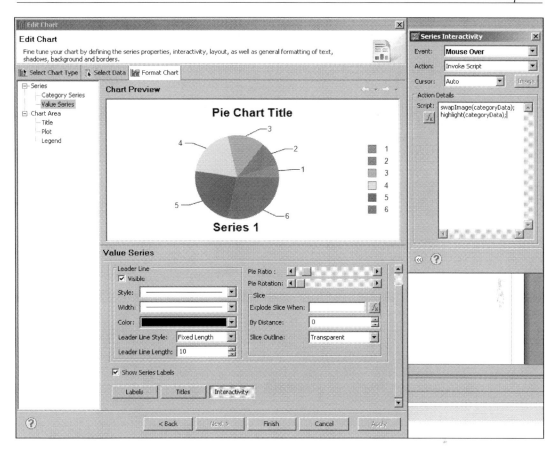

16. Click **Finish**.

17. In the **Report Editor**, select the Chart instance. Under the **Property Editor**, choose **Bookmarks**. Use the following bookmark for the Chart.

    ```
    "Chart-Main"
    ```

18. Under the **General** tab in the **Property Editor**, enter NewChart as the name of the Chart .

19. Select the report's root element. Open the Script editor, and in the report's `initialize` event, use the following code. It is important to note that this code executes on server side, before the browser ever sees the final BIRT report. What this code does is find the single chart instance in our report and duplicate it 20 times. For each duplicate, it will explode the pie slice for the matching category name, and name it so that our swap script can find it. Remember, this code executes and is completely unaware of any of the code in either of the two text elements or in the chart interactivity.

```
var reportDesignHandle = reportContext.getReportRunnable().
getDesignHandle();
var re = reportDesignHandle.findElement("NewChart");

var pieChart = re.getReportItem().getProperty("chart.instance");

for (var x = 1; x <= 20; x++)
{
    importPackage(Packages.org.eclipse.emf.ecore.util);
    var chartCopy = EcoreUtil.copy(pieChart);

    var outerSeries = chartCopy.getSeriesDefinitions().get(0);
    var innerSeries = outerSeries.getSeriesDefinitions().get(0);
    var pieSeries = innerSeries.getSeries().get(0);
    pieSeries.setExplosionExpression("valueData == " + x);
    pieSeries.setExplosion(5);

    var eih = reportDesignHandle.getElementFactory().
newExtendedItem("chart-" + x, "Chart");
    eih.getReportItem().setProperty("chart.instance", chartCopy);
    eih.setBookmark("\"Chart-" + x + "\"");

    re.getContainerSlotHandle().add(eih);
}
```

20. Save the report. Preview it. When we mouse over any of the Pie slices, we will see the chart appears to let the slices "jump" out, and the corresponding row will be highlighted in the table. The same thing happens when we mouse over any of the rows.

Multiselecting parameters and binding them to a dataset through Property Binding

As we have discussed Expressions, now would be a good time to discuss Proeprty Binding. Property Binding is a mechanism in data sources and datasets that allows us to override values at run time through scripting. For example, let's say we need to change the value of a data source to point to a production database in a runtime environment, but want it to point to a development database while we are designing the report. Property Binding could be one way to accomplish this. We could set a report parameter, or a system environment variable, and using Property Binding, can change the JDBC URL on the fly. Property Binding will replace the value at runtime.

In the following example, we are going to look at using Property Binding to change a dataset's SQL query to use a multiselect parameter, to allow a report user to select multiple customers from a database and see their orders:

1. Create a new report called `multiSelect.rptdesign`.

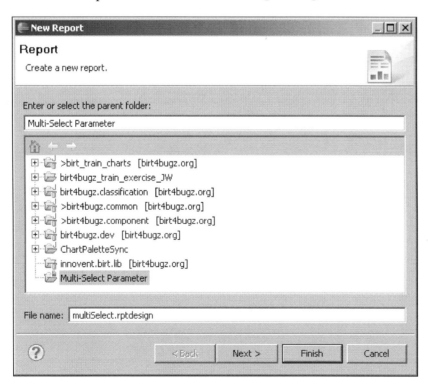

2. Add in a data source for Classic Models.

3. First, let's create a dataset that will be used in our multiselect parameter. Create a new dataset called `setGetCustomers` using the following query:

```
select
        CUSTOMERS.CUSTOMERNUMBER,
        CUSTOMERS.CUSTOMERNAME
from
        CUSTOMERS
```

4. In the **Data Explorer**, right-click on **Report Parameters** and select **New Parameter**.

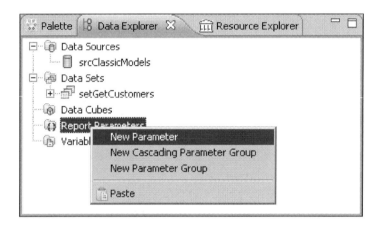

5. In the **Edit Parameter** dialog, set the parameters as shown **next**. Be sure to check the **Allow Multiple Values** checkbox.

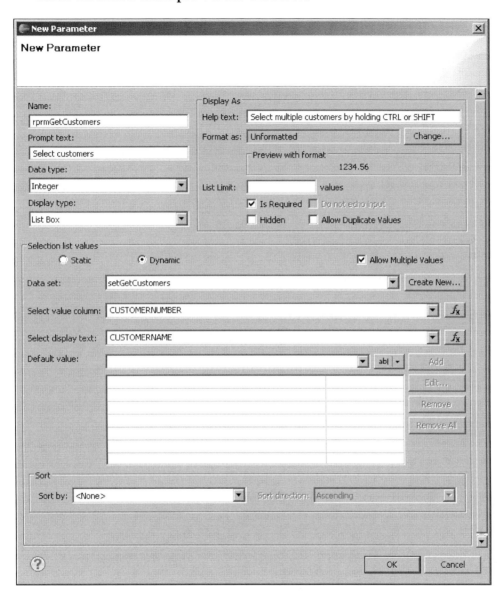

6. Now we need to create the main query that will be used in the display of our report. Create a new dataset called `setGetCustomerOrders`, using the following query:

```
select
        CLASSICMODELS.CUSTOMERS.CUSTOMERNAME,
        ORDERS.ORDERNUMBER,
        ORDERS.ORDERDATE,
        ORDERS.STATUS,
        ORDERDETAILS.PRODUCTCODE,
        ORDERDETAILS.QUANTITYORDERED,
        ORDERDETAILS.PRICEEACH
from
        ORDERS,
        ORDERDETAILS,
        CUSTOMERS
where
        CLASSICMODELS.CUSTOMERS.CUSTOMERNUMBER = CLASSICMODELS.
ORDERS.CUSTOMERNUMBER
        and CLASSICMODELS.ORDERS.ORDERNUMBER = CLASSICMODELS.
ORDERDETAILS.ORDERNUMBER
```

7. Drag `setGetCustomerOrders` over to the **Report Designer**.

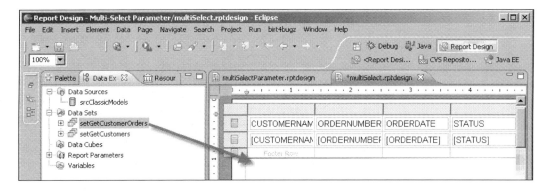

8. In the newly created table, right-click and choose **Insert Group | Above**.

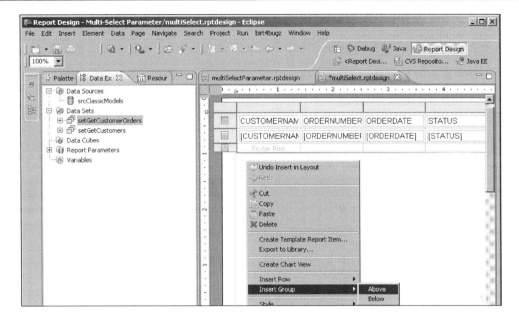

9. Call the new group `grpCustomer`. Set the **Group On** drop-down list to CUSTOMERNAME. Click **OK** when finished.

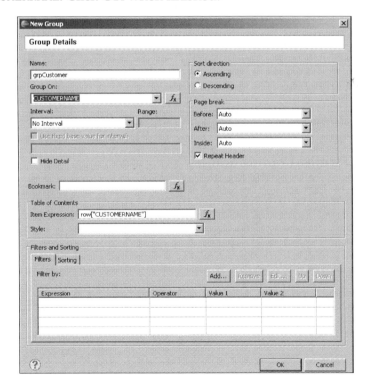

10. Right-click the table, select **Insert Group | Below**.

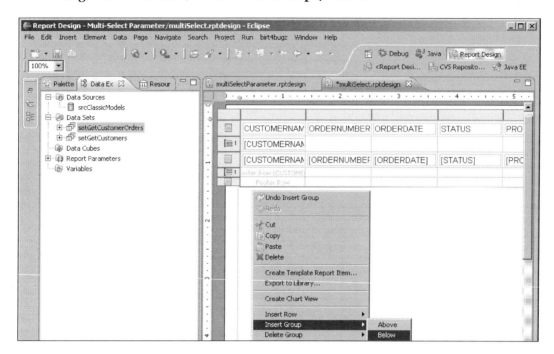

11. Call the new group `grpOrderNumber`. Set the **Group On** expression to
ORDERNUMBER.

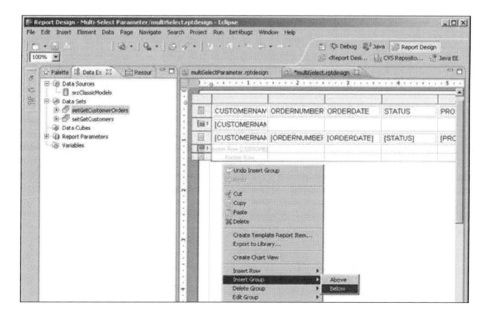

12. In the detail row, delete the CUSTOMERNAME and ORDERNUMBER fields.

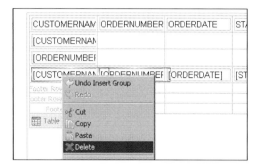

13. In the grpOrderNumber header row, move the ORDERNUMBER field to the second column.

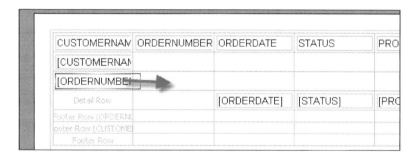

14. Move the ORDERDATE and STATUS data report items from the **Detail** row to the grpOrderNumber **header** row.

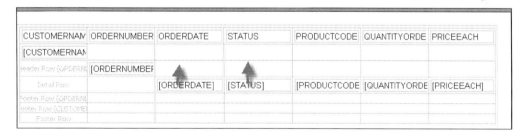

15. Select the PRICEEACH column, and right-justify.

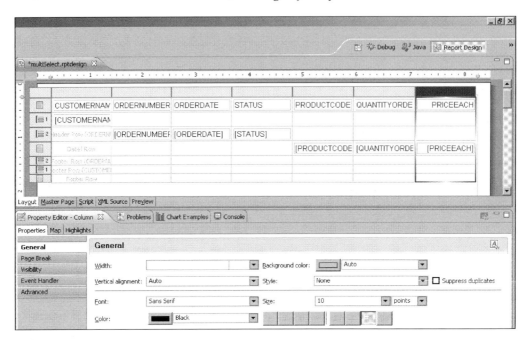

16. Now that we have the basic report, we need to set the filtering. In step 6, we did not add in a question mark noting a parameter binding in the query. This is because the parameter binding in the WHERE clause is going to be added in the Property Binding section of the dataset. Double-click on setGetCustomerOrders in the **Data Explorer**.

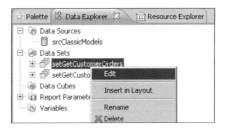

17. In the dataset editor, select the **Property Binding** section, and click on the Expression editor button next to the **Query Text** text area.

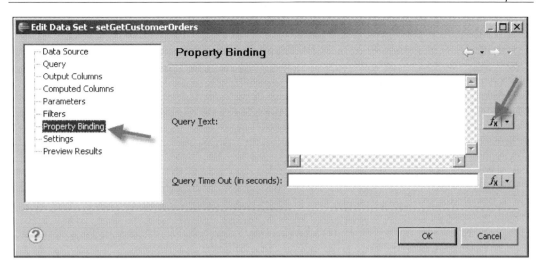

18. Use the following as the Property Binding expression:

```
//the base query as defined in the Query Section of the edit
dialog. Notice the space at the end
//of each line. Be sure to put a space at the end of the very last
line
SQL = "SELECT CUSTOMERS.CUSTOMERNAME, "
+"        ORDERS.ORDERNUMBER                 , "
+"        ORDERS.ORDERDATE                   , "
+"        ORDERS.STATUS                      , "
+"        ORDERDETAILS.PRODUCTCODE           , "
+"        ORDERDETAILS.QUANTITYORDERED       , "
+"        ORDERDETAILS.PRICEEACH "
+"FROM    ORDERS          , "
+"        ORDERDETAILS, "
+"        CUSTOMERS "
+"WHERE   CUSTOMERS.CUSTOMERNUMBER = CLASSICMODELS.ORDERS.
CUSTOMERNUMBER "
+"AND     ORDERS.ORDERNUMBER       = CLASSICMODELS.ORDERDETAILS.
ORDERNUMBER "

//append the IN statement for our multi-select parameter
+"AND CUSTOMERS.CUSTOMERNUMBER in (";
```

```
//iterate over the multi-select parameter, and append the values
to our query
for (x = 0; x < params["rprmGetCustomers"].value.length; x++)
{
      if (x > 0)
      {
            SQL = SQL + ", ";
      }

      SQL = SQL + params["rprmGetCustomers"].value[x];
}

//close out the IN statement
SQL = SQL + ")";

//return the new SQL statement
SQL;
```

19. Run the report.

Using the MultiSelect parameter in an Event Handler

When we run the previous report, we can select either a single or multiple customers, and it will filter down. Now, the drawback is that we have to maintain two copies of our query—one in the query editor under the dataset editor and the one in the Property Binding expression. We can accomplish the same thing if we use an Event Handler and have to maintain only a single copy.

1. Repeat steps 1-16 in the previous example.
2. Open the Script Editor, and using the **Outline** or the **Data Explorer**, select setGetCustomerOrders. In the Script Editor, choose the beforeOpen event.

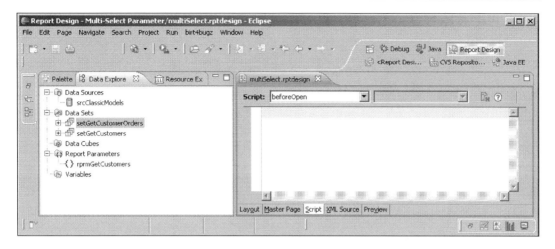

3. Use the following JavaScript for our Event Handler:

```
//get the original query from the edit dialog and append the IN
statement
SQL = this.queryText + " AND CUSTOMERS.CUSTOMERNUMBER in (";

//iterate over the multi-select parameter, and append the values
to our query
for (x = 0; x < params["rprmGetCustomers"].value.length; x++)
{
        if (x > 0)
        {
                SQL = SQL + ", ";
        }

        SQL = SQL + params["rprmGetCustomers"].value[x];
}

//close out the IN statement
SQL = SQL + ")";

//set the queryText to our new modified query
this.queryText = SQL;
```

4. Save and preview the report.

Using the Event Handler, we now need to maintain only a single copy of our query. This works in both examples because a multiselect parameter is an array of objects. We need to iterate over this array and append the values.

Using the Innovent Custom Script Libraries for query binding

In the last two examples, we modified a query at runtime to use a multiselect parameter. However, there are some issues with both approaches as we are modifying a SQL statement at runtime based on user input, which can lead to some security issues such as SQL injection attacks. This is not really a desirable condition, especially if these reports are going to be Internet facing. Fortunately, BIRT has the ability to allow for functionality to be extended, and to address this concern, we created a BIRT extension to do real time parameter binding to a SQL statement. In the following example, we are going to use the Innovent Solutions BIRT Functions Library in a SQL statement to bind a multiselect parameter.

1. Go to the BIRT Functions Library website located at `http://code.google.com/p/birt-functions-lib/`.

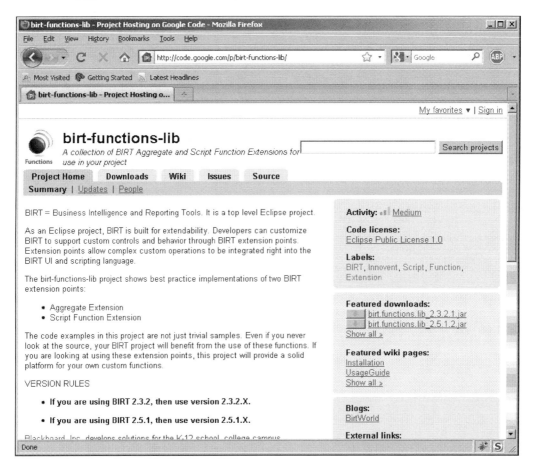

2. Make sure BIRT is closed before we perform this step. Download the `birt.functions.lib` JAR file that is appropriate for your version of BIRT. In this example, we will use 2.5.x. Copy the JAR file to the **BIRT | plugins**.

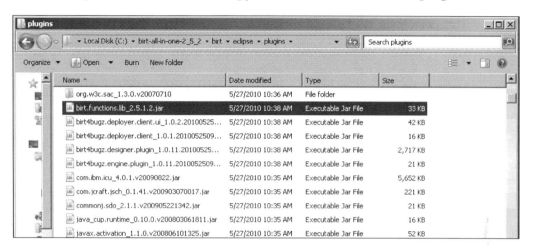

3. Complete steps 1-16 from the *Multiselecting parameters and binding them to a Data Set through Property Binding* exercise.

4. Open the Script Editor and using the **Outline**, select the root of the report. Select the `beforeFactory` event from the drop-down list.

5. If we open the Report Item Palette, it will have changed to the Script Editor palette. Under the BIRT Functions section, there will be a new category called CustomFunctions. Here we will need the BindParameters() function. This is an initialization function that will replace anything with a special marker in our query with a report parameter. Double-click on BindParameter(), and as a parameter, use the reportContext variable.

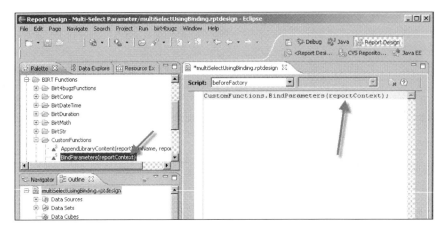

6. We need to edit our query to utilize our multiselect parameter. From the **Data Explorer**, double-click on setGetCustomerOrders.

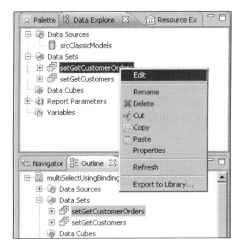

7. The next line is a special token that the `BindParameters()` function looks for and inserts a report parameter into any marker prefixed by a $. The name after the $ must match a report parameter name. Add the following line to the end of the query:

```
/* BIND and CUSTOMERS.CUSTOMERNUMBER in ($rprmGetCustomers) */
```

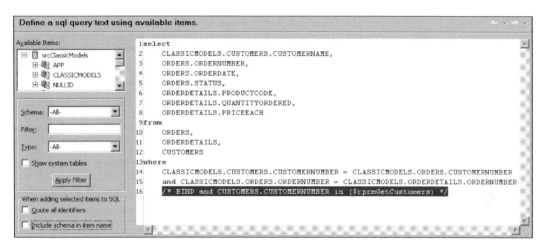

6. Save and preview the report.

Using this example, we now have a only single query to maintain and the `BindParameters()` function will take care of checking for SQL injection and not allow invalid characters. The BIRT Functions Library has all sorts of neat functions such as the `DisplayParameters()` function that will add a table to the beginning of each report showing what parameters were used and their values, `BirtLogger()` that will work the Report Engines logging utility to add messages during report execution, and `SetChartPalette()` that will synchronize different charts color palettes. All these functions and more assist report developers. These are just some of the examples along with the BIRT Controls Library that showcase some of the functionality that BIRT lets us extend to go beyond the out of the box features.

For more information on BIRT Extension Points, see my article on the Aggregation Extension Point at http://www.ibm.com/developerworks/opensource/library/os-eclipse-birtextpts/index.html?ca=drs-.

More scripting examples

If one is looking for more examples on scripting in BIRT, he/she shouldn't look furthur than the Report Examples View and Chart Examples View. Both contain example reports that utilize scripting to demonstrate different techniques such as dynamically adding visibility rules, adding in dynamic maps, and scripted data sources.

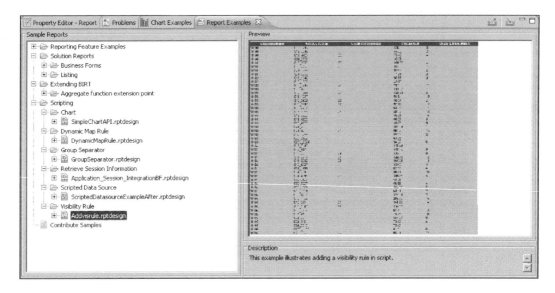

Summary

In this chapter, we looked at some of the scripting capabilities that BIRT has to offer with Expressions and Event handlers. We looked at the different report contexts that are available for accessing properties and methods in BIRT report designs, adding and removing report elements dynamically, and finally we looked at how to use Java objects as Event handlers.

This touches on the BIRT API, which is a large topic and beyond the scope of this book. But it gets the reader familiar with some of the things that are possible with the scripting and API environments that BIRT provides. More information can be gathered from the Eclipse website and newsgroups, the BirtWorld blog, and my website.

The final part of this book will look at deploying BIRT reports.

10
Deployment

So far in this book, we have developed a bunch of reports. While some of these reports were intended to be used for our own purposes, some reports may be intended for use by other people. How do we get these reports to the users who need to run them? That's the question that deployment seeks to answer.

With BIRT, deployment is a large topic. Some people consider the BIRT Viewer that comes with the BIRT Runtime as the deployment endpoint. On the contrary, BIRT deployment is a much larger product due to the fact that the BIRT Report Engine API is available to embed into Java applications.

In this chapter, we are going to look at two of the different deployment options available. We will look at the BIRT Viewer for J2EE that comes with the BIRT Runtime and that is embedded into the BIRT Eclipse IDE. We are also going to look at a basic Java application that implements the Report Engine API to run reports. We are also going to look at the command line tools that come with the BIRT Runtime for executing reports.

Everything in this chapter uses utilities from the BIRT Runtime installation package, available from the BIRT homepage (`http://www.eclipse.org/birt`).

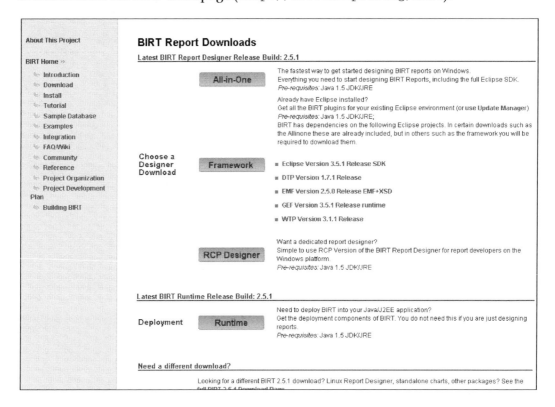

BIRT Viewer

The BIRT Viewer is a J2EE application that is designed to demonstrate the implementation of Report Engine API to execute reports in an online web application. For most basic uses, such as for small to medium size Intranet applications, this is an appropriate approach. The thing to keep in mind about the BIRT Web Viewer is that it is an example application. It can be used as a baseline for more sophisticated web applications that will implement the BIRT Report Engine API.

Installation of the BIRT viewer is documented at a number of places. The Eclipse BIRT website has some great tutorials at `http://www.eclipse.org/birt/phoenix/deploy/viewerSetup.php` and `http://wiki.eclipse.org/BIRT/FAQ/Deployment`.

This is also documented on my website in a series of articles, aimed at introducing people to BIRT (`http://digiassn.blogspot.com/2005/10/birt-report-server-pt-2.html`).

Let's not go into details about installing Apache Tomcat as this is covered in more depth in other locations, but we will cover how to install the Viewer in a Tomcat environment. For the most part, these instructions can be used in other J2EE containers such as WebSphere. In some cases a WAR package is used instead. I prefer Tomcat as it is a widely used, open source J2EE environment.

Under the BIRT Runtime package is a folder containing an example Web Viewer application. The Web Viewer application is a useful application if one requires basic report viewing capabilities such as parameter passing, pagination, and the ability to export to formats such as Word, Excel, RTF, and CSV.

Name ▲	Size	Type	Date Modified	
about_files		File Folder	11/1/2007 4:08 PM	
ReportEngine		File Folder	2/3/2008 7:40 PM	
WebViewerExample		File Folder	2/3/2008 7:40 PM	
about.html	5 KB	Firefox Document	11/1/2007 4:08 PM	
birt.war	34,772 KB	WAR File	11/1/2007 5:29 PM	
epl-v10.html	17 KB	Firefox Document	11/1/2007 4:08 PM	
notice.html	7 KB	Firefox Document	11/1/2007 4:08 PM	
readme.txt	5 KB	Text Document	11/1/2007 5:29 PM	

In this example, we have Apache Tomcat 5.5 installed into a folder at `C:\apache-tomcat-5.5.25`. To install the web viewer, we simply need to copy the `WebViewerExample` folder from the BIRT Runtime to the web application folder at `C:\apache-tomcat-5.5.25\webapps`.

Name ▲	Size	Type	Date Modified
balancer		File Folder	2/3/2008 7:49 PM
jsp-examples		File Folder	2/3/2008 7:49 PM
ROOT		File Folder	2/3/2008 7:49 PM
servlets-examples		File Folder	2/3/2008 7:49 PM
tomcat-docs		File Folder	2/3/2008 7:49 PM
webdav		File Folder	2/3/2008 7:49 PM
WebViewerExample		File Folder	2/3/2008 8:22 PM

Accessing the BIRT web viewer is as simple as calling the `WebViewerExample` context.

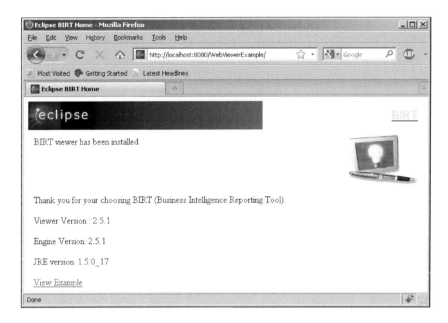

When copying the `WebViewerApplication`, we can rename this folder to anything of our choice. Obviously, `WebViewerApplication` is not a good name for an online web application. So, as shown in the following screenshot, let's rename the `WebViewerApplication` folder to `birtViewer`, and access the Birt Web Viewer test report. When we click on the **View Example** link in the preceding screenshot, we can see the report viewer as shown here:

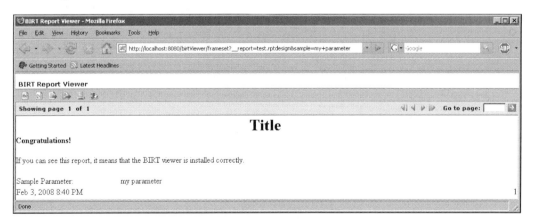

More information on installing the BIRT Web Viewer can be found at
`http://www.eclipse.org/birt/phoenix/deploy/viewerSetup.php`.

Installing reports into the Web Viewer

Once the BIRT Viewer is set up, deploying reports is as simple as copying the report
design files, libraries, or report documents into the applications context and calling it
with the appropriate URL parameters.

For example, we will install the reports from the "Classic Cars – With Library"
folder into the BIRT Web Viewer in the "birtViewer" subfolder. For these reports to
work, all dependent libraries need to be installed with the reports. In the case of the
example application, we currently have the report folder set to the root of the web
application folder.

Name ▲	Size	Type	Date Modified
documents		File Folder	2/3/2008 8:40 PM
logs		File Folder	2/3/2008 8:38 PM
report		File Folder	2/3/2008 8:38 PM
scriptlib		File Folder	2/3/2008 8:22 PM
webcontent		File Folder	2/3/2008 8:21 PM
WEB-INF		File Folder	2/3/2008 8:51 PM
index.jsp	3 KB	JSP File	11/1/2007 5:29 PM
test1.rptdesign	57 KB	RPTDESIGN File	11/1/2007 5:29 PM
test.rptdesign	5 KB	RPTDESIGN File	11/1/2007 5:29 PM
ClassicCarsLibrary.rptlibrary	25 KB	RPTLIBRARY File	9/7/2007 5:20 PM
Customer Orders.rptconfig	3 KB	RPTCONFIG File	9/7/2007 5:28 PM
Customer Orders.rptdesign	34 KB	RPTDESIGN File	9/7/2007 6:28 PM
Employee_Sales_Details.rptD...	25 KB	RPTDESIGN File	2/3/2008 12:18 AM
Employee_Sales_Guage.rptD...	60 KB	RPTDESIGN File	2/1/2008 12:38 PM
Employee_Sales_Percentage....	43 KB	RPTDESIGN File	1/27/2008 7:33 AM
EmployeeSalesPerformanceR...	60 KB	RPTDESIGN File	1/29/2008 9:49 PM
StringLength.rptconfig	3 KB	RPTCONFIG File	2/1/2008 5:07 PM
StringLength.rptDesign	5 KB	RPTDESIGN File	2/1/2008 5:07 PM

Accessing reports in the Web Viewer

Accessing reports is as simple as passing the correct parameters to the web viewers. In the BIRT web viewer, there are following seven servlets that we can call to run reports:

- `frameset`
- `run`
- `preview`
- `download`
- `parameter`
- `document`
- `output`

Out of these, we will need only `frameset` and `run`, as the other servlets are for Engine things, such as the preview for the Eclipse designer, the parameter dialog, and the downloading of report documents.

Out of the two remaining servlets, `frameset` is the one that is typically used for user interaction with reports as it provides pagination options, parameter dialogs, table of contents viewing, and export and print dialogs. The `run` servlet provides only report the output feature.

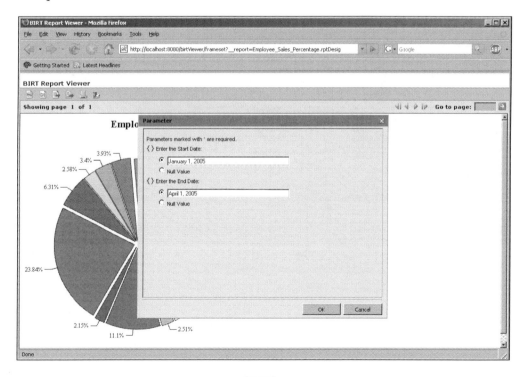

There are a few URL parameters for the BIRT Web Viewer.

- __format: The output format, either HTML or PDF
- __isnull: Sets a report parameter to null, parameter name as a value
- __locale: The reports locale
- __report: The report design file to run
- __document: The report document file to open

Any remaining URL parameters will be treated as a report parameter. In the following image, we are running the Employee_Sales_Percentage.rptDesign file with the start and end date parameters set.

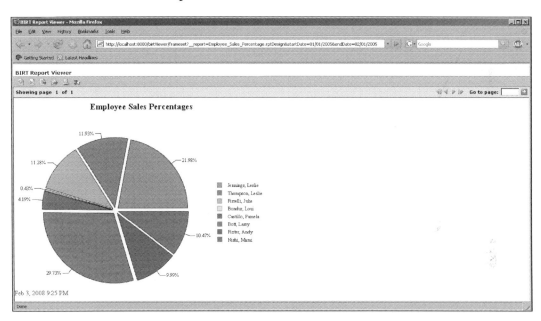

More information on BIRT Viewer's usage can be found on the Eclipse BIRT Viewer page at http://www.eclipse.org/birt/phoenix/deploy/viewerSetup.php.

Command line tools

The command line tools that come with the BIRT Runtime are useful for scheduled report execution. Under Windows, calling the batch file using the Window Scheduler or the AT utility makes unattended report execution simple. In the case of the Unix, there are tons of Cron daemons available. Scheduling report execution without the need to interact with a GUI application is convenient.

In the Runtime folder, the batch or script files are located under `ReportEngine` folder. The prerequisites are that we must have a Java implementation greater than 1.5 and must have preset the `BIRT_HOME` environment variable to the location of the BIRT runtimes root folder.

More information can be found in the `ReadMe file`, and on my website at `http://digiassn.blogspot.com/2006/07/birt-birt-report-scheduling-without.html`.

First, let's create a batch file called `runReport.bat`. The file will be simple and only have the following lines:

```
Set BIRT_HOME=C:\birt_runtime\birt-runtime-2_1_0\
C:\birt_runtime\birt-runtime-2_1_0\ReportEngine\genReport.bat
-runrender -output "c:\birt_runtime\birt-runtime-2_1_0\ReportEngine\
sameples\output.html" -format html "C:\birt_runtime\birt-
runtime-2_1_0\ReportEngine\samples\Hello_World.rptDesign"
```

While this example is for BIRT 2.1, the same steps will apply to any version of BIRT, including 2.5.

To Schedule this file to run, we go to **Control Panel | Scheduled Task** and create a new scheduled task. We set the command to run to `C:\birt_runtime\birt-runtime-2_1_0\ReportEngine\runReport.bat`. We select the appropriate time, and set the directory to start in to `C:\birt_runtime\birt-runtime-2_1_0\ReportEngine\`. Finally, we also set up the scheduled task to run as a dedicated report user. The following screenshot illustrates the values used under scheduler:

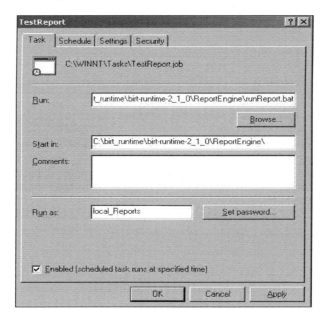

Now, we can schedule BIRT reports to run without needing Apache. This cuts down on system overhead. There are a few caveats to take into consideration. If our BIRT report hits a database, the appropriate drivers will need to be included in the `ReportEngine\plugins` folders. For example, if the report uses JDBC to connect, the JDBC drivers will need to be installed under the `ReportEngine\plugins\ org. eclipse.birt.report.data.oda.jdbc_<version>` folder.

From this exercise we can learn a few interesting things. People are unaware of the fact that Java classes could be invoked from the command line. For example, if one sets a environment variable called `BIRTCLASSPATH` like:

```
SET BIRTCLASSPATH=%BIRT_HOME%\ReportEngine\lib\commons-cli-
1.0.jar;%BIRT_HOME%\ReportEngine\lib\commons-codec-1.3.jar;%BIRT_
HOME%\ReportEngine\lib\com.ibm.icu_3.4.4.1.jar;%BIRT_HOME%\
ReportEngine\lib\coreapi.jar;%BIRT_HOME%\ReportEngine\lib\dteapi.
jar;%BIRT_HOME%\ReportEngine\lib\engineapi.jar;%BIRT_HOME%\
ReportEngine\lib\js.jar;%BIRT_HOME%\ReportEngine\lib\modelapi.
jar;%BIRT_HOME%\ReportEngine\flute.jar;%BIRT_HOME%\ReportEngine\lib\
sac.jar;
```

then he/she can run the following command from the DOS prompt and get the parameters that the `ReportEngine` class is expecting:

```
java -cp "%BIRTCLASSPATH%" org.eclipse.birt.report.engine.api.
ReportRunner

org.eclipse.birt.report.engine.impl.ReportRunner

--mode/-m [ run | render | runrender] the default is runrender
for runrender mode:
we should add it in the end<design file>
--format/-f [ HTML | PDF ]
--output/-o <target file>
--htmlType/-t < HTML | ReportletNoCSS >
--locale /-l<locale>
--parameter/-p <parameterName=parameterValue>
--file/-F <parameter file>
--encoding/-e <target encoding>

Locale: default is english


parameters in command line will overide parameters in parameter file

parameter name can't include characters such as ' ', '=', ':'
For RUN mode:
we should add it in the end<design file>
--output/-o <target file>
--locale /-l<locale>
```

```
--parameter/-p <parameterName=parameterValue>
--file/-F <parameter file>

Locale: default is english


parameters in command line will overide parameters in parameter file

parameter name can't include characters such as ' ', '=', ':'
For RENDER mode:
we should add it in the end<design file>
--output/-o <target file>
\t --page/-p <pageNumber>
--locale /-l<locale>

Locale: default is English
```

This is a major break from the paradigm of compiling and running software in other languages.

Report Engine API

Embedding the Report Engine API into our application requires a little knowledge of the inner workings of BIRT. The API is beyond the scope of this book, but we will get a little view of how to create a simple report executor application.

For this application to work, we need to have Java 1.4 or higher set up for BIRT 2.2 and below, and Java 1.5 set up for BIRT 2.3 and above, and have the BIRT runtime set up and visible in our classpath. We will use the Apache Commons CLI to handle the command line options. The following does not take into account parameters; it simply demonstrates how to instantiate the Report Engine API.

```java
package com.birt_book;

import java.util.HashMap;

import org.apache.commons.cli.CommandLine;
import org.apache.commons.cli.CommandLineParser;
import org.apache.commons.cli.HelpFormatter;
import org.apache.commons.cli.Options;
import org.apache.commons.cli.PosixParser;
import org.eclipse.birt.core.exception.BirtException;
import org.eclipse.birt.core.framework.Platform;
import org.eclipse.birt.core.framework.PlatformConfig;
import org.eclipse.birt.report.engine.api.EngineConfig;
import org.eclipse.birt.report.engine.api.EngineConstants;
```

```java
import org.eclipse.birt.report.engine.api.EngineException;
import org.eclipse.birt.report.engine.api.HTMLRenderContext;
import org.eclipse.birt.report.engine.api.HTMLRenderOption;
import org.eclipse.birt.report.engine.api.IReportEngine;
import org.eclipse.birt.report.engine.api.IReportEngineFactory;
import org.eclipse.birt.report.engine.api.IReportRunnable;
import org.eclipse.birt.report.engine.api.IRunAndRenderTask;

public class ReportExecutor {
    private static String BIRT_HOME = "C:/birt-runtime-2_5_2/birt-
runtime-2_5_2/ReportEngine";
    private static String IMAGE_PATH = "C:/BIRT_RUNTIME_2_2/images";
    private String reportLocation;
    private String reportOutputLocation;

    /**
     * setupCLIParameters
     *
     * This will setup the arguments
     * @return
     */
    public Options setupCLIParameters()
    {
            Options options = new Options();

            options.addOption("i", "input", true, "The report file to
execute");
            options.addOption("o", "output", true, "The name of the
output file");

            return options;
    }

    /**
     * parseCommandLineOptions
     *
     * Given the arguments passed into main, this method will use the
Apache Commons CLI
     * to parse those options and return a CommandLine object with the
options
     *
     * @param args
     * @return CommandLine
     */
    public CommandLine parseCommandLineOptions(String []args)
```

```
        {
                // First, parse the command line options using Apache
        Commons CLI
                CommandLineParser parser = new PosixParser();
                Options options = setupCLIParameters();
                CommandLine line = null;
                HelpFormatter formatter = new HelpFormatter();

                //Try to parse the command line options, exit the app if
        there is an error
                try {
                        //get the options
                        line = parser.parse(options, args);
                } catch (Exception e) {
                        System.err.println("Parsing failed.  Reason: " +
        e.getMessage());
                        formatter.printHelp("ReportExecutor", options);
                        System.exit(-1);
                }

                return line;
        }

        /**
         * startupPlatform
         *
         * This will startup the Eclipse platform and load any plugins
         */
        private void startupPlatform()
        {
                //initialize the Eclipse platform, plugins, and report
        engine
                PlatformConfig platformConfig = new PlatformConfig();
                platformConfig.setBIRTHome(BIRT_HOME);
                try {
                        Platform.startup(platformConfig);
                } catch (BirtException e) {
                        e.printStackTrace();
                        //we cannot start the platform, exit
                        System.exit(-1);
                }
        }

        /**
         * createReportEngine
```

```
 *
 * This will create a report engine to use
 * @return
 */
private IReportEngine createReportEngine()
{
        //create a new report engine factory
        IReportEngineFactory factory = (IReportEngineFactory)
Platform.createFactoryObject(IReportEngineFactory.EXTENSION_REPORT_
ENGINE_FACTORY);

        //create a new report engine
        EngineConfig engineConfig = new EngineConfig();
        //the location of the BIRT Runtime goes here
        engineConfig.setBIRTHome(BIRT_HOME); //will replace with
configuration file
        return factory.createReportEngine(engineConfig);
}

/**
 * Executes a report with no parameters, only requires report name
to execute
 * @param reportName
 * @return
 */
public void executeReportNoParams(String reportName, String
outputFile, IReportEngine engine)
{
        try {
                //create the report runnable and runandrender task
                IReportRunnable runnable = engine.
openReportDesign(reportName);
                IRunAndRenderTask task = engine.createRunAndRenderTas
k(runnable);

                //Set Render context to handle url and image
locataions
                HTMLRenderContext renderContext = new
HTMLRenderContext();
                renderContext.setImageDirectory(IMAGE_PATH);
                HashMap contextMap = new HashMap();
                contextMap.put( EngineConstants.APPCONTEXT_HTML_
RENDER_CONTEXT, renderContext );
                task.setAppContext( contextMap );
```

```
                   //Set rendering options - such as file or stream
output,
                   //output format, whether it is embeddable, etc
                   HTMLRenderOption options = new HTMLRenderOption();
                   options.setOutputFileName(outputFile);
                   options.setOutputFormat("html");
                   task.setRenderOption(options);

                   //Run the report and close
                   task.run();
                   task.close();
            } catch (EngineException e) {
                   e.printStackTrace();
                   System.exit(-1);
            }
    }

    /**
     * executeReport
     *
     * This method will execute the report and save the the output
file
     * @param reportInput
     * @param reportOutput
     */
    public void executeReport(String reportInput, String reportOutput)
    {
            //startup the platform
            startupPlatform();

            //create a report engine
            IReportEngine engine = createReportEngine();

            //create a run and render task and execute report
            executeReportNoParams(reportInput, reportOutput, engine);

            //shutdown platform
            Platform.shutdown();
    }

    /**
     * @param args
     */
    public static void main(String[] args) {
```

```
ReportExecutor re = new ReportExecutor();

//Get command line options
CommandLine cl = re.parseCommandLineOptions(args);

//get the input file and output file
String reportInputFile = cl.getOptionValue("i");
String reportOutputFile = cl.getOptionValue("o");

//execute the report
re.executeReport(reportInputFile, reportOutputFile);
    }

}
```

Outputing to different formats

The BIRT platform supports a plugin structure based on Eclipse. A part of the BIRT Plug-in Extension Points are the Emitter extension points. **Emitters** are plugins that handle the rendering of reports to different formats.

Out of the box, BIRT comes with several different emitters. BIRT can output to the following format with the default Emitters:

- HTML
- PDF
- Microsoft Word
- Microsoft Excel
- RTF
- Microsoft Powerpoint
- Adobe Postscript

In the BIRT Web Designer, the different output formats are available under the **Run | View Report** menu.

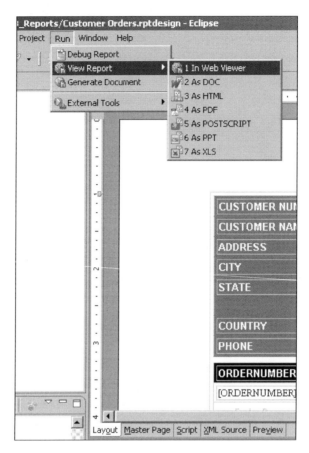

When using the BIRT Web Viewer, we can specify different report formats by using the __format URL parameter. If we specify __format=pdf, it will output in the Adobe PDF format, and if we specify __format=xls, then the Viewer will output in the Microsoft Excel format.

In addition to the URL parameter, there is also an Export dialog available in the frameset servlet.

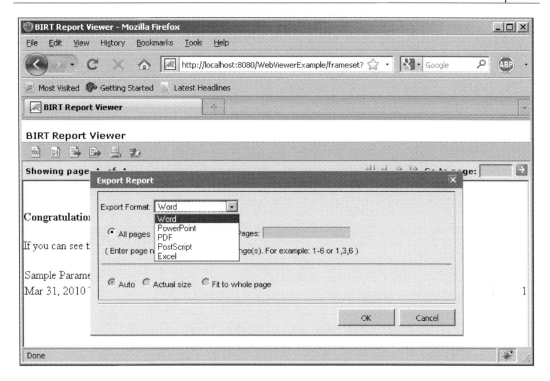

Summary

This chapter gave some brief examples of how to deploy BIRT reports. The main things we saw involved how to use the BIRT Example Web Viewer, how to use the example command line tools, and how to embed the BIRT Engine API into our own custom web application.

In the next chapter, we will wrap up with a practical series of reports around the Bugzilla platform. We will also cover creating a project and some reports from the ground up.

Index

Symbols

A

B

Thank you for buying
BIRT 2.6 Data Analysis and Reporting

About Packt Publishing

Packt, pronounced 'packed', published its first book "*Mastering phpMyAdmin for Effective MySQL Management*" in April 2004 and subsequently continued to specialize in publishing highly focused books on specific technologies and solutions.

Our books and publications share the experiences of your fellow IT professionals in adapting and customizing today's systems, applications, and frameworks. Our solution based books give you the knowledge and power to customize the software and technologies you're using to get the job done. Packt books are more specific and less general than the IT books you have seen in the past. Our unique business model allows us to bring you more focused information, giving you more of what you need to know, and less of what you don't.

Packt is a modern, yet unique publishing company, which focuses on producing quality, cutting-edge books for communities of developers, administrators, and newbies alike. For more information, please visit our website: www.packtpub.com.

About Packt Open Source

In 2010, Packt launched two new brands, Packt Open Source and Packt Enterprise, in order to continue its focus on specialization. This book is part of the Packt Open Source brand, home to books published on software built around Open Source licences, and offering information to anybody from advanced developers to budding web designers. The Open Source brand also runs Packt's Open Source Royalty Scheme, by which Packt gives a royalty to each Open Source project about whose software a book is sold.

Writing for Packt

We welcome all inquiries from people who are interested in authoring. Book proposals should be sent to author@packtpub.com. If your book idea is still at an early stage and you would like to discuss it first before writing a formal book proposal, contact us; one of our commissioning editors will get in touch with you.

We're not just looking for published authors; if you have strong technical skills but no writing experience, our experienced editors can help you develop a writing career, or simply get some additional reward for your expertise.

Business Process Management with JBoss jBPM

ISBN: 978-1-847192-36-3   Paperback: 220 pages

A Practical Guide for Business Analysts

1. Map your business processes in an efficient, standards-friendly way

2. Use the jBPM toolset to work with business process maps, create a customizable user interface for users to interact with the process, collect process execution data, and integrate with existing systems.

3. Set up business rules, assign tasks, work with process variables, automate activities and decisions.

JasperReports for Java Developers

ISBN: 978-1-904811-90-9   Paperback: 344 pages

Create, Design, Format and Export Reports with the world's most popular Java reporting library

1. Get started with JasperReports, and develop the skills to get the most from it

2. Create, design, format, and export reports

3. Generate report data from a wide range of datasources

4. Integrate Jasper Reports with Spring, Hibernate, Java Server Faces, or Struts

Please check **www.PacktPub.com** for information on our titles

Printed in Germany
by Amazon Distribution
GmbH, Leipzig